# Chiriaco Summit
## Built by Love to Last in the Desert

**An American Success Story by**
## Mary Contini Gordon

Foreword by
## Helen Patton

Story Consultant
## Margit Chiriaco Rusche

Epilogue by
## Howard N. Stewart

*Chiriaco Summit: Built by Love to Last in the Desert*

This book researched using *Her-His*tory Method™, Mary Contini Gordon, 2017.

Published by Wheatmark®
2030 East Speedway Boulevard, Suite 106
Tucson, Arizona 85719 USA
www.wheatmark.com

ISBN: 978-1-62787-465-6 (paperback)
ISBN: 978-1-62787-466-2 (ebook)
LCCN: 2016963139

Front cover photos: Joe and Ruth Chiriaco, 1934. Some of subsequent generations around 1929 Ford Roadster from Chiriaco Classic Car Collection. L to R standing—Robert Chiriaco, Cecilia Garcia, Victor Garcia, Heather and Santos Garcia. In car, Margit Chiriaco Rusche. Chiriaco Archives. Photo by Eduardo Guevara, December 9, 2016.

Back cover photos: Joe Chiriaco, the Desert Hunter, c 1932; Ruth Bergseid, The Minnesota Farmer, c. 1931, General Patton Memorial Museum Statue and some of the Chiriaco Staff, 2016, Chiriaco Archives.

ChiriacoSummit.com

To Joe and Ruth Chiriaco:
Pioneers, lovers, and entrepreneurs
Who embodied the true spirit of the desert,
Overcoming obstacles to lay a foundation
For future generations to continue,
*Serving the World on Wheels*

# Contents

Contents

## PART TWO

## Pioneering Courage Pays Off, War Years, 1940s

## PART THREE

## Putting Chiriaco Summit on the Map, 1950s–1970s

### PART FOUR

## Transitioning, 1980s, 1990s

# Contents

# Foreword

### Helen Ayer Patton,
### Granddaughter of General George S. Patton

*You can get something hearty to eat and cold drinks at the Summit. They know how to fix cars—and they care about people too*! So said the many travelers who stopped by Chiriaco Summit and then spread the word up and down what was at first a rough road but is today Interstate 10.

I do not believe it is too lofty a speculation that in a thousand years' time, Chiriaco Summit will still be known as an oasis built upon acts of kindness and courage. As this story unfolds, so colorfully told by author Mary Contini Gordon, it becomes clear that this special desert place is grounded in a humility that comprehends: *There can be no parched land where living waters flow.*

In 1942 my grandfather took command of what would eventually be a million troops in the unforgiving desert all around the Summit. They were conducting very realistic battle drills, preparing for war in the North African desert. While Grandfather expected unflinching courage in the maneuvers, he also saw the value of camaraderie; so he made the Summit café on-limits for his soldiers. There they interacted with each other and the Chiriacos. Later that year he and some troops left to confront the evil antithesis of all the good this great American family has symbolized for decades. I am glad you will have a chance to get to know them as they meld courage and camaraderie through almost a century on these pages.

*Helen Ayer Patton*

Helen Ayer Patton, the honorary chair of the General Patton Memorial Museum at Chiriaco Summit, is the granddaughter of General George S. Patton, the great liberator of Europe, and daughter of Major General George Smith Patton, Korean and Vietnam war hero. She is the founder of the Patton Alliance, organizations fostering leadership development, Veterans' causes, and a cultural awareness that helps prevent the seeds of war from taking root. On March 23, 2017 Helen and Rommel's granddaughter, Catherine, crossed the Rhine together as a symbol of peace and forgiveness. Helen is an award-winning speaker, singer, actor, producer, and director in the US and abroad, whose heartfelt speech and soaring song have graced museum events at Chiriaco Summit.

# Map of Major Locations in the Story

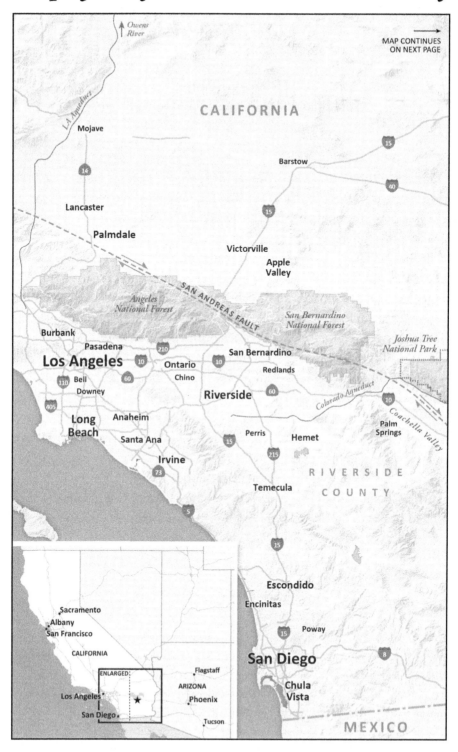

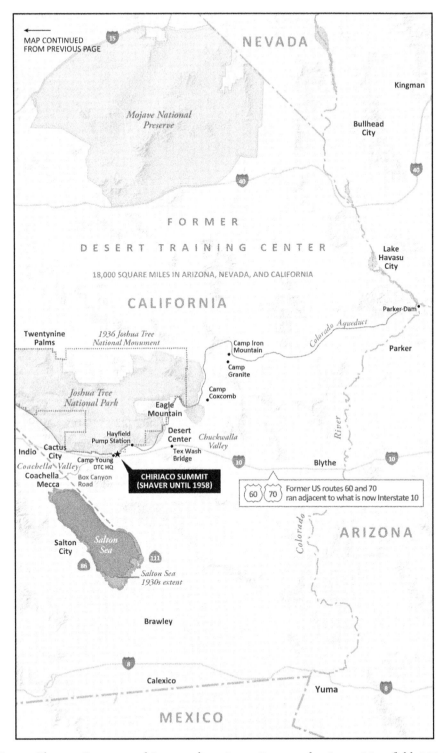

*Map 1: Chiriaco Summit and Surrounding Areas. Cartographer James Mansfield, 2016*.*

---

\*   Unless otherwise stated in Appendix D: Tables, maps are by Cartographer James Mansfield.

# *Preface*

## Why this story matters

"Wine was free, but we had to pay for water." Joe Chiriaco[†] and his thirteen siblings would hear this from their Italian immigrant father from time to time as he recounted his ocean journey to America from Italy. Little did Joe know he would start an enduring business where water was truly scarce.

*Chiriaco Summit* is a historical account of family, foresight, and fortitude fueled by a love that overcame prejudices. It chronicles the development of a small business started by a son and a daughter of immigrants (Italian Joe Chiriaco and his Norwegian wife, Ruth Bergseid); today the business is owned and operated by the second, third, and fourth generations. It examines why this business has lasted in the rural desert for decades when statistics tell us that family businesses, even in populated, popular areas, often fail after the second generation. Some do not make it past the first.

The story starts in the face of no water, no power, no phones, and rudimentary dirt roads. It is told integrating the effects of its historical backdrops on individuals and on the oasis that came to be known as Chiriaco Summit—backdrops including the building of aqueducts, highways, World War II military camps, a national park, West Coast war memorials. The story plays out through economic, social, and political upheavals and through times of prosperity. And yes, there were family dynamics, but success came in spite of them.

The 24-7 challenges are lightened with the courtship of two feisty lovers, the frolicking of children and teenagers in the desert, the youthful energy of a new generation of industrious immigrants, and the juxtaposition of some very imposing personalities, including General Patton, who interacted with Joe Chiriaco.

Chiriaco Summit, born during the Great Depression, endured and grew despite great odds. In addition to its inspiring success story, it is an example of the many small family businesses that contribute to the individual and collective well-being across the many faces of America.

---

† The family at the Summit pronounces their Chiriaco name *sher-ay-coe*. Some other family members pronounce it *Kir-ee-ah-coe*, and some others yet pronounce it *Cheer-ee-ah-coe*. The author took on the Summit family pronunciation and suggests that since this is the Summit story it be read their way—unless, of course, the reader is someone who has been pronouncing it another way for some time.

## How the story was researched and written

This book grew out of the author's involvement with Margit Chiriaco Rusche on a museum project that over time spawned a sincere association between the Chiriaco family and the author—the family wanting to preserve their unique history and the author determined to tell it as the great American success story it is.

Chiriaco Summit can be considered an ethnographic history, based on interview data and observations backed up with additional research. The author conducted interviews with people involved in the story, consulted experts of relevant history and geography, reviewed records, letters, photo collections, and scrap albums from business and family archives, consulted government documents and news media, toured the facilities that make up the Summit, hiked to the 1930s water sources, and visited the Summit many times, including living there on occasions. She did extensive fact-checking by cross-referencing interview, expert, documented, and photographic sources.

This history is real life, after all. Thus it contains vignettes based closely on recollections and documentation. The author asked those who were there to describe the character and personalities of people in the story, to recall at least the gist of any dialogue, to depict events and their settings. She also asked for the thinking behind decisions, behaviors, and actions and any influences that affected outcomes or would have a future effect.

The dialogue is from either a publication quoting or paraphrasing people in the story or an approximate reconstruction based on letters and/or interview data. In many cases, the people interviewed recounted what they believed to be the dialogue. In some cases, they provided the substance of it. Exact dates were sometimes impossible to pin down, so in those cases events are placed in a general time frame. In several cases, the vignette is a characteristic scene based on historical facts and memories from several sources and over several events. These characteristic scenes are composites and so noted. The intent is to bring the reader into the heart of what has made Chiriaco Summit an enduring success.

Many people gave input to this story and are acknowledged in the list of sources and at the end of the book, where their contributions can be most appreciated, but two must be mentioned here: Paul and Shirley Chiriaco. Paul, in his nineties, graciously provided information through interviews, e-mails, and phone calls. His poor eyesight did not deter him; he reviewed selections with a special enlarging machine. His wife, Shirley, facilitated many communications throughout the process. Paul Chiriaco is one of the youngest of Joe's brothers and the only remaining of the fourteen Chiriaco siblings. He is a World War II veteran. His recounting of people, dialogues, and events of decades ago checked out time and again with others and in documented sources. The early chapters of this book are rich because of him.

In sum, this story matters to historians and the general public because it tells of a vision realized against incredible odds. Read on to discover Chiriaco Summit, a desert oasis founded on limited water—but grounded with an entrepreneurial spirit, with a strong work ethic, and by a love that has sustained it for several generations.

# Part One

# Winding Back to the Pioneers, 2014 to the 1800s

*Foresight*

We must build together and make it such a strong bond that nothing
can tear it apart.

(Ruth Bergseid, June 9, 1934)

# 1

## *The Dream Realized, Westbound, 2014*

"While you fill up the tank, I'll run into the store."

"Just get me some cold water."

"And some extra bottles. We're in the desert, after all."

My daughter, who had come from her Canadian home to drive with me to a family event in the Los Angeles area, darted into the Food Mart while I pumped gas at this clean, new pump, installed in 2012.

We were examples of the thousands who experience this state-of-the art travel stop every week; but right off in the distance, anyone could see the way it was— undeveloped desert with no visible amenities. There was a time when any water was hard to get here, let alone cold water.

I discovered the Summit on my many trips to the Los Angeles area from Tucson, got to know the people there, and before I knew what happened, I was writing its fascinating story. I always looked around trying to understand the surroundings and how anyone could eke out a living here, starting so long ago.

We had taken Interstate 10 through the Sonoran Desert, losing sight of the large saguaro cactus with its signature arms as we drove west through the Chuckwalla Valley, and then onward to the heavily irrigated Coachella Valley, date capital of the United States, where we took the easy off-ramp to Chiriaco Summit. Dry-looking brown terrain surrounded us: the Orocopias and Chocolate Mountains to the south, the Little San Bernardinos to the northwest, and Joshua Tree National Park and the Eagle Mountains to the north. Some twenty miles back, we had passed Desert Center. Its traveler services shut down not too long ago. On our way west to the Los Angeles area, we would pass Indio, the closest big city to the Summit, where there is a choice of gas stations, but we needed gas now. Many others thought the same.

A huge eighteen-wheeler truck loaded with metal pipes moved up to the pump nearby, then a camper trailer pulled up on the other side with a couple on a Harley right behind. All six pumps were occupied on both sides, with lines waiting. It was crowded, but the access in and out was so well planned that there were no issues for anyone going through the lines, no matter how large the rigs. Some drivers filled up and moved on. Others parked and then went into the Food Mart, got an ice cream at the Foster Freeze, or went to have lunch at the coffee shop.

I could see the airstrip clearly across from the pumps. It was originally established as Shavers Summit Airfield to train pilots, bring in supplies, and serve as a medivac base for military training camps in the area during World War II. Today it is the Chiriaco Summit Airport, owned and operated by Riverside County, mostly for emergency and recreational aircraft. Often huge trucks, parked between the gas station and the chain-linked airstrip, block that sight. But not today. I could see no planes right now, although aircraft can average sixteen per day. A hundred or more might land on weekends and holidays. From time to time planes would come in for what the pilots jokingly called the $100 hamburger at the coffee shop.

With the tank filled, water bottles stowed, and snacks in hand, we hopped into the car and were on our way down Chiriaco Road to the on-ramp when we noticed an antique shop. We couldn't pass it up. It was a hot afternoon, but we braved the heat, took a few steps from our car, and roamed around for a while in the air-conditioned store. We noted an old balance scale, an old spring scale, some ornate cash registers, wooden furniture from years ago, and a purple glass collection. I bought a small white glass dish. The purple ones were not for sale. In the meantime, my daughter found the Southwest Information Center in the back of the store. She picked up a free map of Los Angeles and vicinity. Just a short walk next door was the coffee shop with a modern-day gift section, but not today. We needed to get moving to beat the Los Angeles rush hour.

As we continued down Chiriaco Road toward the on-ramp this summer day in 2014, we passed one of many dirt roads in the area, some remnants of years gone by. We noticed a sign at the turnoff to this one with an arrow pointing to free dry camping sites. We are a family of campers, but another time. We passed the General Patton Memorial Museum. We had visited it before. Right now we were anxious to get back on Interstate 10 going west leaving Chiriaco Summit, a place born out of a 1930s dream. We drove off from this desert oasis that had

*Photo 1: Chiriaco Summit, Antique Shop.*[‡]

*Photo 2: Dry camp area, mountain scenery at Chiriaco Summit.*

---

[‡] Photos add much to the historical perspectives in this story. The full credits and information for each photo are listed in Appendix D: Tables.

built up over decades based on Joe Chiriaco's 1930s commitment of *serving the world on wheels* and his corollary promise to travelers, which became his slogan: *All the necessities and some of the luxuries.* The meaning of Joe's slogan would grow and change over the years, but it would remain a promise kept no matter the challenges—and there were many right from the start.

# 2

## *Before the Dream, 1928*

The swarthy young man pushed his dark hair away from his forehead. He was beaded with sweat and spotted with sand. It was summer 1928 in the Colorado Desert. The Colorado is actually part of the Sonoran Desert, a desert that stretches from Mexico to Arizona and into California. This California part of the Sonoran or Colorado Desert, as some call it, borders the better-known Mojave. The Saguaro cactus with its picturesque arms is what people think of when they picture a southwestern desert. It populates the Sonoran, but not the Colorado section. It does not cross the Colorado River for some yet undetermined reasons, although the drier Colorado Desert weather may play a part. The lack of rainfall can be extreme in this area, causing water sources to dwindle, but water usually can be found if one knows where to look—as young Joe Chiriaco would come to find out.

### Young Joe the surveyor

Joe was out in the desert as part of a five-man surveying team. He was standing next to a surveyor's transit that looked something like a telescope. The most experienced surveyor, known as the instrument man, used it to measure vertical and horizontal angles. A tarp lay on the ground near the transit. Joe picked up a canteen and took a swig of water. A level lay on the tarp—something the instrument man would use to read elevation. Of course, they all could see with their own eyes that the terrain would make the building of the Colorado River Aqueduct, being planned by the Metropolitan Water District of Southern California, an engineering feat. It would have to go uphill at times and through tunnels. The party chief, the man in charge of this group, was holding a solar compass, more reliable at determining latitude and true north than a regular compass. Back in the 1800s, a law had been passed that this type of compass was required for surveying any public lands. Using all this equipment required an understanding of math and earth sciences, which Joe had learned without a college education. He taught himself advanced topics such as logarithms. The team had two tape men, head and rear. They were usually the less experienced on the team. Joe picked up the steel tape and held it steady a little above a dry expanse of brown with a spattering of yellow-green scrub brush in its path. Another young surveyor, some distance away, pulled the other end taut.

Joe's mind was already on the next step. He shouted impatiently to the man at the other end of the tape, "Tighter so we get it right."

"This is a godforsaken place," the other man grumbled.

The two were taking measurements to be used in deciding the route of the proposed Colorado River Aqueduct in Southern California. The land all around them looked extremely arid. Any water came from one thousand square miles of steeply sloping mountain watersheds surrounding the surveyors. The precipitation varied from year to year, but it was rarely much. In fact, from records available in 1931, ninety-four out of 157 recorded years had less-than-average rainfall. The aqueduct would come none too soon, since the population and the agriculture in the area were burgeoning. Communities, farmers, and ranchers dug more and more wells. They went from artesian wells that were drying up to pumped wells, but it became clear that they all needed another solution to the water problem, and soon. The aqueduct was a must, but it would be a challenge in this mountainous and rocky terrain. And the Great Depression was engulfing the country. But Joe smiled, remembering that he had come upon several springs on his hikes into the seemingly dry mountains.

"Ohhh, there may be some opportunity here," he responded with his Southern drawl mixed with a tinge of Italian accent. It was morning, but they were almost done for the day. Soon the sun's heat would stretch their tapes and make their work inaccurate. The two surveyors pounded stakes in the ground to mark the line they had drawn with the tape. Then they packed up their tools and hiked back to their base camp nearby. There were a number of these camps in the desert for men like Joe working as surveyors in preparation for building the massive Colorado River Aqueduct. It would run from Parker Dam, yet to be constructed on the Arizona/California border, to Los Angeles.[§]

## Vision or mirage

"Yes, opportunity here," Joe mused to himself as he surveyed the desert.

Joe Chiriaco saw what many could not see in this desolate area. He connected the dots on what was about to happen: the aqueduct, a rumored paved highway

---

§   For sources see Appendix E organized by author's research, official documents, and other printed/electronic sources by parts/appendices, in this case sources listed under PART ONE.

to be built, people who needed work, and travelers who would welcome respite as they drove through this dusty place. He saw the whole picture before it was painted. He saw it at a place on a rough dirt road, with no commercial water or power, nor any amenities to speak of. With a lot of pioneer resolve and almost no money, he started what today is a rarity, a fourth-generation small family business, an unlikely long-standing, successful venture in the dry desert along what eventually became Interstate 10. What did Joe see way back then, as the flapper era was ending and the Depression was taking hold? What has sustained his family and its business for eight decades so far? It all started with the partnership between the young Italian fellow, Joe Chiriaco, and the stalwart, beautiful Norwegian nurse he married, Ruth Bergseid, and before that with the influence of family values that came across the Atlantic with their European immigrant parents.

*Photo 3: Colorado River Aqueduct Survey Crew, 1930, Joe Chiriaco, back row, second from left.*

# 3

## Old-Country Influences,
## Late 1800s to 1927

"Wine was free, but we had to pay for water." Joe Chiriaco and his thirteen siblings would hear this from their Italian immigrant father from time to time.

### Italian roots

Joe's father, Vincent Chiriaco, was a colorful character with a sense of adventure, with pride that could get him into trouble, and with the immigrant hard-work ethic that he passed on to his American-born children. Vincent's father, Vincenzo Chiriaco, a teacher, died when the boy was but six years old. When his mother remarried about two years later, her eight-year-old son went to live with an uncle on his mother's side. This uncle was a shoemaker, and Vincent apprenticed with him. At one point in his twenties he decided to immigrate to America. Often, immigrants had contacts in America, and this was the case with Vincent. The Fago family in Italy told him to contact a sister in New York. He did, and that New York Fago sister helped him find a job at a shoe shop in the City.

Vincent arrived in New York City in 1898 at the age of twenty-eight. He had come by ship in steerage from his hometown of Nicastro in the Italian province of Calabria, not too far from Naples. He told little of his journey at sea to his American-born children, except from time to time he would say, "We had to pay for water." So early on, a good thirty years before learning to subsist in the desert, the Chiriaco family was introduced to the scarcity and value of water.

Far away and several years earlier, John Wesley Powell had warned of a need to address the water deficiencies of the American West.

When all the rivers are used, when all the creeks in the ravines, when all the brooks, when all the springs are used, when all the canyon waters are taken up, when all the artesian waters are taken up, when all the wells are sunk or dug that can be dug in all this region, there is still not sufficient water to irrigate all this arid region. Powell, J. W. *A Report on the Arid Region of the United States with a More Detailed Account of the Lands of Utah*, 1878.

He would not be heeded until many years later, in the time frame when Vincent's son Joe became part of the surveying team to plan the Colorado River Aqueduct. At the turn of the century, other parts of the country did heed the call for water. For example, by 1916, New York City imported water from the Catskills system, but that was not yet the case when Vincent arrived in 1898.

Like many big cities in America, New York City was a melting pot with immigrants from all over Europe. Many of them maintained pride in their country of origin, and Vincent was no exception. After all, Italy was the origin of much art and science: Galileo, Michelangelo, Leonardo da Vinci, and more recently Marconi, who in 1897 had sent the world's first-ever wireless communication over open sea.

For a long period of time, perhaps weeks, an Irishman, who the family lore describes as a drunk, stood outside the shoe shop cussing at the Italian shoemakers. It is possible he was calling them derogatory names and making fun of their homeland. Whatever he was saying, it was upsetting to Vincent. The annoyance was building up. One day he started cussing directly at Vincent. In quick reaction, Vincent picked up a tool and hit the Irishman in the forehead. After that the story gets hazy, but this we know: the owner of the shop told Vincent, "Get out of here. This will not be good for you."

## Setting up shop, starting an American family

Vincent had been in New York only about two years, and now he was on the run. He left the shop in a hurry without knowing how seriously he had injured the Irishman. The Fago sister who had helped him find a job in New York helped him again; she told Vincent to be on his way quickly to seek out her brother in Alabama. Almost immediately after the incident, Vincent was on a ship again, this time to Norfolk, Virginia, where he caught a train to Florence, Alabama. There he connected with Frederico Fago, an immigrant who called himself Fred. Fred had bought land in and around Florence. He owned an umbrella shop and a junkyard that someone ran for him. The junkyard was full of iron scraps, things like paper clips, cans, and whatever else he could garner—a predecessor to a similar yard thirty years hence in the desert.

Fred set up Vincent in a shoe shop across the Tennessee River in Sheffield. But Vincent came back and forth across the river. He met Fred's young daughter, Petranella, who had arrived with her family from Italy in 1886 when she was six years old and was now called Paulina. She had been born in Casa Bianca, which was near Nicastro and Naples. It is likely that these two Italian immigrants, born not too far apart, sat on the riverbanks, walked the streets of Florence, and found themselves falling in love. At the age of sixteen, Paulina married thirty-two-year-old Vincent. Sometime after the wedding, Fred brought Vincent back over the river from Sheffield. He moved the umbrella shop to the back of the building and gave his son-in-law the front for his shoe shop. Later, Vincent built a house on the same street as Fred and his immigrant wife, Rosa Gennacarro. Then Vincent also built a small framed structure alongside his house. To add to his income, he rented the front of the addition to a man who put a hot dog stand there and moved his shoe shop to the back. Like many immigrants, he worked hard enough to become independent and with that to take on more and more responsibility.

And what responsibility! Vincent and Paulina raised fourteen children in Florence, seven boys and seven girls. After Joe, her second child, was born, Paulina got phlebitis (then known as milk leg, thought to be linked to breast-feeding, thus the name). The doctor told her having more children could be fatal, but she had twelve more. The children would come into the shoe shop on a regular basis to watch their father or to listen in on conversations with customers. It was hot and busy but also fun. The shop had windows and doors so did not feel closed in. It smelled of leather but was never dirty. Once in a while, Papa would make things for the children out of scrap leather. There he'd sit winding a leather strip around a bobbin he got from Paulina's sewing discards. He had been making leather yo-yos for years. He'd say to his children, "I've been making these before they were sold at Woolworth's. This should be my invention." The children agreed with him, never mind that the yo-yo had actually been invented in Ancient Greece.

Joe saw how his father made do with little. He did most of the work by hand. He nailed or sewed the soles. Joe and the other children would watch him poke holes with an awl and then sew with a threaded needle, hole after hole, shoe after shoe, with steadiness, exactness, and perseverance. Vincent never owned or used a sewing machine. Eventually, though, he did buy one machine—a sander to buff shoes. Factories had taken over making new shoes, so 90 percent of his business was repair, but he was very capable of making shoes from scratch, including shoes for special circumstances. Joe wrote a memoir in his adult years remembering that his dad had made boots for an airman whose feet were arched sideways as well as a shoe for an elephant that needed it for an act in the circus that came to town.

*Photo 4: Vincent Chiriaco's shoemaking tools brought from Italy in 1898.*

Vincent could speak enough English to get by in the shop, but he never learned to speak it fluently. Joe heard Italian and English in the shop and at home, and like the four oldest children became bilingual, which would be important for Joe in the desert years later. As Joe got older, he read newspapers to his father in English and listened to his dad read Italian newspapers to him. Saturday nights, his dad would be finishing up shoe repairs for farmers who came to pay him with butter, eggs, chickens, rabbits, and other wild game. Interesting people stopped in. This was the segregated South, but Vincent's shop was open to all. One regular was an educated black man who came to discuss Italy and other parts of Europe, the arts, and music, which Vincent and this man both loved. Joe and the other children listened in.

Paulina had more finesse than Vincent. The Fago family had sent her to a Catholic school. She spoke English well and was the lady of the home. There were many big families in the area, but most were not as big as the Chiriacos'. With over a dozen children and Vincent in the shop for long hours, she needed and had excellent help in the home. The oldest sisters helped, but in addition, Paulina had black servants. One of these was Jessie Thomas, a middle-aged midwife and nurse who assisted at all fourteen births and helped bathe, feed, and supervise the children. The children called her Aunt Jessie, which was a Southern term of respect. Jessie had had some fame. Before she worked for Paulina, she had been Helen Keller's nurse at Ivy Green, the Keller home in Tuscumbia across the river. Jessie was a teenager at the time and Helen just a baby, before she lost her sight. Sometime after Jessie retired, the University of North Alabama, then Florence State Teachers College, invited Helen Keller to a ceremony in her honor. The college also made sure Jessie was there. Helen Keller brought Jessie on stage to recognize her for her loving care of so many children over so many years.

## Discipline and kindness

Paulina handled some of the discipline of the children. As was done more readily and with more acceptance in those days than today, some sort of corporal punishment was administered if any of the fourteen misbehaved. Paulina would get a switch from the peach tree in the backyard and the children would feel it on their legs. Sometimes she would say, "Wait until Papa gets home." She said that in the tradition of the time, that the father was the ultimate disciplinarian in the family. But in reality Vincent was rarely angry at the children, so his punishment was light in comparison. In some cases, she would put the children in a room to think about their behavior. They would think for a while and then escape out a small window. She said nothing about the escape, just looked for improved behavior. She encouraged the children to be polite, kind people, which the children became to varying degrees. Paul, her twelfth child, was one who took her lessons to heart, starting as a youngster.

Many years after Aunt Jessie had worked for the Chiriaco family, about 1938, Paulina asked Paul, who was about fourteen years old at the time, to take some food to her dear servant, who was then between ninety and one hundred years old. Jessie Thomas was probably born into slavery, so it was not surprising that her exact age was unknown. It was the usual hot, humid Alabama summer, but Aunt Jessie's house was cool. She had all the shades closed. Paul did not just drop off the food and scamper away. He stayed to talk with Jessie. He knew he was not just doing an errand.

"I saw your husband yesterday," he said, trying to make conversation.

Jessie just smiled politely. When Paul did not go on, she explained, "Master Paul, you must have seen my son on one of his deliveries."

"Oh, Uncle Jim?" Jessie's son, Jim, had a business using a horse and cart to deliver goods to people in town.

"Yes, Uncle Jim." Jessie said kindly. "My husband died years ago."

Paul smiled at Aunt Jessie's sharpness.

Mother Paulina's lessons and Father Vincent's hard-work ethic would both matter to making the inhospitable desert hospitable for others so many years in the future—the desert that Joe would make home and where some of his siblings would come to visit and to work. His brother Paul would be one of those.

*Photo 5: Joe Chiriaco as a young man in Alabama, c. 1926.*

Paul was nineteen years younger than Joe and not yet born when Joe graduated from high school in 1923 and went to work for the Wetumpka Water District near home in the cotton town of Wetumpka, Alabama. Joe learned some surveying on this job. In truth, Joe was self-taught on many topics, especially those having to do with math and engineering. He was starting to hear the call first to enter the seminary and then more loudly, "Go West, young man, go West."

## Football out West

At the shoe shop, sports was a major topic of conversation. Alabama did not have a baseball team, so the talk was all about football. Joe had played football for the Coffee High School. (The school was named after a confederate officer, Captain Alexander Donelson Coffee. He and his wife donated land for parks in Florence.) Southern football teams had never been invited to any bowl game until 1926, and then Alabama played in the game that some say changed the South.

Conversations of this sort were going on in Vincent's shoe shop and all over Alabama:

"Did you hear, we won! The Washington Huskies lost."

"In Pasadena at the Rose Bowl?"

"Yes, us, University of Alabama, our Crimson Tide team."

"We scored all our twenty points in the third quarter. We won!"

"Now let 'em look down on the South!"

Joe was in on these conversations at the shoe shop, with his buddies from school, and out in the surveying field. As 1926 came to an end, it was clear that Alabama was going to play in the Rose Bowl again.

With the sense of adventure that brought his dad across the Atlantic, Joe said to Bud Collier, one of his surveying buddies, "Hey what do you think about going out to California for the game? We'll have to hitchhike."

So off they went, thumbs up. At one point they got on a vegetable truck. The driver picked up another hitchhiker, who sat in the back. He had won an Olympic gold medal for swimming and was on his way to Hollywood to find his fortune there. All three would make it: Joe in the desert, where his name would be on an interstate off-ramp sign, Bud on political posters, and Johnny Weissmuller, whose name would light up many a movie theater marquis when he played Tarzan. They had all headed the call, "Go West young man."

Joe and Bud arrived in time for the 1927 Rose Bowl game. This time the Crimson Tide played against Stanford, the champions of the Pacific Coast Conference. The game ended in a tie, the last Rose Bowl game to end that way.

Bud came from a family of some money, but not Joe. Bud decided to go to college in California. Joe was feeling a sense of independence. He felt attached to his Alabama family and would remain so, but he wanted to stand on his own. He decided to stay in California. For a short while, he worked at a restaurant in Pasadena, washing dishes, until he heard of a surveying job. Since he had learned some surveying working for the Wetumpka Water District, it made sense that the Los Angeles Department of Water and Power (LADWP) hired him. At the end of 1928 the California Legislature established the Metropolitan Water District of Southern California (MWD) to build and operate the Colorado River Aqueduct. With the LADWP experience, Joe was ready when MWD started looking for more surveyors. Soon he found himself working in the Coachella Valley at a parched, barren spot, only a few hours' drive to the already water-challenged, populated greater Los Angeles area and not too far from Indio or Palm Springs. The huge Colorado River Aqueduct Project was getting underway. MWD was leading the charge. Joe never went back to live in Alabama. Neither did Bud.

# 4

# *Dust to Dream, 1900–1932*

Other than the unreliable rainfall, the earliest sources of water were pushed by water wheels out from open irrigation ditches called *zanjas*, which settlers had dug at the banks of the Los Angeles River in the late 1700s. These ditches brought water to buildings for domestic and business uses and to fields to irrigate crops. By 1900 that ditch water was only trickling in some Los Angeles areas. So settlers began digging wells, which sufficed for some time. And then at the turn of the century the Southern Pacific and Santa Fe Railroads, oil discoveries, the spread of citrus groves, and the lure of the wonderful Southern California climate combined to create a population and business boom. These booms also cried for better roads. Few paved roads existed where Joe was working in the early 1930s. They were dirt, gravel, or wooden-plank roads. Something more needed to be done on both fronts.

## The importance of water

By 1900, a group of influential men looked north to the Owens River Valley, where they started buying land and water rights. Finally, in 1907, voters approved the Los Angeles Aqueduct, which was to bring water south from the Owens Valley. William Mulholland, an Irish immigrant who at first dug the zanjas to carry water, at age thirty-one became superintendent of what was then the Los Angeles Water Agency. Mulholland was a self-taught engineer. He took charge of building the controversial Los Angeles Aqueduct, started in 1908 and completed in 1913. It brought water from the Owens River two hundred miles north of Los Angeles. This newly imported water inspired another land rush in the Los Angeles area and a belief by some that selfish capitalists had stolen the water from the Owens Valley farmers. Stolen or not, the population grew again. Again the water would not suffice.

In the 1920s, while he was still in Alabama, a number of events occurred that set the stage for Joe Chiriaco to become a surveyor in the Coachella Valley. A quick summary of these events follows:

In 1922, seven states signed the Colorado River Compact. It provided for division of Colorado River water among these seven. Arizona declined to ratify the compact, and so the compact stood as ineffective for several years but raised consciousness about water issues.

In 1923, a number of prominent citizens became concerned that the available water would not be enough to sustain continued growth in the desert areas. They met in Fullerton, California, where they formed the Boulder Dam Association, which was actually made up of two hundred civic organizations in Southern California, Arizona, and Nevada. The objective was to advance the construction of Boulder Dam, the All-American Canal, and other water initiatives. Perhaps, critically, the Association carried out a public education campaign about water needs.

In 1924, another group of citizens led by Pasadena Mayor Hiram W. Wadsworth organized the Colorado River Aqueduct Association, made up of representatives from thirty-seven communities in the region. This association sought to organize metropolitan water districts. About the same time, the Los Angeles Board of Public Service authorized William Mulholland, who was by then the chief engineer of the Los Angeles Bureau of Water Works and Supply, to start surveying to determine feasibility of another aqueduct.

By 1925, he and others started large-scale mapping of the desert region for an aqueduct that would bring water from the Colorado River. Not only had the Los Angeles Aqueduct started to become inadequate, the artesian wells settlers had dug back in 1900 and those they had replaced with pumped wells were drying up.

In 1927, the year that Alabama and Stanford tied the Rose Bowl game, the California Senate passed a bill to establish water districts.

In 1928, prior to the passage of the Boulder Canyon Act later that year, Colorado River Aqueduct proponents transported a huge relief map, made of 250,000 pieces of flat board showing 50,000 square miles surrounding the proposed aqueduct route, to congressional hearings in Washington, DC. The map displayed the rugged terrain, including elevations on the aqueduct route. Twelve expert draftsmen had created the map. Since it weighed five tons and was the size of a small room, they designed it to come apart like a jigsaw puzzle. When the Boulder Canyon Act passed later that year, it paved the way for what would shortly become the Metropolitan Water District of Southern California (MWD). The map helped to keep surveyors, construction workers, and engineers on target as they worked on the aqueduct through a very challenging landscape. It would play a role for Joe and his family some sixty years later.

On December 6, 1928, the Metropolitan Water District of Southern California (MWD) was incorporated with eleven member municipalities all on the Pacific Slope: seven in Los Angeles County, two in Orange County, and two in San Bernardino County. None were in Riverside County, which was not on the slope. The slope would be an issue later affecting Joe Chiriaco.

In 1939, MWD published *The Metropolitan Water District, History and First Annual Report*, which presented many of the events and statistics summarized above. Much later, they published a brochure about the Big Map.

Growth in the semi-arid desert region was overtaxing the water resources. MWD was poised to step into action, but it needed employees who could survey the arid desert.

## Aqueduct workers

Joe and Bud were elated after the Rose Bowl, but then reality set in. Bud enrolled at Occidental College. Joe felt he needed a job. While washing dishes at the restaurant in Pasadena, he happened to hear of surveying work with the City of Los Angeles. He worked as a surveyor for the city until the newly established Metropolitan Water District of Southern California needed surveyors for a planned aqueduct. *I have some experience*, he thought, and applied.

The surveying effort was crucial and difficult. The aqueduct would be traversing mountains and inhospitable desert. Joe joined a team surveying in the Coachella Valley, working near and at what would be the Hayfield Reservoir and Pump Lift and close to a place known as Shaver Summit, where MWD also put their reservoir #4 for construction purposes. John B. Shaver had been a Riverside County supervisor in the early 1900s. Shaver's Well, Shaver's Valley, and then Shaver Summit (with no 's) were named after him. The Summit was and is 1,740 feet in elevation, the high point on the road between Blythe and Indio. Of course, the surrounding mountains were higher. For example, the Orocopias reach an elevation of 3,815 feet. Surrounding ranges are higher yet.

Surveyors were paid $90.00 a month (about $4.50 a day), which was much more than other workers, who got about $0.33 an hour, or about $2.64 a day. Of course, these figures are not accurate, because there was no such thing as a regular schedule of eight-hour days for the surveyors and probably not for other workers either. Many of the surveyors traveled on foot or horseback with their bedding and supplies. They made their way on dirt trails, the occasional plank road, or, if near a river, on boats. Sometimes they led horses or mules loaded with food and equipment. Their backpacks weighed about thirty pounds, not counting the surveying equipment they carried.

At one point, Joe made a comment reported later in the March 1998 *Tattler*, a local newsletter: "When we got Model A wagons, we were in the clover. We would just pack them with food and water and take off. You'd be surprised where we went in those cars. The desert took its toll and vehicle repairs were made on the spot."

The surveyors stayed at or near camps established by the MWD wherever they were working. Some camps were better than others. The Coachella Camp had access to a camp hospital, library, and recreation hall. If Joe ever stayed there, it would have been in a two-story dormitory with no air-conditioning. He, like others, might have chosen to sleep on the porch at night. The Coachella Camp was one of the better ones. Others were pup-tent camps with little amenities, such as the Hayfield Pump Camp where Joe often stayed. Sometimes there were no tents, so he and the others slept on the ground, always being wary of rattlesnakes. To sleep in the heat, sometimes they had to drench blankets in water. Usually, they had a cook, such as he was. Joe later told his much younger brother, Paul, about reactions to the grub, recalling a conversation like this one.

*Photo 6: Joe in cap with unidentified surveyors, 1929 Ford Woody Wagon used by aqueduct surveyors, c. 1930.*

"Come and get it."

The surveyors looked at each other and hesitated.

"Man, the food is always so salty," one grumbled under his breath. Others agreed with him, but they were hungry so moved over to the chuck wagon. The cook filled their plates with some meat. They gobbled it down.

"Looks like I made another good meal," the cook praised himself.

"Oh, yes. Was great. Just the way we like it. We are lucky to have you as a cook." A bunch of responses came back all together. The group filled water cups and walked away from the chuck wagon.

"Lucky?" One of the surveyors asked. "How could anyone say that?"

"I meant we are lucky to have a cook." The group went back to work, downing water to quench their thirst, exacerbated by the salt, but they had full stomachs.

MWD hired thousands of workers to plan and then build the Colorado River Aqueduct. Many of the workers had to be trained to use special equipment. Joe probably had a head start because of his Alabama job.

Joe's buddies would notice from time to time that he seemed uncomfortable. One day, one of the surveyors asked, "Are you having trouble breathing?"

"A little. I have a deviated septum."

"Huh?"

"The wall between my two nostrils is slanted." He lifted his head and pointed to the separation between his two nostrils. "So one of my nostrils is smaller than the other. The dryness here makes it worse."

Next day, Joe was out in the field again. Even though it was midmorning, heat waves rising off the desert floor distorted the visibility between the stakes they had pounded into the dry desert earlier. The steel tapes his team were using expanded due to the heat, making their measurements invalid. They packed up to come back at night, when it would be cooler.

Joe's nose condition got worse and worse. Eventually, he ended up with a painful sinus infection while at work. The visiting doctor at one of the camp hospitals decided Joe needed an operation to correct the situation and sent him to a hospital near Indio, where MWD had an arrangement with a Dr. Russell Gray to care for workers. He checked in sometime in early 1932.

Joe woke up after surgery, groggy, and uncomfortable. There was a dressing on his nose. Someone had propped his head up on several pillows. He could see doctors and nurses moving back and forth in the hallway.

*Oh, that is the most beautiful sight I have ever seen*, he thought to himself as he watched a very fair-skinned, blue-eyed, blonde nurse carry a dark black baby down the hallway. She was smiling at the child. *Who is that nurse; where did she come from?* Joe wondered as he fell back asleep.

She came from Minnesota to North Dakota to the Los Angeles and San Diego areas before coming to the Coachella Valley.

## Young Ruth, the nurse with Norwegian roots

The passenger train pulled up at the station in Indio. The train was not air conditioned, so people were glad to get off. They quickly found it was not much better outside. It was 120 degrees that summer day in 1931. The blonde, blue-eyed, fair young woman looked around. She was wearing a black serge wool suit.

"You look like a boiled lobster," a polished but casually dressed gentleman smiled as he walked toward her. "You must be Ruth Bergseid, our new nurse."

"I am; how do you know?"

"Only someone from North Dakota would come here dressed like that."

"Or from Los Angeles. It's cooler there," said Ruth.

"I am Dr. Morris." He reached out to take Ruth's carrying case.

"Let me take your things. Take off that jacket. We need to go inside to claim the rest of your baggage. It's warm there too. I am Dr. Gray's assistant. We are both looking forward to working with you."

Ruth had received her nursing degree in 1927 from the Training School for Nurses at Grafton Deaconess Hospital in North Dakota, and her Registered Nurse Certification (RN) in 1928. She was anxious to see the country if not the world, like her four older brothers, who had moved to Southern California. So, soon after she got her RN, she set out for Los Angeles with her good friend Irene Curran and some other nurses from school to take jobs with a nursing exchange. She set up a well-decorated apartment in the city. From there she went wherever the exchange sent her as a private-duty nurse. She considered herself a bit plump and was constantly trying to lose weight. She knew that the more attractive nurses got the better positions. She worked at homes in Ventura, not too far from Santa Barbara and in La Jolla. She was sent to places like Scripps Hospital in San Diego. By sometime in 1931, the exchange had sent her to the Coachella Valley Hospital near Indio. Ruth had been trained as a surgical nurse and was putting that training to use there assisting Drs. Russell Gray and B. Gene Morris in the operating room. On the floor she tended to all, including many babies.

Male patients tended to become infatuated with her. Some wrote poems. Ruth saved one entitled "My Nurse" by O. H. Judging by where it was placed in a family album, it was probably written in 1929 or the very early 1930s.

*Photo 7: Nurse Ruth with baby, c. 1931.*

When I was sick and lay a-bed, I had the nicest nurse.
Her joyous laughter and gladness, made all my gloom disperse.
She was short and fat and jolly, with merry twinkling eyes!
Her ways were golden and sunny, as the sun that shines in the skies.
I love my little chubby nurse, who was so kind to me,
And if she ever needs my care, I true to her shall be.

Ruth was not actually fat, but not skin and bones. She was an attractive, physically fit farm girl. Her gracious but strong personality and demeanor were a part of that Midwestern farm background.

Joe was waking up. With his eyes still shut, he started to wipe, almost swipe, at his nose.

"No, no, you mustn't do that. Here let me wipe it." Ruth gently took care of the post-op discharge. She looked at the chart she was carrying and then asked, "So Joe, how are you feeling?"

"Like someone punched me in the nose, of course." He looked up and recognized the nurse from the hall. He looked at the nametag she was wearing. "Miss Bergseid, right?"

"Yes, now you rest, Joe. I will be back soon."

*Photo 8: Ruth at the Bergseid Farm in Rollag, Minnesota, on a trip back home,*
*young cousins in the background, c. 1931.*

But Joe kept on, "Am I OK?"

"The doctor will be here soon, and he will answer all your questions." Ruth was ultra-professional, and although she would have liked to tell Joe that the operation had been successful, she knew that was not her place. But she was curious about him. She noticed his strong-looking, tanned arms.

"No hard work for you for a while. You look like you work in the sun."

Painfully but determined, he turned his head so he could see the pretty nurse better. Dark brown curls showed at the nape of his neck. "Well, that and I am the son of Italian immigrants. Where does your family come from?"

Over the next few days, Ruth and Joe started to find out that they had some things in common, especially being first-generation Americans from large families.

"My mother came from the Numedal Valley in Norway."

"What was her name?"

"Margit Lien. Her whole family came to Rollag, Minnesota, when she was about five years old. I was born in Rollag too. I am number eleven of twelve.

"Well, I am the second of fourteen. My father was a shoemaker," Joe said, telling a little of his family story.

*Photo 9: Bergseid Children: Back row, L to R: Christian, Joe, Thomas, Selma, Harry; Front row: Ruth, George, Gerhard, Ted c. 1912. (Three children died in early childhood.)*

*Photo 10: Chiriaco children. Back Row, L to R: 5. Lucille, 1. Rose, 2. Joe, 4. Ella, 3. Stella; Middle row: Mother Paulina, 11. Mary, 7. Cecilia, Father Vincent, 6. Golden, 8. Devio; Front row: 9. Vincent, 10. Arthur, Florence, Alabama, 1922. Not born yet: Paul, John, Charles.*

*Photo 11: Youngest three Chiriaco Children—12. Paul, 14. John, 13. Charles., c. 1939.*

## Love sprouts in the desert

Back in the field, Joe could not stop thinking about the striking blonde nurse. When he returned to the hospital for a post-op checkup, there she was with Dr. Gray in the examining room. Right after the appointment, he said to her, "I'll pick you up at eight. Be ready."

By this time, Joe had saved enough for an old vehicle. Ruth was ready when he picked her up in his slightly used Ford Model A. They went to dinner, which started their courtship. At first they went on group dates with friends to picnics and parties. Many of these friends were from the nearby desert city of Mecca, with its vineyards, train stop, and lots of activity for those days. Eventually they went on drives by themselves. Even though their destinations were near by today's standards, their excursions were exacerbated by routes through mountain terrain, dirt or gravel roads in the rural desert, and roughly paved roads closer to cities. There was plenty of time to talk on these outings.

Sometimes they would drive to the Salton Sea, actually the largest lake in California. The Sea formed in the desert when the Colorado River overflowed in 1905 into the Salton Sink, 227 feet below sea level. The Sea was the place to go. There they would meet their friends from Mecca.

They'd sit on the pier and eat hamburgers and ice cream from the concession stands. John Hilton, the famous desert painter, would come there to show his art, paint, and play his guitar. They would look at his paintings and listen to him sing. In this very saline water they went swimming, boating, and fishing. Sometimes they just sat on the beach enjoying the view and each other.

*Photo 12: Salton Sea, view from Lost Palm Oasis Trail in Joshua Tree National Park.*

They took car trips to nearby big cities. Joe often liked to stop in Redlands on the way to Los Angeles. "There's a good ice cream shop here. Let's get some cones," he would suggest.

Sometimes Ruth would remind Joe, "Let's stop in Banning at that little place that makes those wonderful toasted cheese sandwiches."

She would ask him, "You like driving, don't you, Joe?"

"I like cars. I raced Model T's in Alabama, but I never owned a car there."

As they got to know each other better, some conversations tuned to family history.

"Your dad came from Norway, didn't he? Herbrand Bergseid, right?"

"Yes. Father came in the 1880s, when he was in his twenties."

"Why did he come?" Joe asked.

"He was not going to inherit the family farm—he was the ninth child—so he set out for America. He worked as a farm hand and saved to buy 160 acres in Rollag, Minnesota. I grew up there on that farm."

"What did he plant?"

"Corn, wheat, and soybeans. He ran some cattle." Then Ruth smiled. "But it was dangerous."

"Dangerous?"

Ruth laughed. "Prairie fires. Big ones. One of those fires brought my parents together. My mother married my father after he saved her from what looked like an inferno. She was standing in the middle of a grassy plain when he rushed in to scoop her up."

"My parents met here too—but in Alabama," Joe said. "Nothing dramatic like that. My mom was the boss's daughter."

Whenever they could get together, they took drives or just talked. In a short while they were comfortable enough with each other to share some of their more private stories.

"The holidays are coming. I would like to visit my brothers in Ventura," Ruth said. Her brother Harry was working for the post office in Bell, near Indio, but three other brothers were about a two-hour drive away.

"Oh, I thought we could be together." Joe sounded disappointed.

"That would be nice. Father did not think much of holidays, so the family did not have celebrations, not even birthdays."

"Christmas?"

"No, but this was not a religious issue for Father; he just did not like festivities, but I love them."

"That must have been hard," Joe said.

"My father always thought he was a step above the Lien family. Mother worked all the time. She took care of almost everything in the home. Father worked the farm."

"My father was sometimes difficult too. He had a short temper. I have a little of that," he admitted and then quickly changed the subject. "How did your brothers get to California? I hitchhiked out with a buddy."

"Well, when the Liens and Bergseids came to Minnesota, they saw it as the Promised Land, but as some of my brothers became adults they began to think of California as the place to be. Father was very hard on the boys, so I guess they wanted to get away. But also three of my brothers were soldiers in the Great War." She was referring to World War I, not yet so named.

She continued, "On their army travels they went through Ventura, California. It's a beautiful coastal town, you know. After the war, they came back. They are doing well there."

"Doing what?"

"Building residential and commercial properties. My brother Tom invested in oil. He helped the others get out here. He paid for my nursing school. Father's farm did not make a lot of money. He tinkered and invented things, but never registered a patent. He liked to sit and read. Well, maybe he was more of a dreamer than a farmer. I came here partly because of my brothers. I can't wait to introduce you."

"By the way, when's your birthday?" Joe asked. The young couple found that they were both born in 1905.

"March eighteenth," Ruth answered.

Joe laughed. "You're older. Mine is September twentieth."

Soon, Joe and Ruth were talking about marriage and a life together. Joe shared a plan he was making. "You know that flat spot in front of the gravel road at Shaver Summit?"

"Yes, there's nothing there but a watering trough for some sheep—and that reservoir that MWD put nearby for aqueduct work."

"Water! That matters. But, well, that gravel road—soon it will be paved. I'd like to buy that flat area, spruce it up, and start a stop for travelers."

"That would be fun, but how do you know the road will be paved?"

Joe smiled. "One of the benefits of working for MWD. You hear things. I heard talk about the road. From what I am hearing, it is going to happen, and soon. It will be a highway replacing the road that goes by Shaver Summit. In the meantime, a travel stop can serve the construction crews that are building the aqueduct."

"You mean the people who live in those tar-paper shacks."

"Yes, there are about seventy-five of those homes. Those families are a captive audience."

"That little store is already serving the workers, and they have a gas pump," Ruth said.

"You mean Utopia. There isn't much at that stop. We could put in a real café with two gasoline pumps. Besides, our place would be easier to get to from the highway."

"But Joe, we need some money." Joe was silent. He had been putting money away, but not enough.

"I have been saving," Ruth offered. "I will be your first investor. Oh, and my brothers can help build our café."

By April of 1932 they were writing letters to each other, hating to be apart. Ruth often wrote during breaks on her night shift at the hospital. Some of her letters documented her attitudes toward work, which would never wane.

> I really think a person should get up early in place of sleeping until the
> sun is up. (April 24, 1932)

By the end of April 1932, Joe and Ruth were engaged, but they had one issue to resolve before they could get married. Joe was Catholic. Ruth was Lutheran. They both thought they should be the same religion. Ruth went to a Catholic Mass and then told Joe, "This service is so much like my Lutheran Service. I will become a Catholic."

Nevertheless, the marriage needed to wait. By October of 1932, Ruth was living at her brother Harry's home, helping run the household and caring for his three children when she was not working. His wife, Delia, was terminally ill. When Harry first came to California it was to work on the railroad—on the mail train that went from the California City of Albany, north of Oakland, to Los Angeles. When he heard about a job in the City of Bell near Indio, he applied, and so now as his wife was declining he was settled in one place, but still needed help with the children.

> I'm getting wonderful training in washing clothes and taking care of three rascals. Gee I am so weary that I can't even think—come sit next to me and I'll just put my head on your shoulder for a while. (Ruth to Joe, October 7, 1932)

> Honey, you shouldn't tell me of the moon—not long and will [sic] see it together. I'll never forget the big moon over the Salton Sea the night we had the bon fire. Do you remember? (Ruth to Joe, October 26, 1932)

In addition to helping her brother, Ruth continued working at the hospital.

> We are dreadfully busy at the hospital ... I'm in high gear all the time but I do enjoy it. (Ruth to Joe, December 15, 1932)

Joe was working hard, saving money, and thinking more and more about their dream of a business at the Summit, even though the nation was feeling the effects of the Great Depression.

# 5

# *The Partnership at Shaver Summit, 1933*

*Stocks Soar. Low Market Scare. Optimistic on Recovery. Stocks Collapse.* Headlines went back and forth in 1929, but then on October 29, 1929, the word *crash* started dominating newspapers, radio broadcasts, and conversations. By March of 1930, the Great Depression had taken hold. By 1932, over 20 percent of the workforce was unemployed. Joe Chiriaco was not one of them. Neither was Ruth, who continued as a nurse at Coachella Valley Hospital. Joe was still working on surveys that would define the route for the Colorado River Aqueduct. Out in the field, he heard plans to build more camps in the area for thousands more aqueduct workers. He heard that President Roosevelt was planning the Civilian Conservation Corps (CCC) to employ young men who were out of work. Some CCC camps would be in nearby areas. He also learned more about the proposed Highway 60. It would be a paved, two-lane highway from Phoenix to Los Angeles. And it would go south of the existing gravel road, closer to Shaver Summit.

## Opportunity in the shambles

The Cram family owned ranch land in the area Joe was surveying, grazing sheep right after the rainy season when there was fresh vegetation. Joe and Ruth had driven and hiked on the Cram property to natural springs in Lost Palms Oasis, to a cave-like tunnel fed by yet another spring in the same canyon closer to the Summit, and yet another in neighboring Munsen Canyon, close to the juncture of the two canyons. Joe and Ruth had drunk from these clear, clean spring waters many times. He knew that the water from these locations was already piped to Cram's two troughs on the desert floor for his sheep. In fact, he had seen still another spring. The Crams had watered their sheep at springs as they drove them to the railhead in Mecca. Joe started discussing his plan in more earnest with Ruth.

*Map 2: US 60-70, Sunkist Trail and I-10 (Stops are similar to those on the 1930 Sunkist Trail Map available through Sharlot Hall Museum, Map 39). US 60, replaced in Western Arizona and California by I-10, is not to be confused with CA 60.*

"They already started the paved road that will come right by Shaver Summit. It'll be a good stop on a good highway. I know there is nothing there now, but we can make it a place people can't pass up."

"That old dirt and gravel road has been there since the 1800s." Ruth was learning the history of the area. "And it's the one we take to Mecca and to the Salton Sea."

"We take part of it—from Mecca through Box Canyon to Shaver Summit ..."

"... or going to Desert Center and on to Blythe," Ruth said, finishing Joe's sentence.

They were talking about a section of what came to be known as the Sunkist Trail through so much of the irrigated agricultural land in the desert.

"That road'll still be there." Joe smiled, thinking about the fun they had driving around exploring the desert together. Then he said in a tone that was all business, "This new US 60 is coming from Phoenix, passing right in front of—not behind—where I plan to put gasoline pumps, and then it goes on to L.A.—and it will be paved."

In fact, the Sunkist Trail and the proposed US 60 would have the same exits.

"What about Desert Center?" Ruth asked. "They have been serving travelers for a long time, and they are not too far from us." Desert Center was about twenty miles east of Shaver on the same route. US 60 would go right through it.

"Yes, but construction camps for the aqueduct will be everywhere around Shaver Summit, with thousands of workers. And then there are always the miners and prospectors."

"But only a few of those. It's the workers and tourists we want. "

Joe heard the "we."

Ruth added, "Joe, you'll be competition for places like Desert Center; they have a head start on you." She was realistic but not daunted.

Ruth was right; Desert Center and the Summit would be competitors. Years before Joe showed up, back in the mid-1920s, Steve Ragsdale and his wife, Lydia, purchased the property about twenty miles east of the Summit. They named it Desert Center. They settled there with their four young children and quickly established a small café and gas station. They served aqueduct workers and travelers, some of the same customer base that Joe planned to attract. They were both looking forward to serving CCC workers at camps yet to be set up in the area. The Ragsdales also owned Utopia, the stop near Shaver Summit with one gas pump and a small store that already served aqueduct workers. They would come to own additional properties in the area. Mr. Ragsdale had at one time been an itinerant preacher. He banned any alcoholic drink on all his properties, and that included beer.

Joe was not planning to ban alcohol—and certainly not beer. That would come to matter, especially by the 1940s.

"We can catch up. Remember, I am ready to invest," Ruth said confidently.

During the week, Joe talked with his surveyor buddies. Some of this talk made him think more seriously about starting a traveler's oasis.

"Joe, we'll need to start surveying for those tunnels they're planning to come through these mountains around us."

The mountainous terrain along the 242 miles between Parker Dam and the Cajalco Reservoir near Los Angeles required twenty-nine tunnels, or 92.1 miles of tunnel, which was 38 percent of the mileage between the two points. Early in 1933, MWD opened eight camps in the Coachella Valley, right where Joe was stationed, for tunnel construction workers assigned to the East and West Coachella Tunnels.

Joe frowned. "Hmm, soon we'll have to work inside the tunnels." Working underground did not appeal to him. He decided to make a move soon, even though times were financially precarious.

His courtship with Ruth continued, with weekend visits and almost daily letters to each other on weekdays. In one of those letters, Ruth seems to be writing about tenting somewhere as a nurse in the field. She complains about bugs and dirt and then gets romantic, as she did regularly in subsequent letters.

> I doubt if I'll ever be clean again.... I'll throw a kiss over the mountains and you catch it. (Ruth to Joe, April 26, 1933)

Both Joe and Ruth were working hard, often in uncomfortable situations. Ruth wrote that the operating room was a steam box and then turned playful in the same letter.

> I believe I will take a stroll out to Hayfield this morning to wake you up. Now don't be surprised if I come. I could do anything this morning. Shall soon dress and go on duty—I hear Mrs. Lux strolling about. She must be up and getting breakfast for her hungry crew. (Ruth to Joe, May 25, 1933)

For a time, Ruth stayed at Mrs. Mattie Lux's boarding house. Mattie also rented to other nurses, to doctors, and to some MWD personnel. Surveyors like Joe, however, slept on the ground at places like Hayfield or in tents at other camps.

## Absence makes the heart grow fonder

Ruth's brother Harry, now a widower, was planning his yearly summer trip to Minnesota with his three children. Ruth was planning to go with him.

"How long are you going to be gone?" Joe was not happy.

"Barbara is only seven. The little one is three. Harry could use my help on the trip."

Ruth got her way. Off they went in a new Chevrolet with running boards. It was June of 1933. As they started through the desert, they stopped to attach a water bag so the radiator would not boil over. Harry drove hard, making it in four and a half days. The entire trip seemed hot to the children—no air conditioning, of course. Ruth spent a few weeks in June and July in Minnesota with her large family there. She talked, laughed, pitched hay, drove tractors, and cared for Harry's children.

Ruth received a number of letters from Joe on this trip, all saying how much he wished she would be back soon. The sloppy writing on this one makes it look as though he wrote it sitting on the ground. It brought her up to date on his business plans.

> You know the place I tried to get out by [Shaver's] well. The Union Oil Co tried to get funny and get a lease in both the place I wanted at [the] well and a place at the Summit so I told Cram that I would … give him a better deal. I had a letter from him last night … that we would be able to deal OK. Honey, if I get both places, I'll be starting right away as Cram owns the land at the Summit and of course I'll get that. (Joe to Ruth, July 9, 1933)

Some of Ruth's letters showed her balance between being kind to others and standing up for herself.

> Harry has to take nine more days of his leave—which will be two more weeks here…. If I even mention the fact that I must be back, they all tell me about my duty to the poor motherless children…. They forget that I am losing money…. Also had a letter from Irene [Curran]…. I am very glad she said something nice about you. (Ruth to Joe, July 11, 1933)

On July 14, 1933, Joe sent Ruth a Western Union telegram saying he expected her home the next weekend and that he had acquired the land at the Summit but not Shaver's Well, which was a distance anyway in Box Canyon.

So with Ruth's investment and some money he had saved, Joe leased forty acres from James and Aura Cram. The July 15, 1933, lease agreement gave Joe, as lessee, "the right to use all water developed in Palm Canyon," which meant he had water from at least three canyon springs the Cram brothers had tapped: one at Lost Palms Oasis, one lower in the same canyon from the tunnel fed by Victory Palms Spring, and one from Summit Spring Oasis near the juncture of Lost Palms and Munsen Canyons. However, Joe, his family, and employees referred to these differently from how they became labeled on maps. They regularly referred to Lost Palms as *Lost Palms* or the *East Canyon Spring*, to Victory Palms Spring as the *Tunnel*, and to Summit Spring as the *North Canyon* or *Munsen Spring* (not to be confused with the Munsen Spring much farther up the canyon). In the years to come, Joe would tell his family that they maintained about ten miles of pipeline coming from these springs.

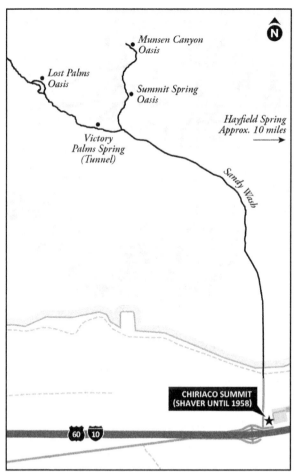

*Map 3: The springs to which Joe and Ruth Chiriaco acquired water rights as part of their 1933 lease agreement with the Crams.*

The agreement also gave him the right to water even farther away, at Hayfield Spring (about ten miles east of the Summit). As rickety as they were, Joe also got the rights to use the pipelines the Crams had laid. He built a storage tank on the flat area on Summit grounds to bank the spring water. Many people would have stood on the desert floor or looked down from some hilltops and seen nothing but empty, desolate, dry desert. Joe and Ruth, both raised by immigrants who had to make their ways from scratch, saw the future and how to get there.

On July 15, Dr. Gray sent Ruth a telegram asking her to come home. He needed her by August 1. The children stayed in Minnesota for the summer. Harry and Ruth made the hot trek back. Ruth was more than ready to get back to the dry desert, get back to her nursing job, and reunite with Joe.

## Setting up shop

With the lease signed, Joe started working at the Summit part time, still surveying for MWD, and saving money for whatever he would need to start their travel stop. For example, with every paycheck he bought some wood for buildings he was planning. Sometime in late summer, Joe collected his last MWD check. He never cashed it; perhaps, as his family believed, so he could still consider himself an employee. At that point he started readying Shaver Summit for business full time.

Joe's first order of business was to secure the water. The sheep troughs near the Summit would not do for the travel stop Joe and Ruth had in mind. Joe's surveying experience helped him understand how to make sure the spring water continued to flow through the Cram pipes to the Summit floor. Joe was a constant learner. He taught himself to connect water wherever it was needed at the Summit to serve his family and the traveling public.

He was in the process of starting a small one-room building when Ruth's brothers came from Ventura to Indio to visit her. She brought them out to the Summit. They were surprised to see their blonde, blue-eyed sister with a swarthy man. Besides, Ruth had a good job, and this man was speculating on something that could go bust in two months. Ruth's very Norwegian businessmen brothers objected to the dark Italian at first, but they soon saw Joe's drive and his love toward their sister and quickly changed their minds. Almost immediately, one of her brothers, Ted, helped Joe build a one-room wooden structure that housed a small café. This same structure served as an office and as living quarters. Once the structure was built, Joe lived in the back. At night he used candles or kerosene lamps, which would be the way at the Summit for their first few years in business. Later, generators were used for refrigeration and lighting.

With the building ready, Joe concentrated on his goal to open the business the same day as the US 60 ribbon cutting, a few weeks off. He believed that with the paved two-lane highway connecting Phoenix, Arizona, with the Los Angeles area, the Summit would prosper despite the Depression.

## In business

How did this scruffy fellow with little to his name have the funds to get started? He lived sparingly so that he added his savings to what Ruth offered. He arranged advances from merchants and wholesalers in Indio. He used his savings and advances for the buildings he needed, for his inventory, including some beer, and for acquiring a small glass-top, ice-cooled unit for sandwich meat and other perishables. Union Oil provided two used glass-top pumps. On August 15, 1933, the same day that US Highway 60 opened, the desert couple opened their travel stop. From the start, Joe's gas station was retail owned and operated. The gasoline companies he dealt with over the years were his suppliers.

*Photo 13: Joe Chiriaco at the Union Oil Station, glass-top pumps behind him, August 5, 1933.*

Ruth continued living in Indio and working at the hospital. When she had been back in Minnesota, of course her family heard about Joe, maybe even seen a photo of him. One day she received a letter from her mother—one that disturbed Ruth so deeply that she reported the contents to her own children years later.

> Ruth, I am concerned about your choice for a husband. I cannot see my fair haired daughter marrying a dark Indian. What future can he give you? (As recalled by Pauline Chiriaco Leedom and Margit Chiriaco Rusche)

She wrote *Indian* knowing full well that Joe was Italian, but in her mind that was not necessarily better. Unfortunately, in the 1930s Native Americans were still not appreciated, and some immigrant groups were disparaged by others.

But Ruth kept seeing Joe. They kept writing to each other. Joe started writing "Shaver Summit" at the top of his letters. He wrote three letters on September 29, 1933, and he printed one very neatly, uncharacteristic of most of his writing.

> Ruth please don't let anything happen just because I'm not in a position to give you the entertainment which you deserve. You know that I'm trying doubly hard because you have inspired me.... Also my darling you know that every couple has their differences and faults.... Let's keep ourselves above the average and not become common.... Ruth, I love you and won't lose you and if you will admit the truth you also love me but there is something trying to separate us but never will.... Boy oh boy is this a beautiful night honey there is no place in the world as pretty as the desert in the moon lite [sic] wish you were here with me.

Joe was trying hard with this letter. Why? Family lore makes some suggestions. Not only did he feel some of the family prejudice against him, but Ruth had other suitors, some more affluent than Joe. Rumor had it that one suitor was a member of the Heineken Beer family who had somehow ended up as a patient at one of the hospitals where Ruth had been a nurse. Could the poem to the "chubby" nurse have been written by him? Ruth's letters and her comments to those who knew her over the years indicated that she was conflicted about Joe at first. She noticed that Joe had an eye for other women, even dating a friend of hers at one point, but she also saw him as very bright and romantic. His printing may have been unusual—but not the romantic closing of this letter and many others.

*Photo 14: Dirt road to mountain springs with remainders of the original Cram pipeline, water storage tank.*

He wrote two more letters that same day. They were in his usual cursive. Sections from these letters make clear that he was working nonstop at the Summit.

Darling, just finishing ... 3000 feet of pipe line.

I piped the water into the house this a.m. we now have ice water at all times.

He had been hauling ice from Indio for some time for his glass-top refrigerated unit. Ice meant they could have some things city folks took for granted such as ice water, cold cuts, and even butter, which had to be served with ice in the summer desert or it would quickly liquefy.

Joe manned the pumps and served customers in the little structure that Ted had helped build. Joe had designed the small, square wooden building to be visible from the highway. It had the advantage of being the only convenient stop for miles. MWD employees, their families, and travelers took a break at what was really a spruced-up snack shop. Little by little he added to his business. He installed a small counter in what he and Ruth referred to as the little café.

Customers could order and eat at the counter or at one of two tables squeezed into nearby space. If they needed a few things before they went on their way, they looked through a few shelves that made up Joe's store inside the café. There they might find bread, canned foods, and snacks such as peanuts, all of which Joe brought in from Indio. If they wanted something cold, they could find drinks, sliced bologna, and ice cream, or other perishables in the small, ice-cooled unit with the see-through glass lid. Joe also stocked a few automotive parts in the store, which came in handy now and then.

Most likely, Joe eagerly showed Ruth how to operate the pumps on one of her visits in an interchange like this showing Joe's know-how and Ruth's carefulness.

"I have to crank the pump like this." Joe started cranking, one crank per gallon until he filled the glass top with gasoline. "See here, each notch on the glass is a gallon." He filled the glass full, to about ten gallons.

Then he started to fill the automobile's tank with a hose. After a minute or so, he pulled the hose out.

"Why are you putting your ear to the tank? Isn't that dangerous?" Ruth asked. This was common practice in those days.

"It might be, but I need to hear if any gas is going in." And then a few minutes later he pulled the hose out and looked down the hole, also dangerous. "I see gas. Looks full."

Done, he calculated the amount he actually used to fill the tank using the gallon notches on the glass multiplied by the price per gallon. Joe collected the money from the driver and put it in a small box. This whole process was not safe, secure, or precise, but it was the way it was. Joe and Ruth constantly learned every aspect of their business and would relearn as technology and business practices changed.

*Photo 15: Glass top of pump similar to ones used at Shaver Summit in 1934.*

Now and then a truck driver needed diesel fuel, but Joe's pumps were strictly for gasoline. In emergency situations, he would sell the driver some of his private stash of kerosene, which could get the truck to the next stop.

One day a German fellow looking for work wandered by. Joe hired him to help as needed. As he worked with Karl Hogenstein, he discovered Karl was a master craftsman.

"Do you think you could build me some cabins?" Joe asked.

"Sure, how many? What do you want in them?"

"Well, I want to rent them to aqueduct workers and travelers. They can be small but need to have a kitchenette, a bathroom with a shower, and one bedroom." From the start, Joe wanted a traveler's oasis, not just a gasoline station or truck stop.

"How many cabins?"

"Let's start with four," Joe said.

"Where do you want them?"

Joe pointed to a barren spot and then said, "Make them portable, so I can move them in case I need to.

Mr. Hogenstein was the first of many wanderers who would lend their talents to the Summit over the decades to come.

In addition to the launch of the Summit business, there was another new, notable business activity in regard to aqueduct workers in 1933. Dr. Sidney Garfield, a friend of Drs. Gray and Morris, opened a small clinic called Contractor's General Hospital between the Summit and Desert Center, with the mission to care for aqueduct workers. Contractors of aqueduct workers, as required by the government, carried worker's compensation insurance for on-the-job injuries. However, Dr. Garfield also treated non-job-related injuries, which had to be paid for by the patients out of pocket. The workers tended to spend their paychecks in Blythe rather than paying the clinic. When insurers were billed, they often came up with reasons not to pay. As a result, Dr. Garfield struggled financially, until Harold Hatch, an engineer who had turned insurance underwriter, came to Dr. Garfield with a proposal. Since Dr. Garfield was interested, Mr. Hatch approached some of the contractors and their underwriters with the same proposal: deducting five cents from the workers' paychecks to pay for the doctor's services in advance. They agreed, and thus Sidney Garfield pioneered a prepaid, preventative medicine approach. Not too long after Contractor's Hospital launched its prepaid services, Henry Kaiser learned of Dr. Garfield's pioneering work with preventative medicine, leading to what became Kaiser Permanente.

The Kaiser Company, as it was then known, was a prime contractor known for large-scale construction projects such as dams and ships. Henry Kaiser, for labor-relations purposes, wanted to provide medical care to his workers. One of his executives knew about Dr. Garfield's preventative medicine plan at Contractor's Hospital. He arranged for Dr. Garfield to provide a similar plan at some Kaiser construction sites, starting with Grand Coulee Dam and then shipyards. Contractor's Hospital is sometimes considered the first Kaiser Permanente hospital. It opened too late to have helped Joe with his deviated septum, but then he would not have met Ruth, his love and life-long business partner. It would, however, play into Summit history one day.

*Photo 16: Gas station, café, store, and cabins, 1934.*

## The Depression as opportunity

Desert Steve Ragsdale, as he had become known, advertised Desert Center. Joe was not deterred by what he saw as direct competition, even though he could not afford comparable advertising. Ruth was even less deterred.

"Joe, you can do it. I hear that Desert Steve is something of an eccentric."

"Yes, but people know him." Desert Steve published his poetry and philosophical sayings in desert publications. They were folksy, appealing to desert souls and getting their attention.

"They will know you too." Ruth from the beginning encouraged Joe, no matter the odds.

His own ingenuity coupled with Ruth's emotional backing made him a constant entrepreneur.

He saw the actual remoteness of the Summit as a chance for more business. He started acting as a bank for aqueduct workers, operating his store on an extensive credit system. He made it easy for workers to buy by putting purchases they made during the week on a tab. On Fridays, workers cashed their payroll checks at the Summit and paid Joe what they owed him. He started having cash and goods delivered to keep up with the volume of business he had developed by then. He also started a delivery service, bringing food, ice, and other supplies to the work camps.

He saw opportunity after opportunity, even where other people saw nothing but a remote, barren desert or useless junk. In 1933 people were coming West from the Great Plains trying to get out of the Dust Bowl that had impoverished them. Many were from Oklahoma, referred to in a disparaging way at the time as Okies. They would come in rickety old cars, trying to get to Los Angeles and then to the San Joaquin Valley for jobs in the great agricultural basin there. Many of those cars broke down at the Summit, beyond repair. Joe did something to help these people and himself. He started buying their dead cars, junking them, and using them for parts. Some of these parts helped the next impoverished souls from the Great Plains. Some drivers came with water bags attached to their car's front end, meant to cool the radiator and to carry water for the passengers, but radiators and other parts still gave out—and often near the Summit. Joe was waiting with the parts travelers needed, so, rich or poor, they could go on their way.

# 6

# *The Start of a Desert Family,*
# *1933–1939*

As 1933 waned, the families started getting used to the idea of Ruth and Joe making a life together. Ruth's mother and Joe's sister wrote to him.

> Josef, both Harry and Ted speak well of you; the only thing is that you are a Katolick [sic] and she is a Lutheran and I am a strong Lutheran; but then I will not stand in the way of your happyness. Be kind to her. Ruth is a good girl. Lovingly, Mother (verbatim, Ruth's mother, Margit Bergseid, November 27, 1933)

> I hope that Ruth makes you a sweet little wife. You deserve it. I never can think to ask but is she a Catholic? If not, have you quit going to the Catholic Church? Are you going to be married in Protestant Church or in both? (Ella Chiriaco, December 14, 1933)

## Together for always

The Chiriaco love story would not always be smooth, but these two from very different backgrounds would make their marriage and business partnership work. Ruth was no small part of that success, partly because she was able to speak her mind to her strong-minded fiancé, assume part of the responsibility for the good and the bad, and then rejoice or forgive and move on.

> Darlin', I am awfully happy to think we will be together for always—to work and build together—and we'll make the wall so strong that it may

never crumble or fall. (Ruth wrote this to Joe before they were married in her letter of December 13, 1933.)

In a letter to Joe on June 9, 1934, just a few weeks before they were married, she wrote:

> Just a few more days now darling and we will be together for always and that will be a long time— [there are] so many things we must learn to be really happy—darling we must be more patient with each other, for if we don't—will never be real happiness. All these we must build together and make it such a strong bond that nothing can tear it apart.
>
> Sometimes here alone I think of how cruel and almost crude we have been to each other. I am almost ashamed to think of us—who we are sane and intelligent enough to know that we shouldn't treat each other with such disrespect—but then love never was smart.

What was going on from Ruth's perspective? The prejudice had subsided, but differences in personalities remained. Ruth was a kind and fun-loving soul. Joe's personality was very different. He could be bombastic. He spoke with a big voice even when unnecessary. As a result, he sounded angry when he was just focused on getting something done. In addition, other women continued to flirt with Joe, and he sometimes seemed attracted to them. But Ruth saw beyond that. She saw his strong work ethic, his high energy, and his entrepreneurial spirit. She experienced his fun-loving, romantic, passionate side on trips with him and in his letters. But most of all, they both were far from family, trying to make something of their lives, and could see that the other would be the perfect life partner. Ruth knew that with Joe, she was so much more than an attraction; she was loved.

So on June 25, 1934, Ruth walked down the aisle to take Joe's hand at the historic St. Vincent Catholic Church in Los Angeles, only the second Catholic Church to be consecrated in the area. Father Joseph Johnson, who married them, was one of the first priests to enter their lives. While the wedding was simple, with only Ruth's brother, Harry, and her friend Irene Curran as witnesses and a few other guests, they had full family approval on both sides.

The newlyweds lived in Indio until living quarters at the Summit were readied. Often, Joe stayed at the Summit overnight. Ruth continued nursing. She cared for ordinary people and sometimes the famous. Spencer Tracy had stopped at the Summit with his wife, Louise, who started feeling ill while there. Of course, Joe directed them to Coachella Valley Hospital. Since Mr. Tracy was not yet as famous as he would be after joining MGM, Ruth and Joe did not get the full impact of the movie star they had just met.

*Photo 17: L to R, Irene Curran, Joe and Ruth, Wedding Day, June 25, 1934.*

By this time, Ruth had become a devout Catholic. The family attended church in Indio, where they got to know Father Michael Lee. Father Lee started visiting the Summit on a regular basis and came to know Ruth and Joe well. He saw how hard Joe worked and was worried about it. He noticed that Joe was not always at Mass.

## The business and family grow

In 1935, US 70 overlaid the same route as US 60 from Mecca through Palm Springs into Beaumont in what became part of Greater Los Angeles. From Beaumont, the two routes separated, but interlaced back and forth with each other all the way into downtown L.A. This meant even more traffic coming by the Summit from the populated L.A. area. The Summit now needed Mrs. Chiriaco's talents and energy.

"Good morning, Ted," Ruth greeted her brother, who had come into the café for breakfast. Ted was helping Joe with some odds and ends at the Summit.

"You work too hard. You never stop."

"That's what it takes. I am invested here." Ruth had quit her nursing job and moved to the Summit.

"For as hard as you work, you deserve more. Look how you are living." Ted would later tell family members that he wished Ruth had a nicer house.

The Summit had water but no electricity. The couple operated on candles and kerosene lamps at first. They slept on cots in the back of the store. Their German shepherd, Flash, accompanied Ruth to the outhouse when she had to go during the night. Life was simple and challenging, but they were happy, immersed in their desert dream, which was becoming reality. In fact, the business was growing. Ruth took care of the store and restaurant. Soon she was offering a full breakfast with eggs, sausage or bacon, and toast or pancakes. For lunch, travelers could get a hamburger or a bologna and cheese sandwich. She had a slicing machine, which made her work easier. The menu grew as she learned what customers needed. Outside, Joe took care of the gas station.

The two were lovers and partners. Joe spoke his mind, but so did Ruth. She never cowed to Joe as others might do. They collaborated to understand what their customers might want.

"Well, if I were traveling through here, I would love to get a cold soda," Ruth said.

*Photo 18: Unidentified men, hay—a constant cargo on the highway, Shaver Summit, 1934.*

"Ruth, don't you think cold water would do?"

"For you, Joe, maybe. But not a car full of kids."

Very shortly they added a soda case, and of course they had to keep it cold—and stocked, or they would sell out. Joe picked up the soda and extra ice on his trips to Indio.

The business had a few employees but was big enough to need more. Joe hired a few in 1935. Some were workers on the Aqueduct. Others were people who were Dust Bowl refugees living in cardboard houses with fences made from the ocotillo cactus. The Depression was ongoing, so they were glad to get work. They pumped gas and worked in the ever-busier store, slicing bologna for sandwiches, making the sandwiches, serving the sandwiches and a few other foods at the counter, and selling goods off the shelves.

Because the Summit was now planning to serve sit-down meals with Ruth's roasts and her other meat dishes, they needed more than the small glass-top, ice-cooled case. Joe, ever the wheeler-dealer, found a used room-size, walk-in box that would keep its contents at thirty-six degrees using a small electric refrigeration unit. It was not a freezer, but good enough. He bought it and installed it in the back of the kitchen. Of course he needed electricity. By now he had a small Kohler generator, which was fine for the walk-in box, but that would not do to support more and more plans popping into his head. He bought a large Caterpillar generator and put it next to the Kohler. By the late 1930s, the Summit had access to power day and night, but that did not mean it was limitless. Like their water, they had to conserve it. The business could exist for a while but not grow much on what the generators produced.

Ruth was a stalwart part of the business. She had traded nursing for cooking on a kerosene stove at the café. Why? Simply put, she had fallen in love. She bustled all day long but still managed time with visitors. She especially enjoyed visits from her family. Harry brought his oldest child, Barbara, to the Summit for an overnight stay in 1935 when she was about eight years old, about a year after the trip to the Bergseid farm in Minnesota.

"Turn around, let me see you," said Ruth to the little girl. "Turn all around, I want to see the whole of you."

Barbara stayed for a week over Easter vacation. She played outside and inside. She ate in the café. She noticed how hard Ruth worked no matter what.

"It's hot," Barbara said.

"Oh no, not yet. It's only April," Ruth said, twirling in the sun.

"Auntie Ruth is so nice," the little girl told her dad. Ruth's gentle but no-nonsense way started to become known across the desert. She emanated kindness and concern to everyone, from infants to the elderly, with family, friends—and travelers.

Ruth gave birth to their first child, Pauline, delivered by Dr. Gray on January 2, 1936. Father Lee wrote Joe a letter right after Pauline was born. Joe's tremendous focus on work still concerned him.

> Forgive a word of advice from an old friend. You have the Faith, Joe, but try and go to Mass whenever the opportunity occurs. It's hard in your position to keep up with the duties of religion, but in the long run you will be all the happier for playing the game as best you can. After all, Joe, you're only a young man and you're all immersed in your business, but God Almighty will last longer than any business, and He's the best friend you have. Forgive this counsel for you see how I still worry about you. (Letter to Joe Chiriaco from Father Michael Lee, Los Angeles, CA, January 9, 1936)

New neighbors moved in close to the Summit in 1936 when a large part of the surrounding area became Joshua Tree National Monument, with headquarters at Twentynine Palms, then a homesteading community. Joe still maintained the water rights, even though the area around the springs had new owners. The Monument, part of the National Park System administered by the National Park Service (NPS), brought new friends, new business, but also new threats. Some hikers inadvertently damaged the pipes. Once or twice someone shot at them, causing Joe to make quick repairs. On the bright side, NPS appointed naturalist, James E. Cole, to oversee the new monument. He came and went so wasn't on site permanently at first, but the Chiriacos did come to know him and even invite him to dinner at the Summit. Thus started their relationship with the park, its leadership, and subsequent rangers. In 1940, when NPS opened an office in Twentynine Palms, he became the first superintendent.

## Towing and mail, opportunities

Now and then, someone would roll into the gas station with extra passengers. A scene something like this would ensue.

"Fill it up?" Joe would assume more than ask.

"In a minute, but can you help these people?' The driver nodded toward the back seat. "I gave 'em a ride here. Been here before and saw how you folks can fix things."

A young couple poked their heads out the back window. "We had to leave our car about three miles down the road. The radiator gave out," they chimed in together.

"I can go fix it after I close the station tonight." In the first years, not too many people traveled past Shaver Summit after dark, so closing for an emergency like this was possible.

Sometimes Joe could fix the car. If not, he arranged to get it to the Summit and then get it towed to Indio to be fixed there. If there was no hope for the vehicle and the owner had a title, Joe bought it from him and put it in his growing junkyard. What happened to people like the young couple if they ended up with no working automobile? Usually, a kind driver stopping for gas took them to a place where they could catch a bus or train or possibly buy a running vehicle.

Always looking for a new venture, by the end of the 1930s Joe bought a 1920s Lincoln tow truck and started towing cars in from the highway to fix at the Summit. He constructed a small corrugated tin shop across from the café where he was himself the mechanic. He removed engine heads, radiator belts, hoses, and fan belts. If he could not fix the vehicles there, he towed them to a shop in Indio.

He continuously thought ahead and did what was needed for the sake of the business. His foresight about towing met with his foresight about portable cabins. By this time, he had fourteen. When the aqueduct work moved further east, he towed eight of his cabins to Indio, where he had a plot of land, leaving the other six on the west side of the Summit. Ruth and Joe moved into one of those six. Good thing; Margit, their second child, was born in March of 1938.

Sometime before Margit was born, the family's wonderful German shepherd disappeared. Flash had protected Ruth in her early days at the Summit and watched over Pauline as a baby. Joe believed he had been stolen. In any event, Ruth no longer had the comfort of Flash's constant vigilance, but she had many, many helpful friends. One of Ruth's nurse friends came to help every time a baby was born.

*Photo 19: Flash, c. 1936.*

Perhaps because of Margit's birth, Joe started looking for even more ways to make money for his family. In 1938, he signed a contract with the US Post Office to deliver mail in rural areas. With his new Chevy truck, he picked up mail in Indio or Redlands where it arrived by train and then delivered it to post offices in Blythe, Needles, Palo Verde, and small desert communities.

## The Alabama family meets the Summit

"Well, Ruth, my dad and two of my sisters are coming. Let's see how they do with our simple lifestyle here."

Ruth had met Joe's family in 1937 when they visited them in Alabama with baby Pauline. Joe rigged up a way to heat baby bottles on the drive using the radiator; he was always clever. While in Alabama, Ruth had formed some impressions of the Chiriacos, which she reflected to Joe.

"Your Dad is coming too? He'll probably be OK here, but some of the others may find life here uncomfortable."

So in 1938, at about the same time Joe moved the cabins to Indio, Papa Vincent, Joe's sister Ella (fourth in birth order), and sister Cecilia (seventh) arrived at the summit. His brother Devio (eighth) had come out earlier. The sisters worked in Indio caring for the eight cabins there, but also spent time at the Summit. Sure enough, life at the Summit was foreign to the sisters. Showering at the Summit was outside under a faucet high up on the sun-warmed, spring-fed holding tank, which Joe had installed right after he leased the property. One day while showering, a whirlwind came through and peppered both sisters with spiny cacti. After that, they stayed in Indio as much as possible.

Papa Vincent lived at the Summit and seemed to enjoy it. He got up early to light a fire so he could make coffee and toast for the family. By the time the coffee was brewing, packs of newspapers had already arrived at the Summit, to be sold throughout the day. Joe, always busy, found time to translate the newspaper stories for Vincent in those early hours. He tried to get him a shoemaking job and even a shop, but it didn't work out. After two years, Ella went on to Washington, DC. Cecilia went back to Alabama, as did Papa. Devio stayed and helped until he was drafted in 1942. Joe found other workers, people who were more amenable to the desert and grateful for jobs in those Depression years.

Joe was generous with those who readily accomplished tasks for him, like Karl Hogenstein. He could see motivation in some of the seemingly unfortunate who wandered by. Bob Howe, a forty-year-old baker, had been walking place to place looking for work. Joe gave him a few tasks and found him to be quite capable. Bob started climbing the mountain as a scout for any water problems. He worked in the café and did odd jobs everywhere on the site. At first he camped out, but in no time he saw a way to build himself a simple structure. He watched for emptied wooden boxes, especially those that had come full of apples. Once he had enough of this wood, he built himself a lean-to near the reservoir, with its fourth side braced against the dirt that had formed against the reservoir wall. In time he became a surrogate grandfather to the children. His wanderlust got to him, though. He would be sitting in the café looking out the window at a faraway mountain when a daydreaming look would overtake his eyes. He would tell Joe that he was taking off for about three weeks, and then he'd walk off. He would be back three weeks later just as he said, settling back into the lean-to he had made for himself by the Summit reservoir. Joe found him completely reliable and always had work waiting for him.

## Entrepreneurs in the desert

As the 1930s drew to a close, Ruth and Joe were firmly in business: two children of immigrants living the American dream. Joe had a firm grasp of the natural desert environment and enough technical savvy to solve problems for himself and for weary travelers. Sometimes Joe's strong personality came across as tough, even rough. He also had a take-charge demeanor that usually served him well, although as time went on some saw it as stubbornness. Ruth tempered that with her welcoming and hospitable manner. She was the grounded constant in the family. She understood people and the political environment. She was kind and gracious, just what was needed for a service business. She was able to learn and adapt to new and difficult circumstances, which she saw as adventure. They both could see the future. Both moved to action, Joe with a little more caution than Ruth; but generally they were both risk takers. Both had the mental and physical stamina needed for their harsh environment. Neither was afraid of hard work. Their combined abilities and attitudes would make it possible for them to profit from the deluge that was about to descend on the Summit. They were about to be joined by thousands, in fact a million, more people.

*Map 4: Desert Training Center, California-Arizona Maneuver Area (DTC/CAMA). CAMA as it was in the 1940s under Generals Patton and Gillam. Stone Map placed at Camp Young by Bureau of Land Management 1985.*

# Part Two

# Pioneering Courage Pays Off, War Years, 1940s

*Fortitude*

They were lucky in some ways—the Aqueduct, Highway 60,
General Patton, the POWs.

But Ruth and Joe had a knack for turning circumstances—
fortunate or not—into good fortune.

(Paul Chiriaco, January 24, 2014)

# 7

## *The General and Joe,*
## *Early and Mid-1940s*

"Run. Mother wants to wash our hair!" Pauline shouted to Margit. The two raced off behind the café.

Just as Joe and Ruth were having more children, the number of customers at the Summit burgeoned. Ruth and Joe worked almost nonstop to serve them all. Some were from the ranks of the traveling public winding off the US 60. Many more came as a result of ramping up for war under the command of General George S. Patton. Joe and Ruth adjusted quickly, becoming a *24-7* operation but managing a *work–life balance* before those terms entered the American vernacular. Their spirited brood brought them joy. Serving their new customers made them proud.

### Before the general—getting ready

On September 1, 1939, Germany invaded Poland, effectively starting World War II, but this had very little effect on Shaver Summit at the time. More locally, earlier that same year, water first flowed from the Colorado River into the Aqueduct. The Aqueduct was completed in 1941, with water flowing through the entire system. This meant that aqueduct workers were no longer needed or living in the area by the thousands, which except for the increasing number of travelers coming off Highway 60 might have had a deleterious effect on the business. Motorists of all kinds stopped for gas, water, food, and other rest-stop amenities. Some aqueduct workers and Dust Bowl transplants remained in the Summit area in makeshift homes they had made from cardboard boxes, fenced with the branches of the ocotillo cactus. The Summit offered some work for these few. The aqueduct ran close to the Chiriacos, but neither they nor families nearby had access to it or to its nearby reservoir.

Joe was always looking out for ways to secure the livelihood of their growing family, especially in regard to water, so he told Ruth, "That reservoir, I am going to see if I can get it. We can use it as a holding tank. That water won't be good for drinking but would be good for other uses."

Once MWD had finished its work on the Colorado River Aqueduct, it no longer needed Construction Reservoir #4 at Shaver Summit. Soon after, Joe started a long string of letters over many years to MWD regarding buying the reservoir. This would not be settled until the 1960s.

Business was good enough so that back in 1940 Joe had added a real kitchen in back of the café. In the café itself he enlarged the counter to an L shape with places for fifteen stools where people could sit and order from an actual menu. The café had a diner feel to it. Ruth was busy, especially in the café and new kitchen. Pauline got whooping cough that year, and pregnant Ruth tended to her in addition to everything else she did.

By February of 1942, Ruth and Joe had four children. The Chiriaco four: Pauline (born in 1936), Margit (1938), Joseph Robert (1940), and Baby Norma (1942)—the last three delivered by Dr. Morris. Baby Norma was born with a hole in her heart, another worry for Ruth. She stayed in the hospital with Norma for a while. That left Joe in charge of the older three. He managed all right, including braiding the girls' hair. He did a fine job braiding, except that he made the braids uncomfortably tight.

A few months before Norma was born, Joe and Ruth heard on their radio that Pearl Harbor had been bombed. It was December 7, 1941. Shortly after, the United States entered World War II. The Summit would play a part starting in 1942. In the meantime, every improvement the family made at the Summit and their nonstop work ethic was preparing them for the masses of new customers to come.

Ruth and Joe were examples of entrepreneurship in spite of what others might consider difficult circumstances. They relied on the pipelines from the springs for water and on generators for electric power, both of which were unreliable. Pipelines froze in winter, gave out due to heat or accidents at other times, and were made of black iron, making them susceptible to rust. There was no commercial water or power, no natural gas, no air-conditioning, but they had propane and the refrigerated walk-in at the back of the café. So ice-cold beer and soda were always available. Joe would drive to Indio, buy the ice for the refrigerator, and haul it back. Sometimes he'd take the older children, who would put their feet on the ice. It would feel so good on a hot summer day. This was not to Ruth's liking, but what she didn't see—oh well!

*Photo 20: Joe holding Margit, Pauline with doll, walk-in dollhouse behind her, c. 1940.*

Even with her four children, Ruth continued to work for the business. She rose early to make eggs, toast, and bacon for breakfast in the café and then started to prepare for lunch and dinner.

Eventually, Baby Norma's heart healed on its own. While Ruth did not ignore the children, they invented much of their fun, sometimes with an uncle who was working on site.

One day Uncle Devio, still at the Summit before he was drafted, went looking for four-year-old Pauline.

"Pauline, come see what I made for you."

Intrigued, Pauline followed Uncle Devio.

"Go in, Pauline, go in. It's for you."

"Ohhh!" Pauline's eyes widened, and she went through the door of her new walk-in wooden dollhouse.

Pauline started to play in the little house immediately, sharing it with her siblings as they grew older.

While Ruth worked in the café and went back and forth to tend to toddler Robert and infant Norma, Pauline and Margit played in the dirt around the doll-house and elsewhere on the premises. Of course, sand would fly everywhere. It smudged their faces, got under their fingernails and between their toes. Worse for Pauline and Margit, who hated hair washing, the sand infested their brown curls. There was no shade except from a few tamarisk trees, so in the summer the children got sweaty, adding to their unkempt look. Ruth was adamant about cleanliness, and the tamarisk trees played a part.

Since the children hated hair washing, they had to be captured for this activity. In addition, it was a bit of a game, a game that frustrated busy Ruth. As soon as the children began to run from her, she would make a switch from a tamarisk twig by stripping the needle-like leaves and switching the children near their legs into the family's cabin. It was 1942. It would be 1953 before Johnson's No More Tears Shampoo came on the market, so they squeezed their eyes tightly shut and bore Ruth's washing in the kitchen sink and vigorous hair brushing. At least their braids weren't as tight as their dad could make them.

Joe was outside with the gasoline pumps much of the day. The increasing traffic warranted it, but also he watched the water lines to make sure no driver went off the road and ran over them. If this happened, suddenly the Summit's water would be interrupted and even stopped. Fixing the system in these rare cases required more than his usual patching of holes with inner tubing and special wire from his junkyard. He had to use pipe from his short supply, a supply soon to be depleted by war rationing. As much as Ruth was particular about cleanliness, he was particular about his water system, and rightly so. While outside at the gasoline pumps, he started noticing what seemed like a small reconnaissance plane flying overhead now and then, but highway motorists got most of his and Ruth's attention.

Ruth's penchant for cleanliness extended to travelers, as did her concerns for proper nourishment and health issues. She saw parents coming in cars with flaxen-haired youngsters, filthy dirty, hungry, with noses running. The tightly packed families were often sweaty, since there was no air-conditioning in their rickety cars. By some estimations, the Depression was waning, but for many travelers, money was still very tight. Some of these people were coming West from the Plains States to start over after being ruined by the Dust Bowl. They had barely enough to make the trip.

"Joe, did you see that?" Ruth would ask. "That family looked like they needed food. What was that dad doing buying cigarettes and beer?"

Joe started her next sentence for her, knowing what she would say, "And the children ..."

"Yes, there were dirty children again today. I have a strong urge to scrub them. And I just hate that the parents smoke in our bathroom!" Versions of this conversation occurred time and time again. In most cases, there was nothing Ruth could do about the cleanliness or the smoking during the quick stops these families made; food was a different matter. On some days, Ruth and Joe directed whoever happened to be working in the café to give away bologna sandwiches to hungry people coming by on their way to escape their unfortunate circumstances. Ruth made many herself.

Frequently outside, Joe kept seeing the reconnaissance plane. Once in a while a car would drive up in a hurry and screech to a stop. Joe could hear some moaning from within. Even if curiously watching the sky above, Joe would take off, calling for Ruth as he ran into the café. Ruth delivered many a baby during those early years.

The word spread: "You can get something hearty to eat and cold drinks at the Summit. They know how to fix cars—and they care about people too!"

## War comes to the desert

In March 1942, the United States War Department officially authorized the Desert Training Center (DTC). Major General George Smith Patton, Jr.[¶] received orders to locate, create, equip, and command a training operation to prepare troops to fight the Nazis in the desert terrain of North Africa. The DTC's mission was threefold: training Army ground and air units to fight in the desert environment, testing and developing desert-suitable equipment, and developing training methods along with tactical doctrines. Eventually, the DTC would expand to encompass eighteen thousand square miles in Arizona, Nevada, and California deserts and become known as DTC/CAMA. CAMA would stand for California-Arizona Maneuver Area. But during the time Joe was watching skyward, the huge endeavor was in early planning stages.

The general was doing his own reconnaissance from the air and on the ground. One day when Joe was sitting at the café counter gulping down his lunch, someone tapped him on the shoulder.

"Do you know Joe Chiriaco?"

Joe did not look up, just kept on eating. "Yeah, why do you want to know?" As he raised his eyes, he caught the shine from a lot of brass. He quickly added, "I am that person."

This was one of several visits General George Patton made to the café to learn whatever he could from Joe about the area. On one of these visits. Joe said, "I want to join up. Most of my brothers and brothers-in-law are in the service, and the ones that aren't will be soon."

General Patton was emphatic. "No, you stay here, run this business, and let me run the war."

"You know I am Italian, and we are fighting the Italians," Joe felt he had to tell the general.

Patton just looked at him and said, "Don't worry, we know more about you than you know yourself."

---

[¶]  General Patton became a four-star general. His full name did include a *Jr.* regardless that he had a son with the same name and who became a major general.

*Photo 21: Ruth, Lorraine (Ruth's niece—Tom Bergseid's daughter), Ted Bergseid, chief warrant officer with Seabees, 13th Naval Construction Battalion. Served in the South Pacific, Margit Lien Bergseid (seated), 1943.*

The general came into the café almost every day and sometimes had a beer with his staff. One of those times in the first months. Joe offered, "General, I have water rights from the springs in the mountains near here. I am happy to share with your soldiers."

"Joe, that water will not be sufficient. We will have a quarter of a million soldiers right here near you. We'll get our own water"

Joe began thinking about stocking up on beer—a lot of beer.

The general gleaned what he could in his conversations with Joe. In his flights over the desert in the small plane he piloted himself, he could see that the area was devoid of population save for ranches and stops like Shaver Summit. Patton was not one to waste time. He called on experts to understand the harsh environment, people like Roy Chapman Andrews, the famed explorer of Asia's Gobi Desert, and Sir Hubert Wilkins, the Australian-born authority on tropical clothing. But he also called on the locals, who knew the area from just being there—people like Joe. He visited Joe a few more times, asking him for the names of mountains and for the conditions of the environment across the expanse. He learned and saw firsthand that the geography of the area included dry lake beds, rugged, barren mountain ranges, sandy valleys, washes, and plains. Vegetation for camouflage was scarce in some areas but plentiful in others. Temperatures in this American desert could reach 135 degrees. It had enough similarities to the African desert that it would provide a good training ground.

Another local person Patton learned from was John Hilton, the artist whom Joe and Ruth had encountered at the Salton Sea in their dating days. John noticed a few army officers at Steve Ragsdale's Desert Center. John introduced himself. After a bit of chatter, the officers pulled out a map and asked John to show them where to locate a training base for General Patton and his tanks. John made a suggestion and circled it. The officers invited him on reconnaissance missions into the desert with Patton himself. On one trip, the general chose an Arizona campsite near two sets of cottonwood trees. John warned the general that sidewinders, a type of rattlesnake, pass from one group of trees to the other during the night. General Patton stood his ground and made camp right there. Later that night, he had to draw one of his pearl-handled revolvers to shoot a sidewinder attracted by the campfire light. As the world came to know, the general had a stubborn streak. Soon, the general would find that so did Joe Chiriaco.

Patton oversaw the quick establishment of rudimentary railways, a dirt road system, and power lines. He arranged for ongoing supplies of food, water, and equipment. By April of 1942, troops were making their way into the area. Little Pauline and Margit, who were six and four years old respectively at the time, watched streams of military vehicles make their way down the highway day after day. Within a short time, military tents were all around. Patton made sure that his men had what they needed. An example: PFC Ben Beal served as the clerk for the 515th unit of army engineers assigned to water purification at the DTC. He had an office tent with a wooden floor, a desk, a typewriter, and a training book from which to brush up on his typing skills. Soon Ben was keeping records in the tent or was on the road delivering payroll and paperwork to all the camps.

*Photo 22: What is left of an original Camp Young DTC road (center, cut by I-10).*

In April of 1942, shortly after Patton arrived, Joe and Ruth took a loan and purchased the forty acres they had leased from the Crams. General Patton had plans for some of that land. He told Joe either directly or through one of his representatives, "The military is planning an airport here. It will be on part of your land. We will need a square mile but only twenty of your acres. We will pay you five dollars an acre."

Joe thought the $100 offer for his twenty acres too little. Nevertheless, caught up in the sense of patriotism of the war years, he sold it at that price. Joe understood that the military would return his twenty-acre portion after the war at no extra cost to him, but he continued to think, "I gave it away—and at too low a price."

The airport would be under construction for a while, but very soon most else at the DTC was ready for action. Quickly, the soldiers started being acclimated to the same harsh conditions of possible warzone deserts. They ran a mile in ten minutes every day, slept in the heat, and stuck to a ration of small amounts of water. General Patton, himself, lived and worked under similar conditions. They all lived in camps across a large expanse of Southwestern desert. They practiced maneuvers on several bombing and artillery ranges. The soldiers fought with real artillery. Sadly, some were killed in training.

## A gathering place

Very critically for Joe and his family, General Patton established his headquarters on approximately 3,280 acres at Camp Young, adjacent to the Summit.

How did the military acquire rights to this land and Joe's twenty acres at the airport? Lt. Wayne Kessler explains in one of his DTC reports:

> In regard to real estate in the training zone, the DTC policy was not to obtain prior rights from the owner for the use of the property but to entertain damages to the property....
>
> Approximately one-half of the maneuver area is public domain, one-third is owned by Southern Pacific Railroad and the remainder is privately owned. (Kessler, Wayne. Lt. US Army, *History of the Communications Zone, Real Estate*, p. 69, May 11, 1944, General Patton Memorial Museum (GPMM) Archives)

In Joe's case, the military did purchase the twenty airport acres and promised to return it after the war. His troops did maneuver over other land that belonged to the Chiriacos. A consolation was that he made Joe and Ruth's café one of the few places on-limits for his soldiers. Soon the café became a gathering place and remained so ever after. Some soldiers, like Ben, remained too busy to get to the café or to the other place on-limits, the Desert Center café. By the 1940s, Desert Center had grown to include a service garage, a market selling camping gear, a post office, and some cabins with access to a large swimming pool. Chiriaco Summit had also grown to offer similar services minus swimming. For years Joe heard comments that the owner at Desert Center "would like to put that damned Italian out of business." Quite the opposite was about to happen. Joe had foreseen the opportunities posed by the aqueduct and new highway as a young surveyor.

Could he have foreseen the Patton effect on the Summit when he opened the business in 1933?

No, but he grasped unanticipated opportunities as they arrived. Out of business? Hardly.

To understand the scope of the training effort and its effect on the Summit business, one need only look at Lt. Kessler's summary records of the operation. Sixty to a hundred vehicles a day were processed at the vehicle repair and replacement center. The army brought in four hundred tons of ice a day for subsistence purposes. Refrigerated trucks came in daily to the camps loaded with soft drinks and ice cream. Soldiers could consume 1,500 gallons of ice cream in a day. A record day at the main training center post office saw 2,631 mail orders and $2,747 worth of stamps. At the time, first-class domestic postage was three cents. Joe later told his son, Robert, that he gave up his rural mail contract soon after Patton arrived and through the war years because he was very concerned that delivering mail to the soldiers at Camp Young would overwhelm him. He had enough to do serving the soldiers well with his café, store, and gasoline business.

One day there were twenty customers in the Summit café/store. The next day there were three to four hundred people. The café became packed day after day. Joe quickly added employees. Folks looking for work seemed to find their way to the Summit. Joe balanced customer needs and wants with his own needs to keep the business solvent and to support his family. He noted that a number of the soldiers were from the South. He knew they would like pickled pig's feet, acquired them, and served them at the café. He saw the growing popularity of jukeboxes so supplied them to the army to set up in tent concessionaires at campsites. Inside, soldiers could relax with beer, other refreshments, and popular music of the day. Joe would make the rounds with Pauline and Margit, collecting money from the jukeboxes. He did this just in time. Sometime in 1942 the US government halted the production of jukeboxes to conserve labor and material for the war effort.

When the soldiers were readying to go out for maneuvers, they came into the store and bought almost everything off the shelves.

"Everything," Ruth noted, "except soap."

Often she'd tell Joe proudly, "We have sold our entire stock of pies—three times this week." By some reports the pies numbered over a hundred a week. Was this possible? If the café had as many as three hundred customers a day, as also reported, that would be 2,100 for a week. This meant that that if 100 pies were each cut into eight pieces or 800 pieces total, about 40 percent got a piece each week. No matter how many pies or how they were cut, it was a busy place with a lot of pie.

*Photo 23: Jukebox used at café during World War II, General Patton Memorial Museum (GPMM) Display.*

On some occasions, starlet types from Hollywood, known as Brigadears, came on busses with chaperones to Camp Young and to other camps, where dance floors were set up. At first General Patton objected to this idea. Gladys Lloyd "Robbie" Robinson, wife of actor Edward G. Robinson, who came up with the idea, persisted and won his support. Mrs. Robinson's Brigadears numbered some six hundred women between the ages of eighteen and twenty-five and served over a number of years. Some of these young women were starlets, but most worked in jobs that supported the war effort. On the weekends, they boarded busses at their own expense to freezing, temperate, or sweltering desert camps, depending on the time of year. They danced nonstop for hours. Cutting in was expected, since there would be three or four soldiers to every girl. Patton established strict rules: chaperones, no alcohol, no necking. Dancing was not allowed where alcohol was served, but the young men and the Brigadears wandered over to the café to eat and drink beer. The next morning Ruth would come in to clean up.

"The place was ankle-deep in peanut shells," she would tell Joe. Regardless of

Patton's rules, Joe became somewhat concerned about the soldiers being around his family, so in late 1942, he moved his family to Redlands, a city nearby. Besides, Pauline was starting school, so living there would be more convenient for the family. He and Ruth discussed a long-term plan—college for their children. Their home there was close to the University of Redlands, but that would not be the case for long.

## Water and beer

Ruth and Joe impressed water conservation on their children from an early age.

"Pauline, Margit, turn that water off while you are sudsing your hands."

"Don't run the water all the time while you are washing the dishes."

"Help Robert and Norma wash up so they don't waste water."

For Joe, the spring water, though procuring it was tenuous, was a key factor in selecting the Summit. Even though the aqueduct was in his back yard, Joe would wait decades for permission to use its water. Water was also a key factor in choosing the location of the Training Center. The general tapped into the newly flowing Colorado River Aqueduct—some say at first without permission from MWD. In 2015, Ben Beal, at the age of ninety-six one of the last surviving World War II veterans, and whose job it was to handle water-related paperwork for the DTC, remembered that Patton tapped into aqueduct resources and signed papers later giving him permission.

*Photo 24: PFC Ben Beal at Camp Young, c. 1942.*

Patton positioned nonpermanent tent cities near water sources. Thousands of tents in ten different camps, supply depots, ammunition depots, hospitals, chapels, repair shops, stores, postal stations, and aviation facilities peppered the area. Over the next two years, more than one million soldiers would train across the 18,000-square-mile expanse. They would drive thousands of tanks, trucks, and artillery units across the desolate landscape.

Joe continued to watch for drivers who might ruin his water system. Many pipes were exposed about ten inches above ground, which had advantages and disadvantages: Joe could easily see the breaks, the inner-tubing repairs would not melt from contact with the scorching summer sand, but the pipes could be easily damaged. One day Joe noticed that one of Patton's battalions had run into and over the Summit's water lines during maneuvers, destroying some of the pipes. With no hesitation Joe went to Camp Young to complain to General Patton about the damage. But the general was not there. That did not deter Joe. He complained vociferously to the officers who were present. He was amazed at the recklessness of the soldiers who had damaged his pipeline and so started a barrage of comments and questions.

"Didn't they see the pipes? Why couldn't they take a different route? Why didn't they report this?"

Later that day, a jeep with red lights flashing and a siren blasting came down Highway 60 to the Summit. Patton got out and stomped in to the café.

"Who is the SOB who was giving my men a hard time?" He knew full well who it was.

Joe was not intimidated. "Your men destroyed my pipes. Because of this damned war effort, I cannot get new ones. What are you going to do about this?"

Joe Chiriaco, the headstrong proprietor, and General George Patton, known for his unflinching resolve, almost came to blows. Patton stomped out as vehemently as he stomped in. Joe stood undeterred. He was able to draw water for a while from his storage tank—but, of course without being replenished from the oasis, that water would soon dwindle to nothing.

The next day Joe, still fuming but planning his next move, looked to the area of the broken pipes.

His eyes widened. "Ruth, look at that!"

Ruth smiled. "You and the general, Joe—there are two hearts under all that bravado. He knows it's death in the desert without water."

A battalion had started laying 1.5 miles of new steel pipe, better than what had been there before. During his stay, Patton made sure any pipes damaged by his troops were fixed immediately. More and more soldiers frequented the café. The general came by to talk to Joe about rules for his soldiers. These were in addition to those that applied when the Brigadears were on site. He wanted them to act in a gentlemanly way at all times at the Summit. For a time, he required them to wear dress uniforms to the café. When he was convinced no harm would be done if they wore their khakis, he relaxed his dress rules.

Again seeing opportunities and ways to realize them, Joe noticed that soldiers' wives and other family members came to visit, so he acquired some trailers inexpensively from Edison Electric, put them on Summit property, and rented them as well as the remaining five cabins to visitors. The family continued to live in the sixth. To add to the help, Joe hired some of the soldiers' wives on a part-time, temporary basis. So far Joe was not able to serve liquor, but the cold beer was a real draw. Rudy Heimark, who had been delivering produce from his citrus farm near Indio, saw the opportunity with beer. By the early 1940s he was a distributor for Schlitz Brewing Company. With Patton's arrival, he had new customers, including Joe. The café was one of the few places soldiers in the desert could buy beer. Desert Steve continued to prohibit all beer and alcohol on his premises, so of course the soldiers had even more reason to come to the Summit.

Joe was able to get as much beer as he wanted to serve the soldiers at the café. In fact, back when Patton told him that his water would not be sufficient for the quarter million men coming to the Camp Young area, Joe turned his tin mechanic's shop into storage for eighteen hundred beer cans, stacked to the ceiling with no room for anything else. He adapted to fixing cars on the side in the dirt. Joe bought beer from Rudy Heimark and also in Indio by the train carload. In Indio, however, the merchants could not get enough and would run out. Angry and resentful, sometime in the early 1940s they devised a plot to get Joe in trouble. The plotting went something like this:

"You know that law against serving beer to Indians."

"Sure, it's posted—even at the Summit café."

"Well, I have heard that Italian over there say, 'They are willing to fight, why not serve them beer?'"

"Well, he's breaking the law. Let's get an Indian soldier to buy beer at Joe's café and take his photo in the act."

The merchants went through with their scheme. The case went to court, but Joe was acquitted. Since the Indian was a soldier, the army stood up for him. The law finally came off the books in 1953.

Again in Indio, two DTC soldiers got drunk there. The sheriff threw them into his jail. General Patton probably through an envoy, demanded his men back. He would deal with them in his own way. When the sheriff refused, the general drove to the jail in his half-track (a truck-tank combination), trained his guns on the jail, and demanded the two men back. He got them. It is unclear what happened after that, but Ben Beal remembered that later one became an officer, the other a chaplain.

*Photo 25: General Patton's half-track, DTC, postcard reproduction of an Army Signal Corps photograph, c. 1942.*

Sometime after the shouting match over the water pipes, Patton showed up to talk to Joe again.

"You need a liquor license here, Joe. I'll make sure you get one."

Joe later told his family that the reason Patton wanted the café to have a license is that he "wanted a real man's drink. For him beer was not good enough."

Only four months after he arrived, in July 1942 Patton shipped out to Africa, before he could make good on that liquor promise. Major General Alvin Gillam took over. The soldiers continued frequenting the café.

By April of 1943, the military started using its new 570-acre airport, short of the 640 acres of the square mile General Patton had told Joe he needed. It did include what had been Joe's twenty acres. The Federal Aviation Administration (FAA) installed an Air Traffic Control Beacon, which served to keep pilots flying over and past the airstrip on course and from crashing into mountains. It had nothing to do with landing at the airport, but was a favorite feature at the Summit.

Facilities at the Summit stayed the same except for the gas station. In 1943, the Union Oil sign came down, and a Shell sign went up. Joe got a better deal with Shell. He stayed an owner/operator dealer, he just changed the supplier.

Also in 1943, Ruth and the children rejoined Joe at the Summit full time. Seven-year-old Pauline hung around the gas station and the café, where she witnessed her father's ingenuity and her mother's nursing skills. Travelers who had car problems in the desert were fortunate if they happened to make it to the Summit. Joe invented solutions on the spot if necessary. A car that stalled near the pumps was an example. The driver kept trying and trying to restart his car. Little Pauline watched her dad try to solve the problem for the helpless driver.

"Let me see if I have a starter," Joe offered and went to look in the small parts department he had in the store.

She saw her dad came back with a light switch in his hand.

"I don't have a starter, but I can fix this," Joe rigged up the switch to the car. The man turned it on. It worked, and he drove away.

One summer afternoon when Pauline was in the store area of the café, a lady who looked very pale started to ask, "What's your favorite soda—" and then suddenly fainted, falling to the foot of the soda case. Pauline ran to get her mother. She watched her calmly handle the situation. Ruth recognized heat exhaustion and knew what to do.

*Photo 26: **L to R:** Margit, Robert, Pauline at the gas pump, c. 1943.*

Soldiers continued to fill the café all times of year. The children could hear their tanks roaring around in the area, and then one day, it got quiet. In May of 1944 the War Department ordered the Desert Training Center closed. Again Pauline and Margit watched—this time with Robert and Norma—this time for hours, as a seemingly endless military caravan moved the soldiers and equipment out of the area. Thousands of tanks rumbled off the desert dirt and on down the paved road. The children watched until they finally faded out of sight.

The military left a lot behind—for example, tents with wooden floors and practice dummy tanks. Even as the troops were pulling away, another opportunity presented itself to Joe. The soldiers were replaced by Italian prisoners of war who had been given the tasks of demilitarizing the site and taking down the camps. Joe saw opportunity: He took over some of the tents for storage, but that was minor compared to having new customers. Thousands of them had been assigned to Camp Young. They were not allowed unsupervised outside that camp, except for the Summit, which was on-limits for them as it had been for the soldiers. For Joe the prisoners were a welcome opportunity, and this time his fluent Italian would play a part.

*Photo 27: Military tents being removed near the airport, c. 1944.*

# 8

# *The POWs, Uncle Paul, and the Children, Mid- to Late 1940s*

"What's that? It sounds like opera." Joe looked around, and there behind the café were the Italian prisoners in US Army khaki uniforms with a small Italian flag on the left sleeve. They were eating watermelon and singing. They were some of the approximately fifty-one thousand brought to the United States in Italian service units. Italy had surrendered to the Allies in late 1943. It was now late 1944.

Joe loved listening to Italian and even more, hearing it in song. He told them in their own language how well they sang. *Voi cantate bene!* And he went on in Italian to say what a welcome surprise they were here, far from any concert hall.

*Grazie, grazie, grazie.* Several stopped singing long enough to say thank you for Joe's compliment and take another bite of watermelon.

Again in Italian, he told them he could see that they liked watermelon and asked if he should order more?

*Si, si, va bene.* The prisoners stopped their singing and eating altogether for a moment to tell Joe,

"Yes, yes, OK."

Here it was, so many years later, and the Italian Joe spoke as a child in Alabama was a factor in his connecting well with his new customers. Watermelon and opera became mainstays around the family. Service-unit prisoners had agreed to support the Allied cause, so in many places such as Camp Young the US Army gave them a lot of freedom. The children sat right with the Italians, digging out watermelon seeds with their fingers and sometimes singing along with them.

The POWs were not the only new faces. Some of Joe's family, especially one of his youngest siblings, showed up off and on to help out in the middle 1940s.

## A marine comes by

In 1944, Joe's brother Paul, who was nineteen years his junior, came to the Summit for the first of his many visits. Paul was a marine newly stationed in December of 1943 at the Mojave Marine Corp Air Station in the small town of Mojave, north and east of Los Angeles. As soon as possible, he hitchhiked a ride to the Summit with a deputy sheriff who knew Joe.

During the ride, the deputy laughed. "Don't tell Joe who you are. Let's see if we can pull one over on him."

The two walked into the café and up to the counter, where Joe was sitting. Paul immediately recognized Joe and thought the gig was up. They both sat down, the deputy in official garb and Paul in his marine uniform.

"Hey Joe, this young marine here says you know him."

Joe looked at the young man and said to the deputy, "I don't. Who is he?"

"He says he's your brother."

Joe, for all his bravado, became silent and embarrassed. *Which brother?* he wondered to himself.

"Joe, I'm Paul."

The Italians nearby came over and flocked around Paul, speaking very quickly in Italian. Joe interpreted. And so began a strong relationship between two brothers at the opposite ends of the sibling line; Joe was number two and Paul was number twelve. While he was stationed in the area, Paul visited from his Marine base every other month or so and stayed three to four days. Besides the prisoners, he interacted with the children, adding his influence to their childhood desert experiences.

It was a dark winter night in the desert in early 1944, soon after the marines had sent Paul to the desert. Paul had always been fascinated by astronomy. Now he was in the perfect place to observe the star-studded sky. He knew that the desert atmosphere with its clear, clean air and low humidity did not interfere with seeing what many call falling stars or shooting stars—informal terms for meteors. He had heard that meteor showers were expected in the Summit sky while he was visiting. Some meteor showers are debris left behind by comets orbiting the sun, which the earth scoops up at specific times each year. These showers are predictable. Perhaps Paul had heard about the Quadrantids visible in early January every year in the Northern Hemisphere. While he loved the science, his purpose with the children was the wonder of it all. He took Pauline and Margit outside to see "stars" shooting across the sky.

"Twenty-five, twenty-six, twenty-seven, twenty-eight ..." Pauline was the youngest fourth-grader at her school, because she had been born in January. She was proud of how she could count and was letting Margit, her first-grade sister, know. "Twenty-nine, thirty, thirty-one ..." She continued pointing to stars as they popped out. No meteor shower yet, but lots of stars. Very soon she was counting into the forties.

Margit couldn't count as well as Pauline yet. She pouted a bit. Paul said, "Let's play a game. Pauline, you stand with Margit. Let's start counting stars and see if you two together can count more than me."

The threesome kept counting as they waited a while for the meteor shower. It started getting chilly.

"There is nothing like the desert darkness for stars," he told the girls. "But it is getting late." With that, he led them back inside to warm up and prepare for bed.

The Quadrantids are sometimes visible much later than Paul was willing to wait that night, but they would see meteor showers and even comets many times in the Summit sky over the years to come—as would subsequent generations.

Paul took advantage of what the desert offered night and day. The MWD canal at the Aqueduct's Hayfield Pump station was seven miles from the Summit. On some visits Paul went there to swim. Years ago, the Chiriacos had befriended the families of MWD maintenance workers posted there to care for the pump. Like them, the Chiriacos had special permission to swim at Hayfield. They preferred swimming there rather than at slimy Reservoir #4 near the Summit. There was no security, not even fences around either the Summit reservoir or the Hayfield canal back then. Life in the desert was still simple and unfettered.

On one of his visits, Paul suggested that Joe bring a troubled brother, Vincent, out from Alabama to the Summit. Vincent was the ninth in the Alabama family, so older than Paul, yet Paul took a protective stance toward him. Vincent was alcoholic and irresponsible. He had served in the navy in the late 1930s and then came to work at the Summit in 1941 and 1942. Joe had fired him back then—but now, about two years later, after listening to Paul advocating for him, he decided to give him another chance. Vincent worked in the café and outside, but not always to Joe's liking.

## Contrasting work ethics

"Let's go, Vincent," Joe called to his brother.

"Just a minute. I need to put a few more things in the truck."

"The truck was supposed to be packed last night." Joe was impatient. He wanted to get going before it got too hot.

Joe drove the truck for a while, kicking up dust as he shifted the old pickup truck on the unpaved road as it became sandier, bumpier, and steeper. Vincent had packed the truck with tools, pieces of inner tubbing, and hay-bale wire for repairs just in case. At one point the brothers hopped out of the truck. Joe opened a large water-collection barrel he had put there in the dirt.

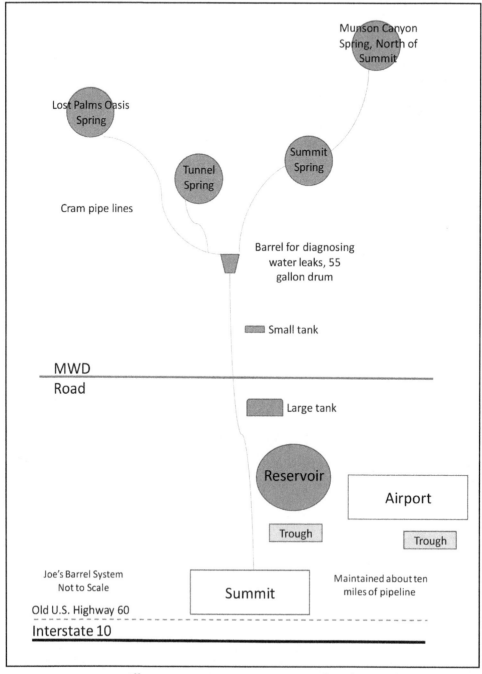

*Illustration 1: 1940s Pipe-connection barrel.*

"Look here, Vincent, see the water is just trickling from the spring at Lost Palms Oasis."

Joe pointed to two intakes. "See here, I connected the Palm Oasis and Tunnel lines to one intake here. The line coming from Munsen comes in here—the other intake." If he suspected a leak, he used the barrel as a diagnostic tool. He could immediately see which line from which canyon was not flowing properly. If there was no obstruction in the barrel, then the problem was down at the Summit, and they could avoid the arduous hike to the springs—but that was not the case this time.

Since the pipes were above ground, Joe could see holes, cracks, or loose joints. In warm weather, the desert heat affected the joints and started leaks, which was probably the situation today.

"OK, Vincent, we are going to have to look for the leak somewhere between here and the Oasis."

They took the truck as far as possible through a wash. When the ground became too sandy in places, too rocky in others, they got out to walk. Joe and Vincent grabbed a few repair items from the truck, backpacked them, and started hiking. They looked at all the pipes along the way. They passed the tunnel and saw no leaks coming from its pipes.

"Keep an eye out for rattlesnakes. Do not put your hands under any rocks." They were pulling themselves over and between large rocks, which today would be called bouldering.

They made their way up a steep-sided, rocky ravine past fan palms and a few willows. They came to waterfalls. They were near Palm Oasis and still saw no leak. They clawed over huge boulders, pulled themselves up over ridges, and passed many types of cacti.

"Vincent, gold miners found this spring a hundred years ago. We're lucky they left it unspoiled. We're close to the source. See those trees."

They were approaching Lost Palms Oasis in what was then Joshua Tree National Monument. A California native, the fan palm grows there—over one hundred of them. This is the palm tree that often sports many dried fronds hanging down. As fronds die, the tree grows taller and sprouts new ones. Why do these trees grow here? Water, of course.

The Coachella Valley is surrounded by seven mountain ranges. The water flow has created many canyons with palm oases. In addition, the palms reach down through faults to get their water. Branches of the San Andreas Fault cut through the surrounding mountains. Joe and Vincent could hear the trickle of water just as hikers in the area today sometimes can. If they were lucky, they might see bighorn sheep. The sheep drank at any time of day or night from the pools made by trickling creeks or springs.

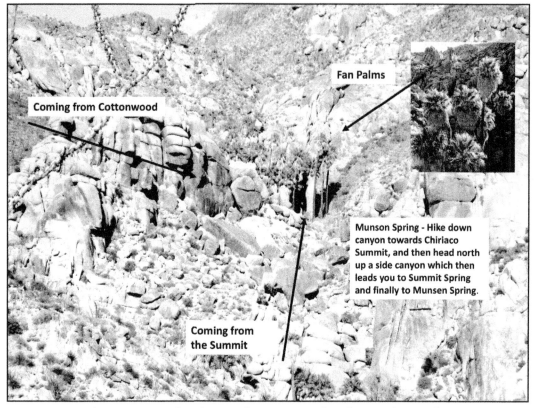

*Photo 28: Lost Palms Oasis with routes Joe took with inset of Fan Palms.*

Finally, close to the water source, they saw it—precious water seeping out of the above-ground pipe.

"Vincent, hand me the wrench." Joe huffed as Vincent fumbled for the tool and finally found it. Joe wound a piece of inner tubing around the seepage and tied it tightly with the wire. For years, until the Summit got a more modern water system, he would constantly be repairing the pipelines coming from the springs in this way. Signs of these repairs remained decades later.

Paul came back and forth for more visits. Sometime in 1945, while Uncle Paul was visiting, the family heard loud noises as they were preparing for bed. They sounded like shots. The children jumped up on their beds so they could see what was happening. The younger ones had to stand on tiptoe to peer out the high window in the room. The window was small, so the four children crammed together to see out. It was as though they were watching their own fireworks display. Joe, Ruth, and Paul explained to the children that the ammunition site across the street had caught on fire. They were seeing trace bullets shooting into the sky every which way. Such bullets have a pyrotechnic component that makes the trajectory visible to the shooter—and everyone else. This type of bullet also creates a fireworks show in an explosion such as the one the children witnessed. This was a dangerous situation, but fortunately the Chiriacos were far enough away. As the night went on, the family watched hundreds of firefighting vehicles come to battle the inferno.

*Photo 29: Remains of a Chiriaco pipeline repair.*
*Photo by great-grandson Anthony Leedom, 2011.*

Vincent was still there and still difficult. Paul, in contrast, was one for being helpful and keeping peace. One evening, Paul and Vincent were eating at the counter when a driver came in with a flat tire. Joe came in and said to Vincent, "Sorry to interrupt your dinner, but go help that driver."

Vincent responded, "Hell no. Make him wait."

"Forget it. I'll do it myself," Paul said as he got up to go outside.

At the end of his visit, Paul flagged down a Greyhound bus coming by the Summit. He was headed back to the Marine Corp Air Base in Santa Barbara, California, where he was stationed in 1945. A group of young men boarded at the Riverside stop. By this time, Paul was stretched out asleep on the back seat in his marine uniform, so he was easily recognizable to the group. They gathered around him and started talking all at once. The bus driver pulled over and stopped the bus. He thought Paul was being attacked.

"It's just the way they talk," explained Paul. "All talk at the same time."

The military had lifted restrictions for the Italian prisoners of war and classified them as noncombatants. They were free to travel. Quite the contrary to any attack, the Italians were excited to see a friend.

Back at the Summit, Joe found he had lost a friend. It was almost Christmas Day in 1945 when news about General Patton reached the Summit.

Joe went inside to look for Ruth. He was shaken. "Ruth did you hear..." His voice broke. "General Patton died."

"What?"

"There was an automobile accident—in Germany. He did not recover from it." Joe was almost in tears. He considered the general a friend and was honored to have known him. He wanted to create a special remembrance for him and for the men who had trained all around him, who had died in battle, and some who even died in training. Dummy tanks remained in the area. They were made of pipe covered with canvas to simulate the form of a tank. They had been powered with jeeps underneath. Joe had an idea about how to make the remains onto a meaningful memorial but did not get to it right away. The growing family and business took most of his attention.

## Blurring work and play

The Chiriaco children worked and played at the Summit, sometimes blurring the lines, especially since they lived right with the business all around their little cabin. While the soldiers were there, the children could see them coming and going all over the Summit and adjoining areas. Now they could see the Italian prisoners around their home and in the distance as they worked to remove the signs of war.

The business was doing well enough that the Chiriaco couple asked a carpenter they knew to build an actual house in 1944. The carpenter used two of the remaining cabins, joining them with a living room that he constructed in between. Now the family had a kitchen, dining room, living room, two bedrooms, and bath with a shower. The narrow children's bedroom had four cots lined up in a row. At bedtime, when the weather was hot, Ruth sprinkled the sheets with water, her own type of air conditioning. Pauline made up stories for the brood as they fell asleep. Later Joe added a screened-in porch where the children slept in the summer. No matter the season, the girls spent hours there making paper dolls and doll clothes. Sometimes Robert stayed off to the side drawing houses for the dolls. More often, he was out watching Dad fueling or fixing the generators, carrying things for Mom, or just hanging out in the café. Four cabins were left for renting.

The family continued to eat at the café unless it was a holiday. In that case, Ruth set an elegant table in their little home. She had good taste and could instill elegance and proper manners with very little. Inside their small house the family lived closely, comfortably, and with some style due to Ruth's artistic bent. She papered the walls herself but supervised the children and employees to paint some parts of the home. The home extended to the outside. Ruth and Joe allowed their children enough freedom that the Summit itself and the adjacent desert became a fascinating playground and intriguing learning lab.

The burgeoning business at the Summit existed side by side with the youthful energy showing itself in adventure after adventure, whether with animals, at the abandoned airport, at recreation areas like the Salton Sea—or whether outrunning danger or just plain exploring.

Since Flash had disappeared, the family had no dog, but they had chickens, homing pigeons, turkeys, and a horse living on Summit grounds. By the age of five or so, the children took charge of feeding the animals. The strong muslin feedbags had cute prints on them. Ruth turned those prints into curtains, skirts, and dresses.

Ruth had stayed in contact with Dr. Morris. The doctor was about to put down his aging horse, Toyjo, when Joe found out. Hard-nosed Joe could not stand the idea of euthanizing the old horse so took him to the Summit. All the children rode him until he died of natural causes.

The abandoned airport became a playground. Like other children of the era, the children had a few toys, but generally found opportunities for play in whatever was around them. After the DTC closed, the airport site became federal property. The airport office stood empty for a while. In the meantime, the children commandeered it as a playhouse.

"Ohhh, look!" six-year-old Margit said to herself as she bent over to pick up a scrap on her way to the airport office one bright day. She could see abandoned tents nearby. She watched the windsock blow back and forth. She smiled in the direction of the beacon light past the end of the runway and inactive at the moment. She was taking in all the scenery when a glittering scrap caught her eye. She picked it up, turned it around in her little hand, held it up to the sun, and experimented looking through it.

"Ohhh, everything looks yellow!" She put the first of these treasures in her pocket to take home.

It was the first time Margit had ever seen plastic, probably some scrap that had something to do with the airplanes. From then on, on her own or with her brother and older sister, Margit looked for colored plastic any chance she got and eventually saw the world as yellow, blue, or some other color. Sometimes she found two pieces of different colors and put them together to get even more colors, like green or purple. The two older girls also had fun finding medals that came off uniforms. Years later, anthropologists and historians would collect and study artifacts strewn throughout the Desert Training Center camps. Some artifacts would find their way to a museum honoring General Patton and his troops later established on these very grounds. Right now, the two girls were just having fun, not yet understanding that they were holding history in their hands. Not all their fun was sanctioned, certainly not by Ruth. In the café, they found gum under the counter and cigarette butts here and there. They tried both—and yes, when they were in elementary school! Ruth was too busy to know, or she would have been so horrified that the tamarisk branch would have come out.

On some occasions, Pauline and Margit took Robert and Norma along on their jaunts to the airport.

"Come on, Robert. Walk faster."

"I think he is too little to do this."

"He's four. He can do it."

Margit and Pauline started skipping over from the café to the airport ahead of Robert and Norma.

Suddenly, they all stopped for a moment and looked up. Mr. Hogenstein, before he left in the late 1930s, had built a wonderful pigeon house, which gave the birds some freedom. The children watched them swarm overhead in a large flock, light on the cabins for a few minutes, and then swarm back to their sturdy home.

"How beautiful!" Pauline swooned as the all-white flock of pigeons flew overhead. The white was common, but their flight did seem choreographed. Even as they watched the graceful swarm overhead, they felt no qualms about eating the birds. Maybe tonight, Ruth would prepare a few as squab, a delicacy elsewhere and normally very young birds, but here it was just desert food, which Ruth would cook long enough to tenderize older meat.

The two older girls started running toward what looked like a jungle gym holding up a windsock. They called it the tetrahedron, as Joe had taught them. They scampered up the pipes making up the four triangles. Robert followed with no trouble. Two-year-old Norma toddled around at the base. Both older girls started showing off.

"Look at me. I'm swinging."

"Me too."

Robert perched, ready to jump.

"Robert, be—careful," chimed in his older sisters. But Robert hit the ground before the last word. He was fine.

Toddler Norma started climbing. "No, No, Norma, not you," Pauline and Margit shouted in chorus as they climbed down to stop her, just in time.

Between all the Summit chores, Ruth and Joe took the children on little trips. Sometimes Ruth alone would take them for ice cream or to the Salton Sea, where they swam and played on the beach. The children were at ease with her, but not always with Joe, who was sometimes a lot of fun and at other times could fly off the handle. He had not heeded Father Lee's advice. His life was mostly work. He took the children with him on his rounds; some they liked, some not so much.

They did enjoy trips to the water lines, even into the tunnel. Joe had put a gate over the entrance to keep animals out, but some bats did make it in. The bats did not concern the kids except for knowing enough not to swim in the pools there

One time when Margit was about nine years old, she got more fun than she bargained for on a jaunt to Lost Palms Oasis to help her dad check pipes. As Dad maneuvered his Chevy panel truck through the sand on the way up the hill, she giggled at the rough bumps and turns. Joe did not believe in four-wheel drives. At one point, as usual, they had to get out and start hiking. Margit was good at keeping up.

"Stop, stay still, Margit."

They were climbing over a boulder just for fun. Margit froze as she saw a rattlesnake on the sand right below her. Joe started to pull out his gun, but the snake slithered on. They waited for it to get far away and then hiked uphill a bit more. Suddenly Joe grabbed Margit's hand.

"We need to get out of this canyon now!" He pulled Margit along as he ran downhill, grabbing the keys out of his pocket. Margit looked back to see why they were running.

"Keep your eyes ahead," Joe commanded and dashed straight to the Chevy. He tossed Margit into the passenger seat, raced around to the driver's seat, and started the engine quickly. He again maneuvered through the dry dust, trying desperately to get out of it before it became mud. They made it to the bottom and onto Summit pavement just in time.

Joe had noticed a big gray ball in the sky and saw water coming their way from higher up. The water was coming after them faster and faster and getting higher and higher. The water had gone from a trickle to a raging river and back to a trickle in a short time. They had just averted being trapped in a flash flood—a rush of water that could slam anything in its way against trees or boulders or carry it swiftly and turbulently away.

Joe taught the children about their natural environment by using experiences as examples. In this case, he would have explained to Margit and the other children, "Water here in the desert is precious but dangerous. You will not be able to cross a flash flood. The water will race down fast and deep. Get out of the area. If you can't, get up high on a hill or on a big boulder, or even climb a tree if there is one. If you are with people who have a car, they need to drive it out fast. If the water catches it, it might be tossed over and swept away like a boat. These floods are very treacherous here in the desert because the soil does not hold water well and there are no storm drains to catch the water." He used big words with the children.

Joe continually found teaching moments; some were as he worked on cars. Car repair was not a favorite activity, at least not for Pauline and Margit. In the mid-

1940s, Robert and Norma were too small for car duty, but they got their chances later. Some of the cars Joe worked on presented him with frustrating quagmires of problems. He reacted by growling at whoever was helping. The children learned to work with their dad regardless of his demeanor, which helped them later with all sorts of customers. They also watched him grasp opportunity after opportunity.

Throughout the mid-1940s, the prisoners were on site. They seemed a happy lot, interacting with the family and visitors whether they spoke Italian or not. Uncle Paul came and went several times in those years, participating in the business and family activities—especially with the children.

A harsh environment? Yes, but full of family, friends, adventure, and new opportunities again on the horizon.

# 9

## From War to Peace, Late 1940s

The Summit and the nation as a whole worked at transitioning from war to peace in all aspects of life at the end of the '40s. This meant spending and living without the restrictions of the war years. At the Summit, Joe and Ruth spent on some new ventures. The children frolicked more freely as the signs of war disappeared from the area.

### No vacancies

The soldiers and their visitors who had rented units at the Summit were gone, but travelers were looking for overnight accommodations by the time they reached the gas station. The trailers and rental cabins were not enough, so in 1946 Joe and Ruth decided to put up a six-unit, cement-block motel across from the café and near where the tin auto repair shop already stood. Ruth outfitted the motel beautifully—this time no muslin feedbags. She went to Palm Springs to contract with the interior designers at Desmond Department Store. Their design included drapes and bedspreads in desert colors. The work crews assigned to the area or the traveling public would find rooms that were simply but nicely furnished. Each had a shower and bath. The motel was just about ready to book guests when Margit and Robert engaged in a little but expensive mischief that almost delayed its opening.

Joe bought a beautiful and pricy neon sign for the motel, high enough to be seen at a distance from the highway. Eight-year-old Margit told Robert one evening as they were playing outside after dinner, "I bet I can throw a rock over that sign."

"No, you can't. It's too high," her six-year-old brother firmly replied.

That only made Margit more determined. She looked around for a rock that was just the right size. "OK, Robert, I am ready,"

*Photo 30: Chiriaco Motel, late 1940s.*

She aimed, and off flew her rock right at the neon sign—at it, mind you, not over it.

Both children covered their mouths to stifle screams as they saw the gaping dark spot in the beautiful neon. Now what? The two accomplices said nothing for a while but eventually fessed up. The sign got repaired and just as Joe and Ruth hoped drew people to the motel.

The word got out that the Summit had an affordable yet classy place to stay. Again Joe's vision and Ruth's industriousness paid off. The motel turned out to be an excellent business decision. For the many years the motel was open, it often had no vacancies.

## Fowl ventures

Like the rest of the world, the desert was susceptible to illnesses, especially before the advances yet to come in medicine, some just around the corner. Thank goodness for Ruth.

Toyjo's rescue was an act of kindness. Not so when Joe took on some turkeys and then increased the flock to about one thousand. He planned to make an eating business out of them, which meant he would have had to meet health department regulations for commercial-grade meat—but before he could complete the process to comply, a huge deluge overtook the area in 1946, making the turkeys sick.

Ruth was outside when she sensed something ominous in the sky. A funnel started to descend from a cloud.

"Come in to the café—hurry!" Ruth yelled to the children and anyone else in earshot. "A tornado is coming!"

The wind started blowing furiously. Rain poured fast and hard. The swirling storm airlifted turkeys every which way out into the desert, some never to return. Others ended up waddling in deep puddles. The wind shoved a trailer into the corner of the little house. Ruth was wise to call people into the café, a strong, sound building.

The tornado was actually a microburst, but that term was not in general use in the 1940s. It was over quickly but had done more damage than immediately apparent. A day or so later, Ruth noticed something was wrong with many of the turkeys that were left. They had swollen neck glands, making it hard for them to eat; Joe was on the verge of losing most of his gobblers. Ruth immediately drew on her nursing experience, but also got some help. Uncle Devio, back from serving during the war, was living at the Summit for a short while before he and his family moved to housing for veterans.

"Here, Devio, you hold their heads over this bucket, and I will lance where it is swollen. We have to get some of that fluid out of them," Ruth said.

Devio did so, turkey after turkey after turkey. Pauline and Margit watched.

"Can I do it?" Pauline asked. She and Devio took turns helping Ruth. Although some of the thousand had disappeared, enough of the remaining were sick, making the lancing a long, tedious job. The turkey business never launched.

Pauline never minded helping her mother, even in a tough situation. The turkey operations done, Joe came back into the picture, killing and freezing many of them for their own use. Joe could see that a turkey business was too problematic, so abandoned that plan. From then on, the family concentrated on chickens, again for their own family use. The children collected eggs and helped process the poultry. Almost every week, Joe called the children over to the chopping block.

"Come pluck the feathers," he instructed, and the children did so. Then Joe butchered the meat, with special orders from Ruth to save the giblets and any eggs that were forming for the special gravy she made.

Another rainstorm came, but this time no turkeys. Joe, Ruth, and the children often found solutions that were out of the ordinary. When the baby chicks started shivering out in the elements, Pauline and Margit started gathering them up and taking them to the generator building, which often got quite warm inside. The rickety building was perfect for drying the chicks. Pauline and Margit were proud of themselves; they had saved quite a few of their future meals.

## Uncle Paul on and off duty

Paul was honorably discharged from the marines in January 1946 with the rank of master sergeant. He continued to work for the marines as a civilian in Washington, DC, for several months after that. Then in the fall of 1946, Paul came back to help Joe at the Summit. He stayed from September through November. He had the day shift. Vincent had the night shift. During the day, in addition to his other chores, Paul helped with the water situation. He and Joe repaired the pipes with inner tubes. They climbed to Lost Palms Oasis or one of the other sources. Once in a while there would be a flash flood coming down the mountain; then they'd have to scurry out of the danger zone. But usually they just found palm trees and rattlesnakes. They'd bring shotguns to deal with the rattlers. The crested quail at Lost Palms showed no fear of humans. Like much else in the desert, their numbers had been affected by the huge number of soldiers, but there were still enough of them to get in the way. They did not scatter when approached. Joe and Paul had to push them aside to get to the break in the pipes.

Paul commented to Joe on repair trips, "This water is a big deal."

"Yes, and people just let the water run from the faucet while they fill up."

This really annoyed Joe, who had installed a faucet near the gasoline pumps to accommodate customers. Sometimes he would see customers splashing water on their radiators to cool them. Sometimes he saw them helping themselves to water in a sloppy way, just letting the water run while talking to someone. At times Joe would see the flow get sluggish and know that the supply was diminishing. Even when there was just a trickle coming out of the spigot, some individuals did not understand that they were wasting water needed for the next customer. Joe cared that people needed and stopped for water, but he just could not allow it to be wasted. So he came up with a way to save water and make money. He removed the faucet and sold water in gallon jugs for twenty-five cents.

Paul reported to Joe shortly after, "One man bought six jugs of water for his radiator. I gave him his money back when he returned the jugs. You know, I think people from the East do not understand the importance of water in the desert."

Joe scowled, "You gave him his money back? The water costs us."

Joe started charging a fee for the water and a deposit for the jugs. He was not about to lose water or money or any opportunities that water presented. He also started selling radiator bags, which were more expensive, anywhere between one and five dollars.

Joe made one allowance for using extra water. In the 1940s, the family installed evaporative coolers, sometimes known as swamp coolers. Except during the summer rains, the coolers made the heat more tolerable for the Chiriacos and their customers. The Summit got something else that made life a little easier. Sometime in the '40s, phone service had come to the Summit. It was a party-line service. The Chiriacos eagerly waited to hear one long and three short rings. That signal let them know the call was for them. The older children were hoping for a call from a friend and a lengthy chat, but sometimes they needed to give the phone over to a truck driver who needed help.

If a truck broke down, the driver grabbed his sleeping bag and hailed the next truck on the road for a ride to the Summit. There were many trucks on the Los Angeles to Phoenix run at night so the driver usually waited for just a few minutes. Once at the Summit, the stranded driver called the repair unit. Before the Summit had a phone, the other driver would contact help once he reached a place where he could make a call. If stranded overnight, the driver of the hapless rig slept in the café on the floor behind the counter. Often Paul was at the counter in the evening. He would write letters, catch up on paper work, and talk to truck drivers, those stranded or those coming and going. He was amazed at their stories, including some about his home town far away in Alabama.

In addition to regular Summit work, Paul unofficially helped out with the children. Sometimes during the day while on duty he had to act as coach.

Norma ran into the café, cute as a button but with a very messy face peeking through her tussled blonde curls. "Uncle Paul, Robert—Robert—he is ..."

"What's he doing this time, Norma? Throwing dirt, huh?"

"He, he ...," she started but noticed people looking at her.

"Go find your mother and get cleaned up."

"Normal kid stuff." Paul shook his head, talking to himself as he went to go find Robert.

Robert was outside playing in the dirt with toy cars. "Are you annoying your sister again?"

Robert looked up with no answer. Paul bent down, played in the sand with him, talking to him all the while. The teasing lessened, maybe due to Paul and maybe due to growing up. In any event, it seemed that the extended family played their parts, no matter how small, in rearing the children. That was not left to chance.

Paul saw Ruth as a kind, hardworking soul who went out of her way to please all at the Summit. He saw Joe as a tough but protective taskmaster. Joe was good with customers but had little patience with slacking workers, which was how Joe saw his brother Vincent, even this second time around. Business was growing, so he hired a few more people. Scruffy Bob Howe was still working for Joe. Now, portly Charlie Lily, quite the Dapper Dan, joined the staff. Bessie Parker came on as a waitress. They proved to be good workers. Joe hired some other people who were not so good.

Joe and Ruth treated their employees like family, even providing living spaces for them. They started to develop a little employee village behind the café, at first with the four cabins still left from aqueduct days, a few simple trailers, and even some left-behind military tents, although the tents were mostly for storage. Bob preferred his lean-to by the reservoir, so he stayed there.

*Photo 31: Uncle Paul with Norma, 1946.*

Paul spent time talking with workers during his visits. He especially liked talking to Bob Howe, who told fascinating stories about his World War I service and about his travels, which were almost always on foot. Once in a while a worker gave him pause. George Boch, who told Joe he had been a German engineer, settled himself in a run-down trailer on airport property, not on Joe's land. He was basically squatting. George was interested in just enough work to pay for food not already stored in his secret caches. Before the soldiers left Camp Young, they buried huge cans of food in the desert. They did this rather than transporting them or giving them away. George knew where the cans were and dug them up from time to time. Joe gave him a job, to clean out an oven that he planned to put back in the café kitchen. George was legally blind so did not see a black widow in the oven. He spent several weeks in the hospital but recovered. Joe, feeling responsible, continued to give him work now and then.

On one encounter George asked Paul, "You know those balloons that the Japanese sent to the Pacific coast during the war?"

Paul did know. "Those are dangerous."

"I found one of those balloons near here. It still has a bomb connected to it."

Paul asked hesitantly, "Where? Where is the balloon?"

"I'll show you. I can hardly see anymore. I want to examine that bomb to see how it's made before I lose all my sight. I need someone to come with me to dismantle it. Will you come?"

Shocked, Paul responded instantly, "Absolutely not!"

One of these balloons had tragically made the news. The only World War II casualties on US soil happened in Oregon in 1945, where a pregnant woman and five children were killed when they saw such a balloon and, thinking it was a toy for play, unwittingly detonated it. Over the years, some but possibly not all were found and made inoperable by experts. To the best of anyone's knowledge, George did not pursue his balloon plans. He stayed safely at the Summit the rest of his life doing odd jobs.

Soon after the balloon scare, Paul left the summit and went with his brother, Vincent, to San Bernardino. Both went to look for work. Joe had again fired Vincent—sort of. Actually, Joe hated firing anyone. He didn't have to. He just kept the pressure on, never letting up on his expectations. He outlasted employees who couldn't measure up. So it was with Vincent—now looking for a different opportunity. Paul too wanted to experience a different type of work. Besides, as Paul would later recount, Joe had "a hell of a temper, but mellowed in later life."

Every day, Paul suggested that they pound the pavement. Vincent wanted to stay in California. Paul planned to return to Alabama but stayed to help Vincent find work.

"Surely there are a lot of jobs here," he encouraged Vincent.

"Today is not a good day to look for a job," Vincent would respond.

Eventually, Paul used the cash he had left to buy a train ticket, except for one dollar he got in change. With that he bought a bag of apples. The apples were his only food on his trip back to Alabama. Vincent went to work for Devio's construction business in Pomona, but eventually he too returned to Alabama.

## The bond so strong

A waitress was buzzing around the café in the early morning serving travelers and some of the prisoners of war. Charlie Lily was sitting at the counter when Ruth spilled a cup of coffee right in front of him. She started wiping up almost as though she was angry at the cup, asking a series of questions as she scrubbed back and forth.

"Where's our other waitress?"

"Bessie's off today," the waitress said.

"I mean the other woman."

"She'll be in later," the waitress explained.

"And Joe?"

Charlie answered a bit sheepishly, "Working on the pipeline."

Ruth caught something that bothered her in Charlie's voice. She left the café and made her way along the pipeline toward the springs. She was not far when she saw tire tracks going up and then turning to go down. She went back to the café.

"Where's Joe?" she again asked Charlie. This time he sat her down and told her what he knew.

"OK, then, I am going to Colton. Good thing Joe taught me to drive," she snapped and left the café for the second time.

An hour or so later, Ruth, with the children in tow, was back. She told Charlie that she would be gone for the rest of the day. Colton was about one hundred miles away toward Los Angeles.

"I know what you are planning. I am all for it," Charlie told her.

Ruth loaded the children into the car, drove to Colton, and parked in front of a motel. It was a cool day, but she cracked the windows open. "Pauline, you be in charge here for a few minutes," she said and marched up to the door, knocked, and made her way in.

A while later she emerged with a determined look on her face. Ruth had done what she had planned, stand up to Joe and anyone who would threaten her marriage with the only man she loved. She drove back home and resumed her everyday life. The missing waitress never came back to the Summit. The affair was over. This event could have destroyed their family life and the Summit business, but Ruth was not going to let either happen. Instead, this bump in the road increased their attention to each other, making their marriage and business partnership even stronger—strong enough to quickly pay off the loan on their property

## Ownership

Joe and Ruth had leased the land at the Summit back in 1933 and then bought it through a loan in 1942, right around the time that General Patton came into the area. Finally, on April 18, 1947, they paid off the last installment of their loan of $11,000 on the original property they had purchased from James and Aura Cram. Now their investment was solid. But how could that be?

Their main customers, the soldiers and the POWs, were gone. Yes, but they had also cultivated the traveling public. Gasoline rationing ended after the war, encouraging more travel. That meant the Summit survived and even needed more help, especially in summer and early fall. A local paper summarized the traffic statistics at the end of the 1940s in *The Survey of Records* furnished by the Arizona and California inspections stations near Blythe. The *Survey* reported that from 1948 to

1949, passenger car, bus, and truck traffic together increased 14.2 percent through the California–Arizona Highway 60 checkpoints near Blythe.

Joe started advertising in the café window for couples with a trailer. They would sign up for a few months now and then. What about the twenty acres of airport land? At the end of the war, the military divested itself of excess facilities. The airfield, including Joe's acreage, fell into that category. The War Assets Administration turned the airport over to the County of Riverside Aviation Department.

*Photo 32: Ruth and Joe Chiriaco, 1940s, Shaver Summit.*

Riverside County administered it for civil use and called it Shaver's Airport. Joe did not get the land there back. *I was right*, he thought. *I gave those acres away.*

Ruth and Joe started buying more land every chance they could, but not at nearby Eagle Mountain, where a new community was forming. In 1948, Henry Kaiser founded the Eagle Mountain Iron Mines, with a city for workers on site. He built four hundred tract homes there. Eventually, the community had trailers, boarding houses, churches, a store, a bowling alley, a movie theater, and other amenities for the miners, including gas stations. At the peak, the population was four thousand. The population lived in small tract houses built by Kaiser.

Even though Eagle Mountain was self-sufficient and thirty-eight miles away, the miners occasionally visited the Summit. While he was happy to sell his goods to them and had some good friends among the Eagle Mountain crowd, Joe was unhappy about the drunkenness, drug abuse, rowdy behavior, and profanity of some. Like his concern when Patton first arrived with his soldiers, he did not want bad behavior around his children. Fortunately, there were also exemplary, capable folks from the mountain whom he would hire as the years went on and who would help in crises at the Summit in the decades ahead.

## A playful view of life

Sick or well, sun, rain, or snow, night or day, no matter what, the children remained creative and positive in their desert playground. Their parents kept making a good life and living among the storms, whether high winds smashing through or throngs of customers coming by.

Even when they were sick, life was interesting for the children at the Summit. In 1946, when she was in third grade, Margit came down with rheumatic fever and was kept indoors for months. Penicillin had been discovered in 1928 but was not readily available until 1945, in time to help cure Margit. Even with the medication, the doctor ordered complete bed rest for Margit until her symptoms improved. Ruth cared for Margit but also had to continue working in the store, so Margit and her parents developed a way to communicate when Margit was alone in the house

Margit was an avid reader. When she needed help, she held her book up to the window by her bed. The window was situated so it could be seen in the store. As soon as either parent saw Margit signaling them, one went to her immediately. After six months of being indoors, Margit started asking to go outside. In early summer, Ruth made a day bed for her under a tamarisk tree. Not too long after, the doctor gave his OK, and Margit was back adventuring in the desert. She returned to school in the fall, going right on to fourth grade after missing most of the third.

The whole family made the best of the desert climate, hot or cold.

"Look, look!" It was January 25, 1949. One of the four Chiriaco youngsters woke up the others. They all scrambled to the window. They marveled at something very rare in the desert. Snow had fallen overnight—and a lot of it. All four dressed quickly, pulling on overcoats as they ran outside. The desert can get very cold at night, so they were prepared with the right clothing. In no time, they rolled three balls, stacked them, made a face on the top ball, and stood back to admire their work.

"He's not done." One of the children ran inside and came back out with a few pieces of winter garb. Ruth followed a few minutes later.

"That's a good snowman. Dad's hat and scarf look good on him." Ruth smiled. "No school today," she added as she turned to go back in. She felt a touch of her Minnesota roots.

*Photo 33: Chiriaco Four with snowman, Edison trailer, cabin, and tamarisk trees in background, Chiriaco Summit, January 25, 1949.*

The snow probably had little effect on the traffic by the Summit that day. Even though the National Weather Service recorded it at three inches at Hayfield Pump Station, most likely it melted quickly. Joe and Ruth did not get a snow day; they had to work. In fact, Joe had to deal with pipes that froze and burst.

*Photo 34: Pauline and Margit with ice sculpture as a result of a burst pipeline, Chiriaco Summit, c. January 25, 1949.*

Winter turned to spring and then the usual hot summer. The business was stable. Military customers had been replaced by prisoners of war, then by the traveling public, and also by miners. Margit beat the dangerous rheumatic fever. The animals were healthy. And the teasing between Norma and Robert had subsided.

Did the children see their environment as harsh? One day ten-year-old Margit and six-year-old Norma went to visit one of Norma's classmates. The little boy lived with his family at the Sweeney stump ranch in the middle of nowhere. A stump ranch grows up haphazardly, usually as a place to eke out a living by raising a few animals. The Sweeneys, however, were uranium miners, with their stump ranch as a base of operations. The Sweeney mom drove the girls the twelve miles from the Summit to the little ranch. She fed the children lunch. For dessert she served them her delicious store-bought peaches sprinkled with sugar.

Later when they were older, Margit and Norma commented to each other, "The Sweeneys live so simply."

"Kinda like us."

"But we don't have those peaches."

All these desert children, including the little boy, seemed happy. Life looked normal and full of adventure to these desert youngsters with treasure of all sorts all around.

Sometimes, the youngsters explored the desert away from their familiar structures and grounds. Sometimes these adventures got the best of their curiosity. One day as they were becoming teenagers, the two older girls and their friends chanced upon what looked like a disturbed piece of earth.

"Look at that sign," Margit said to Pauline. "I wonder who is buried there."

Winifred Moore, Pauline's friend, and Eileen Heimark, the beer distributor's daughter and a school friend of Margit's, were on this jaunt. The four girls stood at the gravesite, some with reverence, and some with sheer curiosity

"Buried—oh this is scary!"

"I think it is interesting. I wonder who the person is."

"We'd better run home and tell Mom and Dad that we found a grave." The four rushed back to the Summit. They burst out the news and couldn't understand why Joe and Ruth were laughing so hard.

"Girls, girls, *Latrine* is not a name. It is not a person who is buried there."

By the end of the 1940s, Robert and Norma were about nine and seven. No matter the season, they would go off on their own, hiking onto old military campground, owned by the federal government and administered by the Bureau of Land Management (BLM) since before General Patton arrived. They loved to go the soldiers' amphitheater, where Gladys Lloyd "Robbie" Robinson, who started the Brigadears, also helped arrange entertainment. They used the eroding seats built into the hillside for steps as they ran up and down the hill. They explored barren campsites outlined by rocks that the soldier builders had put there to mark perimeters years ago. The older children were busier than the younger two by now, but occasionally all four would head out exploring—pulling a red wagon with eggs, bacon, a frying pan, and some jugs of water. They might go several miles away, even into Joshua Tree National Monument, build a fire, and cook.

Did their parents worry? No one was worried about child predators. There were no rules about making bonfires, although perhaps there should have been. In the 1940s, fire regulations were vague. Today, backcountry campers planning to be on public land need to obtain a free permit at the trailhead at Cottonwood Spring, and then fires are limited to a portable stove. No ground fires are allowed outside of official campgrounds. In those days, other than rattlesnakes and dehydration, both of which the children knew how to avoid, their huge backyard was a safe playground. They may have been lucky with the bonfires.

## It's not just luck

Soon after he had returned to Alabama, Paul moved to Washington, DC. He found the new experience he was looking for. He started a lifelong career with the Federal Trade Commission. Over the ensuing years, he and his wife, Shirley, continued to visit the Summit. He would tell people:

Joe was lucky in some ways—the Aqueduct, Highway 60, Patton, the Italian prisoners.

Both he and Ruth were hard workers. Joe understood supply and demand. He saw need after need and hauled what customers wanted out to the Summit. He might have gotten it for five cents and sold it for ten cents. Eventually, he had merchandise delivered, but in the early days he hauled everything out there.

Paul understood and told others how hard it was for Joe's family in war years to get not only what they needed themselves but also supplies for customers.

Sometimes it was hard to get simple things like toilet paper, nylon stockings, cigarettes, meat, or black pepper. Food was rationed. In the café at times they used eggs for protein.

But Ruth and Joe had a knack for turning circumstances—fortunate or not—into good fortune.

*Map 5: Shaver Summit as of the end of the 1940s. Motel to the right. Aerial photo sent by Greyhound Bus Co. in the 1950s.*

Landing

Airplane Parking

Chicken Coop

Generator House

Old Cabins

Laundry

Old Cafe

Junk Yard

Gas Station

Ruth and Joe's Home/Office

Trailer Park

Old Highway 60

55 Ford Tow Truck

Garage

Brick Motel (Late 1940s)

Telephone Line

# Part Three

# Putting Chiriaco Summit on the Map, 1950s–1970s

*Family*

You can't **a-Ford** to miss *Shaver Summit*.
Don't **Dodge** *Shaver Summit*.

(Joe Chiriaco, on tailgates of his vehicles, early 1950s)

Shaver Lake, in Central California, gets confused with us.
Let's change to *Chiriaco Summit*.

(Ruth Chiriaco, 1958)

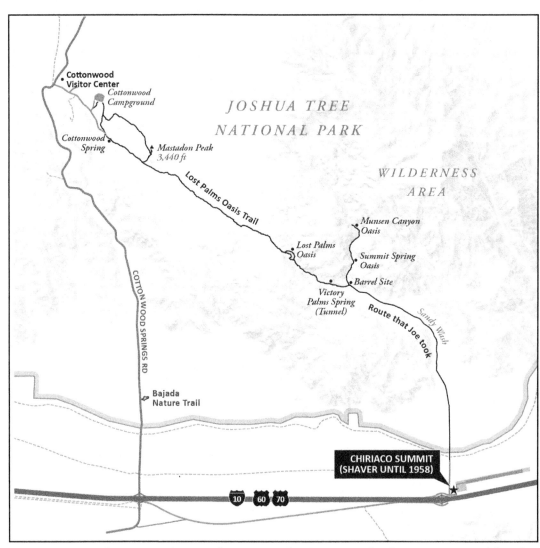

Map 6: *Lost Palms Oasis Hiking Trail, Cottonwood to Summit and Joe's Pipe Repair Trail, based on a Joshua Tree National Park trail map. (Joshua Tree National Monument became a national park in 1996. Visitor Center established in 1964.)*

# 10

## *The Chiriaco Four, Early 1950s*

An operatic voice poured out from the open windows into the desert on a Sunday drive into the brown hills. As was typical, the family sat happily in their Ford. Several jugs of water and a picnic basket shared the car's trunk. Ruth had packed fried chicken and potato salad. The family kept one jug of water in the back seat. Even though it was springtime, they held to their strict, two-point family rule:

1. Never waste water.
2. Never go anywhere without water.

The lifting of gas rationing at the end of World War II, the Korean War, and the Cold War all had effects on the Summit. But so did the post-World War II traditional family life and the national feeling of prosperity. All four of the Chiriaco youngsters rolled up their sleeves to cook, clean, wait tables, fix cars and generators, pump gas, and help with the pipes. In between they enjoyed picnics in the hills, adventures at the airport, noisy air-raid drills, and a contest at the county fair. By the middle of the idyllic '50s, the oldest of the Chiriaco youngsters was gone.

### Family fun, unity

Weekends were busy at the Summit, so the family worked many of their Saturdays and Sundays until they got some special help. In 1950, Mattie Lux came to live at the Summit after her husband died. Since Ruth's early nursing days when she rented a room from Mattie, the two had become good friends. Mattie needed a place and an income and found both with her friend at the Summit. She lived there in a trailer from 1950 to 1955. She became such a part of the family that the children called her Mom Lux. She cooked, sewed, ironed clothes, did housecleaning, and helped with the motel. Ruth added Mattie's tacos to the restaurant menu. The Summit life was a boon for Mattie but also for Joe and Ruth. With Mattie and the other employees, they could relax a bit. Often, Ruth alone took the four youngsters on weekend excursions. On rare occasions, Joe joined the family on outings. Years later the children remembered different aspects of those excursions. Joe's singing, Sunday drives, conversations, hikes, picnics, and nature lessons are merged from their children's memories into this composite scene in what was then Joshua Tree National Monument.

Joe was humming and singing *My Blue Heaven* as he navigated the bumps and curves on the dirt road. His lovely voice was a match for that of the famous crooner Gene Austin, who recorded that hit in 1928, when it charted for twenty-six weeks. Now it was 1950, but the tune was still a favorite of Joe's. Ruth sat next to him in the front seat, mesmerized. She loved his singing. The family was on the way to a picnic at Cottonwood Spring, which bubbled out of the earth and then trickled along on the surface like a little creek.

Three of the youngsters were together in the back seat. One was up front. Pauline was a teenager. Margit, Robert, and Norma were twelve, ten, and eight. Dad stopped singing, and now he and Mother were talking. The back-seat chattering stopped.

"We need to start thinking about college," Ruth started the conversation.

Why would a desert couple who labored manually think about college? Actually, there was never any question about this. Ruth, of course, was well educated. Joe saw that families all around him were planning for college. That was certainly the case with the Heimarks.

"Pauline is already fourteen and ahead in school," Joe said proudly.

"Yes, all the children will go."

"Of course."

All four always knew that school mattered and that they would leave the Summit for college. They liked the idea, but it was more than the words that kept their attention. Mom and Dad had a beautiful way of talking. The cadence of their voices came across like music—one with a Southern accent mixed with a tinge of Italian and the other a Midwestern accent with a hint of Norwegian. On some of these trips, Joe would get stubborn, but not for long.

"When we get back, I need to finish fixing that car," Joe said.

"Not tonight. We will be back too late."

"But Ruth…"

"Now Joe, promise me you will come in after an hour—no staying outside all night."

No answer.

"Promise me, Joe." A firmness came through the cadence.

And he promised. The children smiled, knowing that Mom could talk to a wall and make it answer. Their dad could be a very solid wall.

After a while they had to park the car and start walking. Their goal today was Cottonwood Spring, which had been part of Joshua Tree National Monument since 1936. On the way they explored. They walked by an arrastra, a crude drag-stone mill for pulverizing ore used in the hopes of finding gold. Joe explained that this had been a gold mining area at one time, that water was necessary to process gold, and so hopeful prospectors came to places like this.

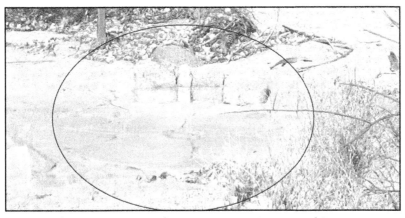

*Photo 35: Remains of an arrastra near Cottonwood Spring.*

"Ohhh, this looks like part of a pot." One of the youngsters bent over to pick up a shard.

In the 1950s, people were still pot hunting, later much frowned upon.

Joe stopped to explain again, this time that the Cahuilla Indians had come to the springs in this area for centuries, that they had they left bedrock mortar and clay pots.

*Photo 36: Bedrock mortar left by Cahuilla Indians, Joshua Tree hiking trail near Cottonwood Spring.*

Soon they were near the spring itself. The fan palms were in sight. All four youngsters started running. One after another put a toe into the trickle of a stream. It was cold. There was some giggling for a while. Joe watched, smiling. Ruth put down a big sheet.

"Look, a canary," one of the four said, pointing as the bird flew out of a palm.

Joe handed the picnic basket he was carrying to Ruth, then gathered the children around him, saying, "See what a bright yellow they are."

"With black wings. Look, there's another one." They all became enthralled with the birds.

"But it's gray, not so pretty."

"It's the mother bird. The male birds are usually brighter. It's nesting time." Joe looked up and pointed to a nest.

Some of the desert inhabitants tended to use the term *canary* for any yellow bird. The bird the Chiriaco family saw that day was probably a Scott's oriole, a hooded oriole, or a lesser goldfinch.

As they walked around the area, they saw more birds: a roadrunner, a mocking-bird, and some quail. All the birds scattered as the family walked by.

"Lots of quail here, Joe."

"They have made a good comeback since the soldiers left. They're scared of people again. The rest of the desert is getting back to normal too."

"Could you come back this week and hunt some?" Ruth asked. "I'll make them for dinner."

Joe nodded yes. Stuffed quail was one of Ruth's specialties.

One of the children picked up a rock. Joe used this as an opportunity for a reminder: "Don't throw stones at rattlers."

"I'm not."

"Well, just in case any of you are thinking about that, remember they were here first. And if you miss, you might make the situation worse. Freeze and then back away slowly. Don't startle them." Joe, however, carried a pistol. If a rattler threatened any one in his party, he would not miss.

"Come and eat before the animals get it all," Ruth called. The four kids all scrambled to get a good place on the sheet. They were hungry after all the hiking, so they downed their food in no time. The family explored some more after lunch into the late afternoon. As the sky started to show signs of early evening, they made the short walk to the car and climbed in, except for Pauline.

"Can I drive?" she asked. Joe had been teaching her to drive on dirt roads and the airport runway since her birthday a few months back, not uncommon for a fourteen-year-old in the desert wilderness.

"Not this time. It's getting late. Get in," Joe ordered. "I'm driving." While he was demanding when the children helped him fix cars, he was patient as a driving instructor, so Pauline pouted a bit as she moved toward the car.

All in and they bumped down the dirt road as a bright full moon was rising. "I have to do a few things on that car," Joe said with his charming accent. "You and the older girls are going to wash dishes anyway."

"They'll be done when we get home since we started closing earlier. Mattie and the Carpenters said they'd handle it."

Jim and Vera Carpenter came in their trailer to work at the Summit off and on for years. Jim was another example of Joe's dichotomy of being demanding yet forgiving. This burly guy had served prison time but was making a new life for himself as a mechanic. As long as he did his work well and stayed out of trouble, he had a job with Joe. He proved himself to be an excellent mechanic. His wife, Vera, was a reliable cook and waitress. She acted in a calm, decent manner. The Carpenters eventually moved to Texas and did well there.

## Family working together

After the troops and prisoners left the area, the Summit business slowed down for a while. Staying open late was not worth it, so Ruth and Joe made a business decision. They closed the café at dark and reopened 24-7 when traffic picked up a few years later; however, closing early did not always mean an early night.

On some weekend nights or any night when school was not in session, Ruth would go on an all-night cleaning spree. The spree had to be at night—the only downtime the business could afford. The family would stay up to help her. They would move everything in the store area as they cleaned above, below, and in between. Nothing escaped. In the café the stove got cleaned. In the parts section, they moved the fan belts hanging from the ceiling and dusted them. On Monday morning they took US 60 back to school in Indio.

The growing family lived in an isolated desert region. The isolation could have given the Chiriacos a narrow view of the world, one reason Ruth and Joe made sure they all spent time with friends and had activities in the cities that surrounded them. For a while in the early 1950s Ruth and the children lived in Indio. Joe stayed at the Summit. The benefit of friends was one factor in the move to Indio. For example, one of Ruth's good friends from her nursing days, Frances Moore, lived in the area. Her daughter Winifred was a good friend of Pauline's. Margit's best friend, Eileen Heimark, lived down the street. Another benefit: the children took a school bus in Indio daily, which was far easier for Joe and Ruth than driving them every day from the Summit. But Ruth still made the long highway trip—going to work every day at the café and then back to Indio by the time the children were out of school. Summer was different. They stayed at the Summit.

During school days, Ruth, Joe, and the staff handled most of the daytime chores. Summer meant chores for the four youngsters starting soon after they awoke. Most of them got up early to feed the animals, which at different times included chickens, pigeons, rabbits, turkeys, and horses. Especially in summer months, they filled radiator bags for sale with water. Robert checked to see if there was enough diesel fuel for the generators. No matter the time of year, Joe often slept in, especially after a long night tinkering with cars or fixing equipment, such as the generators. Ruth was up by dawn summer or winter cooking breakfast. She routinely prepared pancake batter the night before, but she needed to prepare coffee, eggs, toast, and bacon in the morning.

Sometimes Joe would make it to the kitchen just as breakfast was almost ready. Later family members recapped snippets of conversations between Ruth and Joe about scrap metal and pigeons—and chickens once the children joined them after chores.

"I figured out how I am going to crush all those cars in the junkyard. I am going to get an old roller, the kind that they use on highways to level the asphalt. I'll fill it with water, use a working truck to push it, and run it over the cars. I'll take the cars to L.A. and sell them for scrap metal."

"Good idea, but wait to go to L.A. until you have a big pile."

"Yes, and until the price of scrap metal goes up."

*Photo 37: Roller used to crush junked cars, itself junked in the Chiriaco Junkyard.*

Once in a while a pigeon would fly in with a message tied to its legs.

"Did you figure out where that homing pigeon came from the other day?"

"The message gave me a hint."

Joe always tried to find the owner. Now and then he succeeded.

When the children got hungry for breakfast and could smell it cooking they raced to the kitchen.

"Mother, we are out of table scraps for the chickens."

"Here are some more. Just give them these and hurry back. Breakfast is ready."

"Hey, don't bump into me." One youngster was carrying a bucket full of breakable eggs.

"Mother, look how many we got today!"

Ruth looked them over and took out a few to scramble, but just for the family.

As required by the health department, Joe and Ruth bought commercial-grade eggs, produce, and meat for the restaurant.

About 6:00 a.m. daily, Ruth went out to the counter to start serving early customers. The children followed, carrying their plates. They ate at the same counter as the customers.

On some mornings at the beginning of the '50s, Ruth had especially welcome guests for breakfast. Paul had been recalled to active duty as a staff sergeant with the marine corps from August of 1950 to September of 1951 due to the Korean War. He and Shirley were stationed near enough to the Summit to visit with their baby daughter born during that time. To Shirley, Ruth, some twenty years after leaving nursing, was still an expert on babies and motherhood. Shirley had lots of discussions with Ruth. Shirley also had the benefit of watching her with her tiny daughter. On one of these visits she told her, 'Ruth, you helped me be confident with motherhood."

Well, Ruth had years of experience with little ones, but she was now moving into uncharted territory, being a mother of teenagers.

## Friends—a driving incident

By 1951 Pauline and Margit were in high school, Robert was in seventh grade, and Norma was in fourth. It was a Friday in the fall. They had shopped in Indio with their mother after school for food and supplies before going home to the Summit, which they did every weekend. All four were helping to unload and put things away. They had a fifth pair of hands this evening. Eileen Heimark was spending the weekend at the Summit. Both girls were freshman at Coachella Valley High School. Margit was thirteen and Eileen was fourteen, just a few months older. The next morning, Eileen and Margit were up and out early.

"Everyone is learning to drive, Margit," Eileen said.

"I can teach you. Come on, let's go get the truck and go practice at the airport. That's where I learned." Learning to drive before age sixteen was not unusual in the desert environment, and because driving was a resource that rural desert folk needed, sometimes licenses were granted early. However, for these two, driving was more about a rite of passage than a necessity.

Margit drove the red pickup to the edge of the runway, pointing out how she started the truck and then shifted it. Once on the runway, she put it in neutral and turned off the ignition. "OK, get in the driver's seat, Eileen."

Once settled in, Eileen voiced one of her concerns. "We don't have any cars like this. Ours are all automatic."

"This is all we have. Dad likes stick shifts."

Eileen looked worried.

"You can do it," said Margit. "First turn on the car. No, no, not like that. Put in the clutch."

"The clutch?"

"Yes, right there by your foot. Push it in and then turn the key."

"I did it!" smiled Eileen, and she started to go.

"Oh, now you stalled it. Do you know why?"

"I have to put it in first gear right after I start it—and then go?" Eileen asked remembering Margit's demonstration on her way over to the airport. Margit shook her head yes.

Eileen drove up the runway, made a smooth, wide turn to the right, just about where a plane would have left the ground. Then she went back to the start, and then up and down the runway a few more times with Margit still coaching her. She shifted gears until she had the feel of stick-shift driving—enough for today.

"Wow, you learned fast; now drive the truck back and park it," said Margit.

Eileen looked for a way off the runway that would get her back to the parking space behind the café. There was no fencing around the runway in those years, so she got off where she thought she had a straight shot. She came down the incline off the runway just fine. She saw the chicken coop ahead and made a left turn to get around it. My, she was proud of herself, her first-ever ninety-degree left turn! But she couldn't straighten out, just kept turning. And then bang! She tore through part of the wire fence straight into the chicken coop. In an instant, noise and debris surrounded her. Twenty screaming, fluttering chickens scattered all around the now stalled truck. An image of Margit's father, Joe, overwhelmed her. His temper was legend, from the Summit all the way to Indio. She expected the worst. Without a word to Margit, she turned off the motor, threw open the door, and almost tripped as she started running.

"Oh, no! I killed a chicken!"

She saw the coop's metal roof on the ground and ran faster. She darted up the mountain with no idea where she was headed. Running was all she knew to do right then.

Margit ran the other way to get her dad. Soon Joe was after Eileen in another of his vehicles, bouncing and maneuvering through the rocks and brush. He got out and rushed over to her before she could get much farther.

"I killed a chicken! I killed a chicken," she cried out to him, turning back and forth, not knowing whether to stay put or keep running.

He reached out and put his arms around her. "It's OK."

"But I killed a chicken—and the roof ... Oh, I am so sorry."

"It's OK. It's OK."

Joe told her again and again not to worry. Eileen visited the Summit many times more, remaining Margit's good friend. Joe never mentioned the dead chicken or the metal roof again. She did note that the chicken coop, roof and all, was back together. She never asked whether or not the dead chicken became a dinner. This incident, like many others, showed the children that no matter what happened, you fixed it (pipes, generators, chicken coops) and moved on. As the years went on, the children and their friends, like Eileen, came to understand the tremendous and somewhat singular responsibility Joe carried on his shoulders. Like many others, she respected him tremendously, seeing that his intimidating demeanor masked a kind heart even though it conveyed, "Do not mess with me." They saw that he was policeman and businessman at the same time—all the time. His protective bent extended to family, friends, customers, and employees.

*Photo 38: Pauline, Margit, Bessie Parker, Norma, 1938 Chevy mail truck repurposed for towing, Chiriaco Summit, 1950s.*

In fact, if any of his workers were threatened, Joe would stand up for them. His imposing girth and firm tone of voice came in handy in those situations. One weekend in the early 1950s, teenage Pauline observed such an incident in the café. Two drunks were bothering Bessie, making lewd comments and making motions like they were trying to grab her. At one point she had enough, picked up a wrench, and started to chase them out. Pauline saw that this could become an ugly situation. She ran to tell her dad. Joe ran to the café with a pistol, which he made sure the drunks saw while admonishing them. They left, never to return. Joe made sure that people understood his standards for work as well as for just hanging out. Bessie eventually married a railroad man and moved to live in Barstow.

## Living and learning the business

When Joe broke his arm on a tow job about 1953, he needed help and care. Ruth and the children all moved back from Indio.

Back at the Summit, Joe drove them to their schools in Indio on some days; other days it was Ruth or both of them. Ruth and/or Joe would routinely pick up the younger two in the afternoon and do errands while waiting for Pauline and Margit to be done with their after-school activities such as sports, glee club, and field trips. Finally, on their way home from school, sometimes in the winter dark, the four youngsters would start chanting,

"Who can see the beacon light? I can see the beacon light. Who can see the beacon light? I can see the beacon light." They could see it from quite a distance. They got home by 6:00 p.m., sometimes earlier. They did their homework at the counter in the café. Summit employees would serve the customers during the week, but after school the children still would step in to pump gas, wait tables, help a customer in the store, or help out with other work as needed. They learned to "do it right the first time," which Joe preached. When there was a car being fixed, they would assist Joe with anything from handing him tools to actually putting in parts. Pauline did not like working in the garage where she felt intimidated by Joe. In fact, Joe could easily make her cry there and elsewhere. In addition, she was shy and was uncomfortable waiting tables, so she opted for kitchen duty, cleaning rooms in the motel, anything but being a waitress. One day she saw an ambulance leaving outside of Room 1. Ruth had just delivered a baby there. Pauline missed that experience, but Margit did not. She came running over as soon as she saw the ambulance arrive.

"The cord ..." said the ambulance driver, who had some medical training, as he looked at Ruth. He knew her from having worked with her years ago at the hospital.

"Margit, go to the kitchen ..." Ruth started.

"OK, I'll hurry back with the scissors." Margit started running.

"No, no, he's got clean ones." Ruth looked at the driver, who nodded yes. "Get the white cotton twine—some that has not been unwrapped yet."

Margit did as she was told and raced back.

The driver, with Ruth's help, tied off and then cut the cord. The ambulance took off with a healthy mother and baby.

Joe could be impatient with anyone slow to assist, including his children, but he could also make work fun. Sometimes he would line up his four to make hamburger patties, assembly-line style, singing to keep rhythm: scoop beef, roll balls, pat them down. Other times he made a game out of stocking shelves—who could get done first. Eventually, they'd help close the café and go off to bed, but not always all of them. Pauline, especially, would hang around in the kitchen.

"Can I help?" Pauline would ask her dad as he started to butcher a carcass.

"You can help me put it away when I am done," would be Joe's answer at first. Joe learned to do so many things out of interest and necessity—and he taught his children many of these things. For example, he explained all the cuts of meat to them, and in time they all helped with butchering.

Some evenings would be about preparing for the early-morning baking, the standard café fare—but once in a while Ruth took out a special recipe.

"It's Bob Howe's birthday tomorrow. I am going to stay up and make a Lady Baltimore cake," Ruth announced one night. Bob Howe had become like a grandfather to the children.

Pauline quickly volunteered. "Can I help?"

Over the years, Pauline helped her mother make many of these rich layer cakes filled and frosted with nuts, fruit, and whipping cream.

She helped her dad put many pieces of meat in the large walk-in box, but remained intimidated by him. Robert knew how to handle the generators, the water system, and the gasoline station plus he cooked. All three girls helped clean the house and the motel. They washed the linens in a wringer machine and hung them out to dry. Margit and Norma waitressed. Margit, especially, was developing an ease with people. Once done with their work, they sat together and chatted with an ice cream cone in hand. The family was bonded but not carbon copies of each other. Different talents and tolerances were developing among the children.

## Airport mystery, air sport, air-raid drills

While the children were in school, Joe, Ruth and their employees tended to travelers at the pumps, in the café, and at the six-unit motel, established in the 1940s. Once in a while, something unusual would happen. Joe, ever observant, noted something odd one day in 1953. The kids missed the whole event but heard about it after school.

"What are those two blue sedans doing out there? They look like twins," Joe commented to Bob Howe, who looked up from reaching into his pocket to take out some paper. He dropped tobacco on it and started rolling a cigarette. The two were outside talking. Joe continued, "Look, one is parked by the airport, and the other is stopped on the highway."

Bob agreed that something seemed amiss. Joe went inside for a few minutes. He got on the party line to call Sheriff Tom Cross, who was stationed about twenty miles away at Eagle Mountain. As he came back outside, he looked up and saw a plane coming in for a landing at the Shaver airstrip.

"That's Spanish on that plane. I wonder where it comes from," Bob commented. Bob and Joe waited. The plane just sat on the runway. No one came out. Bob Howe rolled and smoked several more cigarettes. The two sedans stayed put. Sheriff Cross drove up. At that point the door opened, and a man descended the steps to talk to the sheriff.

"We're testing this plane. We were going to test it at the Palm Springs Airport, but they are having a car race today, kicking up a lot of dust. That's not good for the test or our pilot."

Joe could see the man showing Sheriff Cross his watch. Then he went back into the plane. The blue sedans stayed put. No one from the plane or the sedans came to the café or anywhere else at the Summit.

"Who are these people?" Joe asked the sheriff. "Did you find out? Why the Spanish? What kind of a test were they doing on the ground? What was that man showing you?"

"That man is the copilot. The sedans are part of a security detail for a test flight. He was showing me his watch."

"What did that have to do with anything?"

"The watch was something to see—very fancy. I have no idea about the Spanish or anything about the test they are doing. But I did find out who gave the copilot that expensive watch. Howard Hughes—he's the pilot on that plane."

After about five hours, the plane took off.

Besides the famous like General Patton and Howard Hughes, the airport attracted corporate, private, and hobby craft. Summit facilities served them all. On a beautiful February day in 1952, Joe was manning the pumps when an unusual plane pulled up.

"Thanks for the help with the gas, Joe." Robert Dudley had landed his small airplane on the runway and then taxied over to fuel it the gas station. This was legal and common in those days. The airport itself had no fuel service. Joe's station was it.

"You feel safe in that thing?"

"It's an Ercoupe. See the twin rudder."

"But is it safe?"

"It was built to be super safe. It can't be stalled, and it's easy to land. Say hi to Ruth. Lunch was good. It's always great to stop by here."

Pilot Dudley, done getting gas and explaining his plane, taxied back to the runway and took off. He was an example of many who flew in to the Summit Airport for fun and sport.

*Photo 39: Pilot Robert Dudley and Joe fueling plane at Shaver Summit Shell Station, 1952.*

Regular pilots and their planes were welcome, but in the 1950s, unexpected aircraft was a concern. Joe actually had to know something about aircraft.

"Dad, there's a plane overhead," Robert called to Joe.

Father and son scrutinized the plane as it flew above them, noting features such as its heading, approximate altitude, and number of engines. They used an official template provided by the Ground Observer Corps.

"OK, let's go make the call," Joe said as they started to run.

Concerned about effects on the US of the Soviet's first atomic explosion (1949) and the start of the Korean War (1950), the government started the Federal Civil Defense Administration (FCDA) in 1951 and the Ground Observation Corps, also known as Operation SKYWATCH, in 1952. The corps was a volunteer organization of adults and youth with the goal of identifying low-flying aircraft in airspace around US borders, aircraft that could be a threat. There were thousands of observer volunteers at sites on the Canadian, Atlantic, and Pacific borders, many with watch towers. Joe and Robert, even at age eleven, were two of these volunteers. They had no watch tower but were outside so much that they were on watch much of the day. At night, they could hear any aircraft and were outside quickly. The corps command (which was actually the air force) had installed a phone behind the Summit garage, which Joe or Bob used to call in descriptions of aircraft they saw overhead.

"Duck and Cover" was another official Cold War protocol. This one involved every citizen.

"It's a drill," Ruth would say as the youngsters ducked under a table or the counter to the screeching of a siren. They knew what to do from air-raid drills at school. If at night, Joe charged to the pipeline road near the airport to make sure the FAA's air traffic control beacon light was not operating. He knew how to shut it off if necessary. After the drill, the family continued making patties, stocking shelves, washing dishes, mopping up, and cleaning in general—all in preparation for another day of customers. Before bed, Joe would call the four together.

"Here's your ten cents each for washing dishes tonight. Pauline, tomorrow I need you to help me with some typing in the office after school. Now everyone get to bed." The ten cents was not a wage or an allowance, just an occasional treat. The children did receive salaries when they were older and actually on the staff. Joe put those salaries into a savings account for each of them.

## Time on their own

The children gone, some nights Joe would notice that Ruth looked tired. "I'll take the children to school tomorrow and do all the shopping with them. I'll see if there's a movie in Indio they'd like to see. You need a break, Ruth."

"OK, Joe. Do you have that letter ready for that lawyer, Mr. Colby? We could make the move, but I'm not sure we have the money to start over in a new location," Ruth picked up a bucket she had filled with water that customers had left in their glasses. Still in working mode, she went outside to water a eucalyptus tree she had planted. Joe followed her out and back in.

"Yes, but I'll talk to him too. He's convinced that that triangle of property he has—you know, where sixty and Box Canyon Road cross—is a better place than the Summit."

"We'll, maybe, but ..."

"Hmm, I think the water table is better there. No, I can't see the advantages. Even if it is a good deal, I do not want to take orders from anyone. I'm not doing it."

Sometimes the children thought it too hot to go to bed regardless of Joe's orders. By the early '50s, after moving back from Indio, Pauline and Margit started living in one of the cabins, where they would go after dinner to finish homework and set out clothes for the next day. Robert took over another cabin. Norma remained in the house but did stay with her sisters sometimes. The cabins had bathrooms and kitchenettes, but no air cooling of any kind. At one point in the early '50s, Joe decided to install real air-conditioning, but not in the cabins. It nearly killed the generators, so he went back to the swamp coolers elsewhere on the property—like the café. One summer evening, Margit stayed late in the café, sitting at the counter and doing homework in relative cool. Several customers were eating dinner. A trucker was loudly spewing rough, profane language at another trucker.

Joe could be gracious and reasonable until something raised his ire. He hated bad language although he himself used it. He walked over to the counter.

"Shut your mouth," Joe said, staring at the guy.

The trucker stood up. He was big. Joe stood taller.

"You don't say. Maybe I should smash your mouth." The trucker raised his fists.

Joe started to raise his. Margit, a teenager at the time, picked up salt and pepper shakers and threw them on the floor. This stopped both men.

"Finish your food and get out of here," Joe said in his big, blunt tone. He took Margit's hand and walked away. Margit had shocked him back into his good senses—the driver too.

Another hot evening when they were supposed to be in the cabin, all the girls decided to walk on the dark airport runway. They dodged the beacon light. They could feel the heat coming from the asphalt right through their shoes. They walked along singing and laughing, Other than their shoes, they were stark naked.

## The county fair

In 1953, the Shell sign came down, and a Richfield Oil sign went up. There were still just two pumps. Joe found that Richfield offered him a better deal on the gasoline he bought. He was always looking for a way to save and make money. That included being on the lookout for good help, many from the family. Hector Franck was one of those. He came in August 1954, just in time to lend a hand while Joe and Ruth were gone on a short vacation. He was also in time for the county fair.

Hector was the son of Joe's oldest sister, Rose. After serving in the navy, he decided to delay his return to Alabama. He made arrangements to spend summer and fall of 1954 visiting his uncles Devio and Vincent in Pomona and then Joe at the Summit. The visit with Devio was pleasant, but Hector found Vincent still to be a difficult fellow, so he did his best to move on. He got a ride in late summer from Pauline and Margit on one of their trips back from UCLA, where Pauline was registering for the fall term—very much a homebody, she was taking up interior design. Margit was entering her last year of high school. Joe and Ruth asked Hector to help out while they went on vacation. He did, especially with towing and in the café. He was only there two weeks, but while he was there, he got to see the fun side of Summit life also.

Joe and Ruth came back from their short vacation and got back to work,

Joe outside and Ruth in the kitchen, but she had to make room for Margit every morning for a while.

Margit reached in to the hot oven to pull out a tray of biscuits. Bob Howe was sampling them as soon as they came out. "Well?" Margit asked Bob with a hopeful look.

"These are good! Perfect! Fluffy! Better than the ones yesterday and the day before and the day before that, Margit."

Margit had been making biscuits every day for a month. Bob had been her constant tester.

"You're going to win, Margit."

"But that's not all there is to the contest."

Hector came through the kitchen. "Win what? What contest?"

She's in the Farmer's Daughter contest. We're all going to the awards at the Riverside County Fair—you too, Hector."

"I still have to learn to drive a tractor and milk a cow—and practice mending clothes," Margit said.

"I have some things you can mend," Ruth offered.

"I only saw chickens here. No cows," Hector commented as he headed back into the café.

But Margit had a plan. She tended to leave nothing to chance. She prevailed upon her boyfriend, who lived on a farm in Hemet, for tractor lessons. The cow was a trickier situation, but Margit had her eyes open for an opportunity. It came with modeling school in Bell, California, which she had to attend with other contestants. Bell happened to be where Ruth's niece and Margit's cousin Barbara lived, now grown up with a family of her own. Margit noted a dairy farm nearby and went to ask if she could learn to milk a cow. The answer was yes. Margit stayed at Cousin Barbara's for several days, during which she learned to milk and model.

The awards day came. Next thing Hector knew; Joe was driving them all to the Riverside County Fair in Hemet. The Chiriacos—minus Margit, who was already there—and Hector were crowded into Joe's new 1954 Ford pickup. The young people were in the back of the truck in the open air. Hector got a full explanation as they flew down the highway through the wind.

"Yes, it's the Farmer's Daughter contest."

"But are you farmers?" Hector wondered.

"We have chickens."

"She has to parade in a bathing suit. I am glad it's not me there."

The only bathing suit practice Hector had seen was at the Hayfield Pump Station. He had ridden in the back of this same pickup when Margit and Robert took him there to swim. He still had dust in his hair from Robert's wild maneuvering over a dried-up lake bed that day. *Yes, Margit could easily win the bathing suit contest*, he thought.

Once at the fair, the whole family and Hector rode every ride and then watched the Farmer's Daughter contests. They witnessed Margit driving a tractor expertly through an obstacle course. At that point she was tied with another girl. But Margit had left no stone or biscuit unturned. The highlight came at the awards ceremony, when she was crowned Queen of the Riverside County Farmer's Fair, quite a thrill for a young girl from the desert and maybe a sign of things to come. Margit seemed to be developing an ease in front of people, gumption, and the ability to learn whatever was needed—all qualities that help a small desert business survive and grow.

*Photo 40: Margit Chiriaco, Queen of the Farmer's Fair, Hemet, CA, 1954.*

When Hector was ready to leave, he asked Joe to stop the bus at the Summit, so he could take it to Blythe. He didn't want the family to know that he planned to hitchhike home, even though he knew that Joe had hitchhiked West so many years before. Hector sat on the side of the road in mountainous territory near the bus station most of the night, fighting to stay awake. That particular night there was not much traffic. A few times he thought he heard a cougar screaming, which gave him second thoughts about hitchhiking. Finally, as dawn broke, a sheriff came by who was taking an elderly woman to a doctor in Kingman, Arizona. He gave Hector a ride to Blythe. From there, hitchhiking was easy on the long way back to Alabama. He would never return to Shaver Summit as it was. It was about to be reborn.

# 11

## *Shaver to Chiriaco, Late 1950s*

The expanding US Postal Service and the Federal Highway Act of 1956 both had positive effects on the Summit. By 1959, the youngest of the Chiriaco Four, Norma, would be seventeen years old and about to join the other three, who had all left the Summit by then. The '50s were teenage years at the Summit and also the years during which the Summit matured as a travelers' oasis. By the end of the decade, it was firmly on the map

### The post office

In the 1950s the postal service was a department of the Executive Branch with a cabinet post. It did not become USPS and independent from the Executive Branch until 1971. Nevertheless, in the 1950s, as after 1971, its mission was the same—to provide postal services to all communities. Joe was part of making sure its mission was carried out in even the remotest of places.

Joe carried mail starting before and resuming after World War II—one of many jobs he took to support the family. He picked up mail in Indio or Riverside and delivered it to small mail stops in desolate areas and small desert towns such as Blythe, Palo Verde, Desert Center, Midland, and the Hayfield Pump Station. When Devio, Paul, or Vincent were around in the 1940s, they had helped with the deliveries. They were gone now. Joe wanted to stop picking up and delivering mail but still enable people far from cities to get their mail.

Since the early 1950s, people could buy stamps at the Summit and pick up or receive mail that Joe picked up in Indio and brought back to the Summit. The post office there was really just a little cupboard in Joe's office, not a full-fledged operation.

One day Ruth commented, "Did you know my brother, Harry, just became the postmaster in Bell?" That was fact but no particular help to Joe's pursuit of a contract post office. He wrote, called, and visited postal officials to make his case. In the process, Joe told postal officials that Shaver Lake, a vacation spot in Central California, got confused with the Summit and caused wasteful redistribution of mail. The officials responded with a proposal that Ruth had already suggested to Joe more than once. "Let's change *Shaver* to *Chiriaco* Summit." By summer of 1958, a rural branch of the Indio post office opened at Chiriaco Summit inside the café.

Pauline, Margit, and Robert helped put together stamp booklets for the new stamp machine. If they did not put the booklets in right, they would bunch up and pop out, making the redo hard—a lesson in doing it right the first time. With the post office came the name change. With the name change came the revision of signs. For years, Joe used his cars as moving ads. His 1953 Fords (a pickup, a car, and a tow truck) and his 1952 Dodge pickup sported clever sayings on their tailgates.

You can't **a-Ford** to miss Shaver Summit.

Don't **Dodge** Shaver Summit.

Joe replaced them with heavy stick-on metal signs on the sides of his vehicles that, like the new sign that identified his post office, proudly proclaimed *Chiriaco Summit*.

*Photo 41: Chiriaco Family (Margit, Norma, Pauline with Baby Michael, Ruth, Joe, Robert), Opening Day, USPO, 1958.*

## The new highway

The name change happened in time for another important event. Just two years before Shaver became Chiriaco, President Eisenhower signed The Federal-Aid Highway Act of 1956, popularly known as the National Interstate and Defense Highways Act (Public Law 84-627), thus authorizing the construction of forty-one thousand miles of the Interstate Highway System. Joe was not a natural politician, but he stayed in touch with the powers that be: California Highway Patrol, County Board of Supervisors, Riverside Airport Commission, Joshua Tree rangers, Caltrans officials and legislators. He had learned in his 1930s surveying days how to keep his ear to the ground. Many of these people stopped by at the pumps and the café. Some he met at events in Indio, Riverside, or other communities. He heard in the news and from his contacts that the new east-west interstate highway would replace US 60 going by the Summit. This could be a disaster for the Summit or a boon, depending on where the east and west off-ramps were placed.

Before long, surveyors were in the area. They stopped in at the café. Surveying had changed since Joe's aqueduct days. Surveyors started using electronic measuring devices in the '50s, but the concepts remained similar. Joe spoke their language, so easily learned more about the upcoming highway. Caltrans was headquartered in San Diego at the time, but Joe knew who was who there. Margit and Robert typed the letters he wrote to these people. Joe went to the Caltrans offices there to make his case for the off-ramps and took Robert along. He kept his contact with officials steady and ongoing. Robert and Margit watched how their father learned everything he could about any upcoming change—in this case especially interchange spacing, the Caltrans standards for distance between ramps. He figured out that the Summit could qualify.

He also kept his eyes open for any related opportunities. In 1958, Ross Dorsett, a retired emergency road service director for the Automobile Club of Southern California, part of the American Automobile Association (AAA), stopped at the Summit café for some refreshments.

"Are you interested in a Club contract?" he asked Joe, referring to an AAA contract.

Joe told him about his towing experience and asked about the particulars of being an AAA Emergency Roadside Service (ERS) operator. After some conversation, Ross promised to send an ERS contract in the mail.

"Ross was sincere and kept his word about a Club contract, and that's the way it's been with us and the club, honest," Joe was quoted in the AAA publication for ERS operators, *Shop Talk,* June 1978. That issue celebrated his twenty years with the club. Was Ross's offer a stroke of luck? Was Joe in the right place at the right time? Maybe so, but with his years of towing, starting with the old 1920s tow truck, he was poised to take advantage of this new opportunity. He signed the paperwork in 1958, making Chiriaco Summit an AAA contract station, just in time for the expanding highway system.

While waiting for the new highway, Joe finally got around to creating a memorial for General Patton. By the late 1950s, only rusting pipe structures were left from the simulated tanks used in the early 1940s DTC training maneuvers. Joe took three of those pipe innards, painted them white, and then set them up with a sign to be seen from Highway 60 and eventually the new Interstate 10. A member of the Joshua Tree ranger's family helped make the sign.

*Photo 42: Joe Chiriaco with Patton Memorial Sign, Chiriaco Summit, Late 1950s.*

## Teenagers

Ruth and Joe drove the children to school until 1953. That year, the Coachella Valley School District, covering cities in the area such as Indio and places like the Summit, bought a brand new White Company bus, which was the standard yellow. The bus driver, Mr. Arch Gratz, who was also the shop and drafting teacher, started his run from Eagle Mountain, where he lived, to the Coachella schools on Highways 60, 70, and 99. The bus made about five stops, picking up fifteen students—all going to Coachella High School except for Norma, who was still in grade school. After school it stopped at the Summit again to drop off the Chiriaco students and let the others stretch their legs. For the Eagle Mountain students, the bus route was a sixty-five-mile trip one way. For the others it was less but still a long enough ride to try the patience of most teenagers. Mr. Gratz knew that.

He announced right off, "I have one rule. I don't care what you do as long as it is at least three seats back from the driver."

No one ever defied Mr. Gratz on this rule or anything else he asked. A few students did homework or talked quietly. Some found time to daydream. Others wrestled a bit or shouted from seat to seat. None did anything really bad or that caused harm. It was a big bus that could seat forty. The fifteen riders were scattered from front to back. A few passed notes to each other, giggling.

Billy Ralph grabbed one of the notes. "What will happen if I throw your note out this front window," he wondered out loud and then shouted, "open the back window."

And sure enough, the scrap flew down the side of the bus and came in the back window. This never failed. Billy was one of the more restless kids, but full of curiosity.

The last school bell rang at about 3:30. By 5:00, Mr. Gratz had everyone home, with a rest stop on the way at the Summit. Once off the bus, the four Chiriaco children hung around to talk to the other students for a few minutes and then took off to do chores and get ready for dinner. Some of those remaining went into the store and bought snacks. Some wrestled in the parking lot; Mr. Gratz saw that as youthful exuberance, not fighting, and so did not stop them. He allowed the kids to blow off steam, but he would not put up with anything clearly wrong. For example, at the Summit stop on one day:

"Come here," he called to two boys. "Whatcha got there?"

The two looked sheepish as they showed their hands full of candy bars.

"And how did you pay for all that?"

The two knew they were caught. Mr. Gratz marched them back into the store and made sure they paid Joe for what they had taken.

The word got out, "Don't mess with Mr. Gratz."

On Friday evenings the kids went to the football games. At 3:30, Mr. Gratz took the kids to downtown Coachella, including Norma, where they were on their own to get dinner, sightsee, or shop. His only rule was to be at the designated pickup point at 6:00 p.m. They were always there. He drove them to the football game, which started at 7:00. Margit absolutely had to be there on time, because she was a cheerleader. Mr. Gratz did the same during basketball season. After the games, they started the long ride home.

By the time Mr. Gratz quit driving the bus, Pauline and Margit were at UCLA. Robert and Norma were seventeen and fifteen, respectively. In that time the students had gone over one hundred thousand miles back and forth to school. The bus never broke down. It was never vandalized. Mr. Gratz came to know what the kids thought about his way of managing both the bus and the classroom.

"Mr. Gratz, you are tough as nails."

"When you say it, you mean it."

"You have the same rules every day."

Morning after morning, afternoon after afternoon, and some evenings, they took that same old ride on what could have been a boring highway. Starting with the fourth seat back, the students created their own entertainment to make their long ride tolerable. This was a lesson well learned for making life interesting, not just bearable, in the barren desert. It was also a recipe for friendships. All four Chiriaco teens rode the bus until each graduated from high school. They got to know some of the kids from other communities well. Robert, especially, started to form some friendships that would come into play later.

After Mr. Gratz retired from bus driving, Joe lined the bus students up to make sure that he collected for everything they bought. He became wary about any of his children befriending kids like the unruly ones. He warned, "Don't behave like them."

Robert would stick up for his bus buddies. "They are good kids."

"I don't like how some of them behave." Joe based this statement on what he'd seen and experienced during the school bus stops at the café, mostly after Mr. Gratz was gone.

Throughout their high school years, their friends from school and surrounding desert areas came to the Summit. They found the Summit so different from their more citified environments.

Sometimes they stayed for a few days, sleeping in the cabins overnight. They participated in the chores and in the unique desert fun. They hung out in the restaurant. They took hikes up and down sandy trails, to the springs, and into deserted military sites. They swam at the Hayfield Pump Station about six miles down the highway. Robert found the Eagle Mountain crowd especially fun. He drove with them over the dirt trails near the Summit and at Eagle Mountain. He may have been the youngest driver in the group. He had a legal license at fourteen, which he did need and did use to help out at the Summit.

Typical teenagers, the friends discovered the walk-in box next to Joe's office. Sometimes the teenagers went in just to cool off. Other times they locked each other in as a joke. They found it especially fun when they locked Pauline and her boyfriend in for a few minutes. Joe was nearby for the rescue. The teens were grateful he was never needed and more grateful that he never knew.

## Power hungry

At times hundreds of people were working in the area, doing manual labor, engineering, and surveying. Robert helped Ruth create luncheon specials for the workers. They put out hearty food like beef or pork roast, stroganoff, and salmon croquette in a cafeteria arrangement. Salmon in the desert? They had a stock of cans.

What were all these workers doing? During the late '50s, work crews came into the area to create or improve utilities. The Chiriacos believed some worked for Edison Electric, bringing power into the desert from Los Angeles. Some others were laying natural gas lines from Texas to California. Some were maintaining the aqueduct. With all the utilities coming their way, one would think the Chiriacos could tap in, but not so. It was the late 1950s, but there was still no commercial gas, water, or power for them. They would get natural gas by 1970, though from the lines being laid. Regarding power, they were not in the Edison customer area. As part of the whole complication for Chiriaco, they were in the Coachella Valley Water District, not the Imperial Irrigation District (IID) area for water—but the Summit was in IID territory for power. Regardless, to get power they would have had to invest a large sum of money for a transformer on their own, not practical at the time. They did have a fleeting chance for commercial power one crazy weekend.

*Photo 43: Joe Chiriaco in generator shed, c. 1960.*

The generators required constant maintenance without delivering worry-free power. Robert, a high school student at the time, kept the generators fueled with diesel. When the generators quit for whatever reason, father and son would stay up all night if necessary to get them back on task. Joe would show his impatience if Robert did not hold the flashlight just right, but Robert continued helping, appearing to take his dad's gruffness in stride.

The Chiriacos got real air-conditioning in the stead of their swamp coolers in this time frame, but it strained the system. For example, Ruth could not iron if the air was running. So in the late '50s when two power company crews, Edison and California Electric (later merged with Edison to become Southern California Edison), showed up on a Friday at the Summit asking for cabins, the Chiriacos were excited. The crews were in a contest to see who could put up power lines between Desert Center and Chiriaco first—by Sunday night! That's how it was in those days—whoever got there first would get the government contract to provide power in the area. This contract involved the right to install a power connection at Desert Center. Commercial power for Chiriaco would almost certainly follow. One of the crews got within a mile of Desert Center when they stopped.

"Someone got an injunction against the project," Joe told others in the family angrily.

"But why?" the family asked.

"I can't say; but well, maybe someone did not want us to get power." Joe suspected competitors.

Desert Center had had power for a long time, but not Chiriaco Summit. Some believed that the old idea of *putting that damned Italian out of business* was still at play. But no one at Chiriaco knew or knows what actually happened. Desert Steve was still in charge at the Center. What they all do know is that again Joe was not intimidated. He and Robert were expert at servicing their generators, big Caterpillars, the best they could buy. They kept them running and running and running.

## Empty nesters

Norma loved horses from the time she first saw Toyjo, but he was long gone. When she was in sixth grade, about 1954, her dad bought her a horse named Patches. Not too long after Patches came to the Summit, a stray, gray donkey wandered in off the hills, befriended Patches, and also joined the Summit population. By the end of the '50s, Patches was Norma's main companion. Margit was at UCLA and Robert at Northern Arizona University (then known as Arizona State College at Flagstaff). Pauline had left UCLA and was already married. Norma rode Patches around the perimeter of the Summit and into the hills.

One very hot summer day in the late '50s, she decided to ride her horse bareback seven miles to Hayfield and go swimming with friends who lived there. It was 102 degrees that day. No matter what Norma did, the donkey followed Patches all the way. Norma was hot, tired, and frustrated by the time she arrived at the Hayfield Pump Station. Mr. Ralph Adams, who ran the station, called her over to a phone and told her to get someone to come get her. Joe showed up with a truck. Joe, Norma, and some of the Hayfield workers tied Patches to the back of the pickup. Once they all believed the horse was safely in tow, Joe started back home slowly down a dirt road that the locals called the Hayfield Road. The donkey followed, untethered. About halfway home, the pickup ran out of gas. Joe and Norma started walking back to Chiriaco, leading Patches. Almost immediately Patches pulled loose and ran off, with the donkey following. As they walked on down Hayfield Road, they could see Patches over on Highway 60, rearing up and causing a ruckus, but there was nothing they could do but walk on. They were too far away, and there were no cell phones in those days. Fortunately, no one was hurt. Later in the day, Patches returned with the donkey following, of course. This was one of Norma's last adventures before leaving home.

*Photo 44: Patches and Donkey, Summit Grounds, 1950s.*

In 1958 the Summit came of age with its new name and rural postal branch. In 1959, Norma left Patches at the Summit and joined Robert at NAU in Flagstaff. As the 1960s dawned, Ruth and Joe became empty nesters, except during the summers.

Which, if any, of the Chiriaco Four would return to stay?

# 12

## *The Second Generation Steps Up, 1960s*

In the spring of 1959, Joe and Ruth agreed: they needed to beef up sales.

"I could use Robert's help. It's only a year and a half and he's done with college," Joe said, and then Ruth stepped in.

"It's been nice Margit's here on her break. She'll graduate in June. Maybe she'll stay for the summer."

"If she doesn't marry first like Pauline did." Joe sounded disappointed but then lightened up. "Not too long, Norma will be done with college too. It's been tight, but we'll be in good shape soon."

"Would you do it again? I mean send them all away to college?"

"Of course." Joe beamed. Every year Ruth and Joe drove their young students to college. Once there, Joe carried box after box up steps in dormitories, sorority houses, and frat pads, never tiring. In Pauline's first year, he maneuvered army cots left over from Camp Young up those stairs. It was as if he were saying with each step, "Look, see, I have children in college!" Ruth and the children could tell it was not muscle he was flexing but pride.

### Daughter Margit comes home

It was second semester of Margit's senior year. She was studying art and political science. She was aware of how much UCLA had opened up her world, but as she overheard her parents' conversation about needing help, she decided right then to come home after graduation. She had dreamed of going to New York to pursue an art career. Robert and Norma were away at Northern Arizona University (NAU). Pauline was living near San Bernardino with her husband, John

Leedom, a citrus rancher. Pauline had just given birth to Michael, the first of her four children. Margit knew she was the one available. Besides, she felt a certain pull to the Summit.

For many years, Joe and Ruth stuck to their decision to close the Summit business after dark. They made that decision after the troops and prisoners had left the area and when nighttime traffic was thin. Now as the '50s were ending, traffic was heavy day and night, so they adjusted. The Summit started staying open all night. By now there was something of a community at the Summit. In addition to the cabins and the motel, new trailers started to occupy spaces. Some Summit employees lived on site in these trailers, which they owned themselves or rented from the Chiriaco business. In addition, snowbirds (people who came from cold climates just for the winter), miners, workmen, and travelers in the area rented on a temporary basis. The old Edison trailers became storage units. Eventually, they fell apart and were discarded.

The increased business and growing community needed Margit's help. She already had the reputation of being good with people. Her political nature would come into play on behalf of the Summit on site and in boardrooms in years to come. The Summit was nothing like UCLA, but it presented a world of opportunity in its own way. In June of 1959, Margit moved back into one of the little cabins, hung some of her artwork, and put on her apron.

Because of its location, local on-duty law enforcement officers frequently took breaks and meals at the Summit café. In fact, Tom Cross had become a good friend of Joe's. Sometimes they would watch TV together in Joe and Ruth's house. Even with increasing traffic, the Summit area was usually peaceful, so law enforcement could usually count on quiet breaks there. In the summer of 1959, a handsome fellow in uniform came in and sat down at the counter.

"What can I get you?" Margit handed him a menu. It had been expanded a few times since opening day in 1933. Joe was not ready to buy a fryer, which would require too much electricity, so still no french fries, but hamburgers held their place front and center on the menu. That's what Dwight Metcalfe ordered.

This young Riverside County sheriff was the resident deputy at Eagle Mountain. He was the only general peace officer in the desert, covering an area larger than the state of Rhode Island, including the Summit. He had replaced Tom Cross, who had left the Riverside County Sheriff's Office, and by now was captain of the Coachella City Police Department. (The city was incorporated in 1946.) Dwight came in to the café again and again.

"This is the best food around," he told Margit.

"Well, Mother is a good cook," she said, smiling. That was true; Ruth was known for her cooking up and down the highway. Now she was cooking breakfast, lunch, and dinner for customers.

The food was not the only draw. Soon Deputy Metcalfe and Margit started dating.

## Joe's self-reliance

One night, while at Eagle Mountain, Dwight got an official call from Joe. It was very late.

"Dwight, there are four young troublemakers here in the café."

"What are they doing?"

"Just hanging around much longer than normal, talking kinda secretly among themselves, and looking around. I have a bad feeling about this."

Twenty-five minutes later, Dwight arrived in his squad car from Eagle Mountain. He could see into the café from where he parked. He was sure no one could see out.

He waited.

And he waited.

He waited some more. Experience told him the guys eventually would come out. One did—to get something out of their car. The deputy intercepted him, immediately working on the possibility that one of the four was carrying a concealed handgun. He had noted that their upper clothing was bulky. Dwight questioned the man, found his answers suspicious, frisked him, handcuffed him, and had him lie on the ground next to the squad car.

He waited some more.

Suspect Number Two came out, and a little later out came Number Three. Dwight handled each as he had the first suspect. Now three were on the ground next to the police car. Joe came out to serve a customer at the pumps. He could see Dwight and the guys on the ground, but went about pumping gas as though nothing was wrong.

"Oh, darn, these guys are juvies," Dwight said to himself. They had no driver's licenses, but their student IDs gave them away. He would have to take them all the way to Riverside, where juveniles were booked. That was a problem. He couldn't leave his assigned beat for that long a trip. Besides, there were four of them and one of him. Dwight decided he needed backup, which was part of officer safety protocol. This was before the days of hand-held radios. To call for help on the car radio, he would have had to take his eyes off the prisoners for too long. Joe was starting back into the café. He could still see Dwight and the three on the ground. Dwight hand signaled Joe to call for help. Joe gave him the OK sign and went inside. Dwight could see the fourth suspect and a waitress inside. Joe seemed to have gone off to make the call for help.

Dwight waited a while longer. He figured Number Four had to wonder why the others were still outside and come looking. Out came Number Four. Dwight was ready for him. He went through the same process with this young guy and took him into custody. It turned out none had a gun, just bulky jackets. From his questioning, Dwight learned that they were runaways from the Midwest, had no money, and were planning trouble. Now what? Still no backup. He called for Joe. Joe came out.

"How soon is the backup coming?"

"Got it covered," Joe answered as he pulled up his shirt and showed his gun. Instead of calling any sheriff's station, Joe had gone to his house and gotten his old eight-inch revolver. Dwight realized that Joe had acted out of his long-standing, desert pioneering self-reliance rather than thinking like a cop, but Deputy Metcalfe still needed official police help. Joe called the Indio office, and they sent the Coachella Valley Unit. Finally, the unit started the kids on the long ride to Riverside.

Later Dwight told Joe, "Those kids ended up in juvenile hall. Well, at least they are getting food and will not hold up anyone."

Dwight was promoted to sergeant and sent to Indio in early 1960, but he kept visiting the café and Margit. On June 1, 1960, Dwight and Margit married at Our Lady of Perpetual Help in Indio. They rented the Indio home Joe and Ruth owned there, the same home Margit had lived in for a short while as a teenager. Until their daughter, Heather, was born on Easter Sunday 1963, Margit (and Dwight on his days off) went back and forth to help out at the Summit. Heather would one day, years hence, take on a significant role at the Summit. In 1965, Dwight left the Riverside County Sheriff's Office. The little family moved back to the Summit. They bought a double-wide mobile home and put it in the little Chiriaco community that was developing on Summit property. Dwight started working for Joe full time.

## Son Robert joins the business

"I wonder if we should stay with Richfield Oil. I think we need more pumps. Two are not enough for all the traffic by here now." Robert started his dad thinking about their gasoline service on his jaunts home from college at Northern Arizona University.

Joe knew traffic would get even heavier once Interstate 10 opened by the Summit. He expected that to be soon. The government was already acquiring businesses and residences in the I-10 path through eminent domain. Construction had already started some miles away. Joe started to prepare for an eventual onslaught of motorists. Careful as usual, Joe investigated and found that the Chevron Corporation helped dealers grow the business, brought in crews to modernize the facilities, and sometimes absorbed the improvements. Other times they offered low- or no-interest loans with a way to pay back through a portion of the dealer's gasoline purchase price. Robert's prodding worked to a point; Joe started negotiating with Chevron but was stubborn on the terms, holding out for a better arrangement. Knowing they had a sweetheart deal, Ruth finally said, "Just do it, Joe." Robert concurred. So in 1960 Joe contracted with Chevron. The new station opened in 1961 with six pumps. One was diesel so he could better serve truck drivers. In the past, if a truck driver was in dire need of it, Joe would sell him some of the diesel he had for the generators. Another pump was for the extra-high-octane gas used in the hot rods of the '60s and '70s. The station stayed put in the same place for now—at the front of the café, but Chevron believed in upgrading, and so did Robert and Margit. More improvements were to come.

*Photo 45: Installation of the Chevron sign, Chiriaco Summit, 1960.*

Robert graduated with a business administration degree from NAU in 1962. He told his family that what he got out of college more than anything else was that he "got to see Highway 66, not just Highway 60." But the truth was he had gained an entrepreneurial bent. Like Margit, he was a friendly sort. Customers clicked with him and liked him. It was another matter between dad and son. Robert was quicker to take risks and start modernizing than Joe, who was visionary but careful. Robert dove right into the business, making his ideas known.

"Why don't we get a new truck?" Robert asked as he helped his dad fix a leaking pipe. They still had to kludge them with inner tubing and bale wire. "This old Chevy is getting rickety, and it's a bear to drive up these mountain paths."

"Just bought a new car for the family. This one is a fine work car. Look at these special sand tires." Joe kicked one of the tires. "And I can keep it running forever."

"I know," Robert sighed, "but we could work faster and safer if we got a four-wheel drive."

"I don't like them."

Robert changed the subject. "I really like cooking in the café. I'd like to go to cooking school."

Joe walked around the car, kicked another tire, and then said matter-of-factly, "Robert, we need you here. You will take over this business someday. Look, we are busier than ever. We just put in that new Chevron."

At one point Dwight and a sheriff friend bought several four-wheel-drive army jeeps from Fort Irwin near Mojave as an investment and stored them at the Summit. Robert suggested to Joe that he buy one of the jeeps, fix it up, and use it instead of the old Chevy for chores around the Summit, but Joe refused for two reasons. Realistically, the jeeps were scrap, good for parts but quite the job to make run. Fundamentally, Joe preferred his old Chevy and did not even entertain fixing one of the jeeps.

Robert joined the air force reserves on May 2, 1963. He was gone six months for training. At the end of his six months, Joe took a Greyhound to meet up with Robert at his training camp in Biloxi, Mississippi. Together they started the drive back home. They stopped in Alabama to visit Joe's parents. The plan from there was to go through Flagstaff, Arizona, where Joe would take a bus to the Summit and Robert would wait to drive home with Norma. She was still at NAU and just about to get out for the Thanksgiving break. On their way into Flagstaff, they were listening to the radio when they pulled over in shock. It was November 22, 1963. President Kennedy had been shot. At the first opportunity, Joe called Ruth. She was wall papering their little house.

When Joe arrived the next day on the bus, the Summit and the whole nation were in mourning. When Robert and Norma arrived for Thanksgiving (November 28 that year), the mood there and everywhere was still somber.

Now home to stay, Robert noticed that some things had not changed. The scrap jeeps were still there. Dwight was good at organization, was very bright, but procrastinated, which did not work well with the Chiriaco family and its business mindset. The jeeps, for example, just took up Joe's space. As the marriage between

Dwight and Margit started to fall apart, Joe and Dwight had several business conversations. They agreed that any jeeps Dwight did not sell would go into the junkyard. In 1967, Margit and Dwight divorced. Dwight left but remained a good dad to Heather. He started a different career, all related to vehicles, ending up as a Department of Motor Vehicles manager by the time he retired. Margit stayed on at the Summit. Most of the jeeps were junked.

Robert continued to struggle with his dad. An example: as they got ready for a pipe-repair trek, they got into a typical argument with Ruth intervening, a sign of trouble to come.

The pipeline car was ready to go. It was actually an old junkyard Chevy with the back seat removed to make space for hauling. It was stocked as usual with tools, rubber tubing, and baling wire in milk crates. It was early on a hot summer evening not too long after Robert finished college. Robert was in his twenties at the time. It had been brutally hot for days, just the weather to cause problems on the line.

"See if the pliers are in the car," Joe said impatiently.

"I'm sure they are. I checked a while ago," Robert said as he reached into the back of the old car and started scrambling among the tools.

"Hurry up."

"Dad, I don't see them, but I know they're here."

"Why are you so slow?" Now Joe's ire was up. He wanted to beat the sunset. It would be cooler in the dark but also much harder to find any leaks.

"Dad, I'm looking."

Out of patience and steaming, Joe reached in to get the tool himself, pushing Robert aside. Robert took this as an affront; now he was also steaming.

"Stop this," Ruth shouted. "We are a family. We need to work together. This is terrible behavior." She pushed her way into the back and reached into the milk carton full of tools. She happened to grab the pliers. She raised them up so both men could see and then with a snap of her wrist threw them back into the milk carton. Like Robert, she had known they were there all along.

"I'll have dinner ready when you return. Wash your hands." She said this curtly and then watched them get into the front seats.

They drove away, apparently leaving their altercation behind them—or if not, they had plenty of time to talk it out before showing up calmly for dinner. Ruth went to prepare the quail Joe had hunted earlier in the day.

## Visitors—family and famous

Joe continued towing, fixing some vehicles but also adding more to the junkyard. Little did he realize; he was training a future tow-truck driver. Pauline's oldest child and Joe's first grandchild, Michael Leedom, came to visit his grandparents and stay at the Summit in the summers now and then. When he was about ten, in the late '60s, he weaseled his way into the tow business, albeit as an observer.

"Please, Grandpa," he would beg. "Wake me up if someone calls for towing."

"Time to go!" Joe would shake the ten-year-old's shoulder to wake him. Time and again, Michael jumped up raring to go off in the middle of the night in an old tow truck with rotating amber lights to help a perfect stranger somewhere on the dark road.

Now and then during the day Michael would see Grandpa grabbing a large glass container of ice-cold water from the refrigerator and start toward his pipeline car.

"Can I come?" Michael would ask. Joe would tell him to hop in, and off they'd go up a dirt road to find the leak. It was easy to see since bees were swarming around the water leaking from the pipe. Joe used rubber inner tube and bale wire to fix the leak as he had done from the beginning. If the old car got stuck on the excursion, Grandpa Joe expertly maneuvered it out of trouble.

Once back, there would be a treat. Maybe the Carnation ice cream truck was there. Maybe there was cold watermelon at the counter on one-hundred-plus-degree days. Maybe Michael made his own suicide drink, a mixture of all the different types of sodas on hand. In the evenings, he sat on the porch with the family gazing at the stars and talking about just anything. Grandpa would send Michael to the café to get ice cream for whoever was on the porch. Anything they wanted! Sometimes it was a ranger from the new Cottonwood Visitor Center. Joshua Tree rangers had lived there since it was built in 1964. They still came to the Summit for the food at the café and to get their mail.

Ice cream was a hit for the tourists too in the hot desert. One day in 1967, an elegant lady stepped out of a limo and came into the café for an ice cream cone. Robert and Joe were the only ones in the store. They looked at each other as she left. They knew they had just served Nancy Reagan and that her husband, who was running for governor of the state, was waiting for her in the limo.

As exciting as the famous visitors were, family on both sides meant the most. Many came, from both Ruth's and Joe's sides of the family.

Devio's family came from their home in Chino, a two-hour drive east of the Summit, many a Thanksgiving between 1947 and 1960 and off and on in following years. His daughter, Dee, so many years later remembered coming to visit with her parents and three siblings. Some of Devio's family would stay in Ruth and Joe's house while others stayed in the small trailers or cabins that were on the property. The children played on the old skeletons of the dummy tanks that were used during the WWII training exercises, rode bikes on the airport runway, and walked with the family each night to watch the sunsets.

The Ventura Bergseids made the four-hour drive to visit their Chiriaco relatives several times a year. Alida, Ted's daughter born in 1953, was one of the youngest of the cousins. He brought her to visit Ruth many years after Barbara started coming.

"Notice how hard Aunt Ruth works," Ted told his daughter, still feeling that his sister should have it easier.

Alida watched her aunt at the restaurant behind the counter. She noticed that she worked hard but she especially noticed that Ruth was talkative and open with everyone. This was different from the Scandinavian reserve little Alida often observed. She liked what she saw and started to emulate her aunt. Like Barbara, she loved and admired Ruth as the family matriarch.

# 13

## Incorporated, Late 1960s

By the late '60s, surveying crews had completed their work for the section of Interstate 10 that would be passing by Chiriaco Summit. *Passing by* is what Joe and Ruth feared. They wanted off-ramps, which would bring more travelers, and which would mean they would need better sources of water and power and legal protection for their business.

### Insuring the off-ramps

Of course Joe lobbied anyone he could in person to make sure off-ramps were put at the Summit. He continued to write letters, which Robert and Margit typed. Margit talked to public officials who had some say in the matter. Joe and Robert continued making trips to San Diego to visit Caltrans officials there so they would not forget why both east and west access made sense at the Summit.

"It's a travel stop with gas, food, and water," they said, and they gave estimates of how many people stopped there.

"There are cabins, a six-unit motel, and some trailers," they said, and they explained that the rooms accommodated travelers and workers. Workers had been constant in the area in recent years, working on power and gas lines and at the Eagle Mountain mine.

"Law enforcement, emergency, and private aircraft land on the runway," they said, tempted to tell the Howard Hughes story.

More letters, more trips, and finally in the mid-sixties, the plans for the one-hundred mile stretch from Indio to Blythe were approved with the off-ramps for which Joe and Ruth had hoped. In addition to all the other reasons, the Summit met the Caltrans standard for distance between ramps. Caltrans set up an office at Chiriaco at the beginning of the construction for this stretch.

One Labor Day after Caltrans arrived, a woman went into labor at the Summit. Yes, on Labor Day. Again Ruth delivered the baby. Again an ambulance came to take mother and baby to a hospital. The route would have been simpler with the ramps. The ramps had been promised but would still take some time. People were starting to wonder, "When is the new highway going to open up by the Summit?"

The highway construction in the area was done in segments: First the segment coming from Los Angeles over the Indio Grade. The Summit was the next contiguous area, but Caltrans skipped it, and instead constructed the highway segment that went by Box Canyon Road, thereby giving access to Joshua Tree National Monument and Mecca. Next they completed the segment from Desert Center to Blythe so Desert Center had off-ramps.

For Desert Center this was not necessarily a good thing. In 1961, Stanley Ragsdale, Desert Steve's youngest son, bought and took over Desert Center after his father retired to a mountaintop cabin in the area. Stanley and his Mormon wife, Crystal, had five sons and one daughter. He maintained the strict outlook of his father, expecting his own sons to do exactly as he said in various operations of the business and his daughter, Suzanne, to wash dishes, take care of clothing, and do laundry. Unlike the Chiriaco girls, she did not know how and was not expected to pump gas. Stanley also maintained Desert Center just as it was, regardless of change going on all around him. Desert Steve used to say that he was on America's longest main street, meaning Highway 60, which went right through his desert outpost. Now motorists would have to get off the interstate to enter what still looked, and in many ways operated, like a 1930s community with its own charm. In the meantime, the Summit, still waiting for its off-ramps, kept updating.

In the late '60s the interstate construction by the Summit finally started, first with excavating the roadbed, eventually grading it, and then asphalting it. Anyone in the café could hear the big loaders, bulldozers, tractors, dump trucks, excavators, graders, and finally the asphalt pavers.

*Map 7: Approximate Construction Sequence of Interstate 10 from Los Angeles to Blythe.*
*Numbers indicate starting points*

Sometime in 1967, an operating engineer who was also an asphalt specialist working on the freeway came into the café. Margit fell for Rudy Baldivid even though, or maybe because, he was eighteen years older. Joe and Ruth were not happy about this, but accepted it. They actually liked Rudy, especially Joe, because Rudy was a man's man. In other words, he could talk easily about traditionally men's topics such as construction. Margit and Rudy were married in Mexico on September 23, 1967, breaking with her family's Catholic tradition. Not only that, shortly after they were married, Rudy explained that he was married with five children. He was not divorced. Eventually he fixed that, and the couple remarried legally, again in Mexico.

They lived in the double-wide at the Summit that Margit had purchased when she was married to Dwight, but did not stay there long. Before they moved they witnessed a movie scene shot in the café with highway construction in the background. The noise from heavy equipment used to level and asphalt the new road did not discourage the producers. It did not bother the customers, who were used to the generators whirring away, but getting there was another matter. The Summit essentially went dead for three to four months while Caltrans detoured traffic as the work crews finally constructed the off-ramps. By then the movie crews were gone. In 1969 the violent biker film *Satin's Sadist*, starring Russ Tamblyn, opened. Since the filming had started some years before the highway was done, the movie showed the freeway still under construction.

Joe used the time well while waiting for the ramps to be completed. He upgraded facilities all over the Summit, getting ready for the deluge he expected with the opening of the new ramps. He upgraded the generators, giving him enough power to finally put in a fryer. Ruth added french fries to the menu. He installed air-conditioning again. It was OK but not great. This time the air-conditioning did not kill the generators, but lights would dim and bulbs might pop when it went on. He and Ruth were excited about growing the business for all travelers, commuters, and tourists as well as truckers. Robert took on a stronger role with the Chevron station, upgrading and moving it a little east of the café in 1968, giving it more space. With this upgrade, Chevron required the attendants to wear their company-issued blue and white uniforms.

The ramps opened on December 4, 1967, with no fanfare, nothing like the day in 1933 when Joe and Ruth first opened their business in concert with the opening of the Highway 60 section by Shaver Summit. Now, about four decades later, I-10, the new interstate, went right through the old Camp Young, with official green signs in both directions that said *Chiriaco Summit*. Motorists wound off onto the newly named Chiriaco Road (a portion of Old Highway 60) through the growing facilities, and then back on. With the ramps and the upgraded gas station opened, the Summit was poised to profit from increased traffic, except for one problem.

Water!

*Photo 46: Interstate 10 off-ramp to Chiriaco Summit.*

## Witching for water

The springs could no longer supply enough water for all the people using the bathrooms at the new Chevron and in the café. Also, these were the days of Lady Bird Johnson's Beautify America Campaign, which carried with it some legislation. Her husband, President Johnson, signed the Highway Beautification Act into law in 1965. In addition to limiting signs on the growing highway system, it also required junkyards along the system to be either screened from view or removed. Joe was not about to remove his junkyard. He and Ruth complied by planting oleanders all around it to hide the rusting treasures from view. This and some new landscaping around other areas visible to customers soaked up a lot of water.

The Chevron, junkyard oleanders, and growing number of travelers kept the Chiriacos negotiating for water. After many letters from Joe over years, finally on July 21, 1965, MWD signed a quitclaim for the area around the reservoir to the federal government. MWD also created a shared right of way with the Chiriaco business so that Joe and his staff could use the District's aqueduct patrol roads for pipeline maintenance. In 1966 Chiriaco Summit received a twenty-year special permit from the National Park Service to continue using the existing pipelines. But these agreements on their own did not solve the water problem. For one thing, after all these years and the same long string of communications with MWD, Joe still did not have clear access to the water in Reservoir #4. By 1969, rainfall in the area became rare. Springs, which had at one time gushed as much as thirty thousand gallons a day, slowed to trickles. Lost Palms dried up for months at a time. Water from the spring in Munsen Canyon slowed to less than one gallon per minute. So for a while Joe, Robert, and Rudy hauled 1,000 to 1,500 gallons twice a day from a deep well at the Gas Company Compressor Station, which was twelve miles away. They also hauled water from Buried Mountain, owned by Mr. Colby of the US 60 triangle. The oleanders, in particular, soaked up a lot of water from the truck. There was no sprinkler system or anything like that for them. When all the hauling got to be too taxing, Joe and Robert contacted James Wright, a well driller.

"Joe, I know a water witch," James told Joe.

Robert listened with concern. Joe thought it worth a try, since they now needed more water than in the past—more than the springs could provide. A few days later, Robert was driving the pickup on the hill to the Summit reservoir area. Joe and James sat in the truck bed. The water witch, also known as a dowser, was in the passenger seat, holding a stick out the window. On the way back down, the dowser started giving directions.

"I can do this from an airplane ..."

Robert looked away, hiding his skepticism.

"... but we're on the ground; drive very slowly, Robert."

Robert complied, moving hardly at all. He was inching toward the trailers. Suddenly, he noticed a jerk from the passenger seat. The dowsing stick took on a life of its own. It had clicked down. Robert stopped driving.

The witch got out and walked around. Robert followed. The stick kept clicking down.

"I can tell by the number of clicks how far down you have to go to hit water."

Joe was excited; Robert did not know what to think of this.

"It's eight hundred to a thousand feet down."

"At Desert Center they don't have to go that deep," Joe said. "But this is very close to the café, the station, and everything else here."

Robert suggested trying another spot, which they did. Again the witch's stick jerked down. Again the dowser got out of the truck and walked around.

"You'll find water about five hundred feet down here."

"I don't like this spot. It's too far from everything." Joe decided to drill at the first spot.

Robert thought to himself, *We have to invest about twenty-five thousand dollars to drill this well. There had better be water down there.*

This was one time Joe was more willing than Robert to take a chance. He knew without water there would be no Chiriaco business. He went to talk with Ruth.

"Joe, it worked on our farm in Minnesota. I even held the stick and felt it vibrating. Go ahead, drill there, Joe."

Joe made arrangements to borrow the money from Chevron to drill the well at the place near the trailers. Mr. Wright's drill went down 1,300 feet but first hit water at eight hundred feet, as the dowser had predicted. The drillers placed the pump at about one thousand feet down, just in case the water table changed. The well started supplying the Summit in 1972. From the start it delivered a tremendous amount of potable water. An added bonus: it came out of the ground at ninety-eight degrees no matter what time of year. No more trudging up the mountain to the springs! Bob Howe turned his attention from checking for leaky pipes to checking on the new well and its pump.

*Photo 47: Bob Howe with Heather, Christmas at the Summit, late 1960s.*

## Joseph L. Chiriaco, Inc.

While Robert had been gone on air force reserve training, Joe had hired Ethel Bagshaw as a bookkeeper. The business had become too complicated for the amount of time he could devote to bookkeeping, especially since he insisted on accuracy to the penny. And now with all the business coming to them from the off-ramps, it was time to formalize the business.

"Ruth, I talked to a business planner. We need to be incorporated to protect us from certain liabilities."

Ruth agreed. "And we need to think about the children taking over after we are gone."

"Yes, right now that is Robert. But we need to start planning for the family trust."

Robert took a strongly supportive role with setting up the corporation. On October 2, 1969, the Chiriaco Summit business became Joseph L. Chiriaco, Inc. Joe officially became the president, Ruth the secretary/treasurer, and Robert the vice president of the company. Joe also became chairman of the board. The Articles of Incorporation stated the corporation's primary purpose as "to maintain, and conduct a garage, service station, general store at Chiriaco Summit, California." In its six pages it stated other purposes, leaving it possible for the Chiriaco business to grow and expand.

They had been buying land over the years and owned more than four hundred acres by the time they incorporated, even though the business was concentrated on seven acres. That seven acres kept them very busy, yet Ruth would suggest a break now and then.

"Let's go to that new movie about General Patton. It's at the theater in Indio." In 1970 when the movie came out, Ruth thought Joe would take a break to see his old friend portrayed by George C. Scott.

"No actor can get into the head of Patton," Joe answered, and he never did see the movie.

## Junkyard or play yard

Oh, what Ruth did not know! While the adults were so busy running the business and making it official, six-year-old Heather and her slightly older cousins used their ingenuity everywhere on the site, especially the junkyard. They trolled the heaps of cars looking for old models with an ignition that could be turned off and on with a thumb. They squealed with delight when they were successful. The cars did not go, but that was not the point. It was the hunt. Now and then they just sat in some of the vehicles they loved, especially a 1932 Cadillac with a beautiful interior and exterior, a green and white jeep, and one of the old tow trucks. The junkyard would remain a resource and a fascination for children and adults as the years went on.

# 14

## *Managing Crises, 1970s*

Joe and Ruth and their family kept up with the news about key issues facing the day through café conversations, radio and TV stories, and newspaper headlines that included such phrases as *mind-altering drugs, body bags from Vietnam, Civil Rights marches,* and *gas prices rising again.*

They had their own Summit headlines that caused questions among themselves. *Where is our son? A halo? How stupid can I be?*

The 1970s were full of crises at home and around the nation. The Chiriacos worked through them all.

### Café to Alaska to coffee shop

In 1970, Margit and Rudy moved to a house near San Bernardino, where their son Chris was born. The house was one that Pauline and her husband, John Leedom, vacated to start a citrus grove in Visalia. Margit and Rudy lived there for a short time. Next they moved to Needles, for Rudy's new assignment, but he would be reassigned again.

The Summit was prospering in 1971 when Margit went there to talk with her mother. "Mother, Rudy has been offered a job on the pipeline in Alaska. They need him while they are building roads up there. But I hate to leave everybody here."

Ruth's eyes gleamed. "Go, Margit, go. You might not ever have another adventure like that."

So a Chiriaco Caravan formed. Ruth and Margit drove Joe's car with little Chris. Joe took Heather in Rudy's camper—a moving van of sorts. Rudy was waiting to meet them in Fairbanks. Joe and Ruth stayed for a while, but as summer ended and the weather started to become ominous, Joe was torn between leaving his grandchildren and making a safe trip back. Tears came to his eyes as he and Ruth said their good-byes. He especially hated leaving the grandchildren, On September 1, they arrived back at the Summit, where Robert had been in charge during their trip—good practice for what was to come. Margit, Rudy, and the children stayed in Alaska for about two years.

At the start of the 1970s, the country was still influenced by the counterculture of the '60s. Some young people, disillusioned with actions of the civil rights movement and the Vietnam War, searched for alternatives with reality-altering drugs, which they believed opened the mind. By 1969, the drug culture became so pervasive that President Richard Nixon declared a "war on drugs." Some of the Eagle Mountain crowd were part of this culture. Joe had been wary of some people there way back to the late 1940s and still was. This iron-mining community was close enough to the Summit for interactions between the communities to take place on a regular basis, which worried Joe. The word around the desert was that life was rough and tumble in the bachelor quarters, involving more vices than just drugs, in spite of the five churches on the mountain. Parents like Ruth and Joe discouraged their family members from spending too much time in the mining community. Suzanne Ragsdale's mother allowed her to go to the movie theater there in her teenage years, but only if she went with her Mormon friends.

In 1970, before the Alaska trip, when Ruth was sixty-five years old, Robert encouraged her to retire. She did so. She kept herself busy with the growing brood of grandchildren who came to visit and work at the Summit as they got older; however, like Joe she could not take a back seat with the Summit business entirely. She went over to check on the café several times a day.

Ruth's expertise was hard to replace. Once Margit and Rudy were gone to Alaska, the Summit did not have their help. Fortunately, Robert had maintained friendships in the area from his school bus days. He hired a number of people from surrounding desert areas to do towing, cooking, and waiting tables. Some did very well. Three from Eagle Mountain even went on to lead roles with MWD. Unfortunately, others, as Dad Joe observed, drank, smoked a lot, and seemed to be on illegal drugs or were waitresses with an Old West saloon mentality—going out to trucks with their drivers. And a great sin in Joe's eyes: these few were not good workers.

Nevertheless, business was booming. Robert lobbied Joe to expand the café, which still had the counter and a few small tables along one wall. He proposed a dining room. At first Ruth and Joe thought they would be better off expanding their grocery section. And then in 1972, while Margit was still gone, at the age of sixty-seven Joe had a stroke, so any expansion was put on hold. For a while Joe had trouble walking, but his feisty, in-charge attitude did not change. Robert stepped up, listened politely to Joe's constant direction, and did what was needed, sometimes in his own way. Ruth took Joe on as a full-time nursing job, caring for him and making him walk. He started using a cane, which would be with him to the end of his days.

By the end of 1972, Margit and Rudy were back—just in time to help out with a few crises and to add appeal to the Summit grounds.

Joe had long noted that Rudy was highly skilled with hands and mind. The Mountain crowd disturbed Joe more and more, but Robert supported them and socialized with them at the Summit and elsewhere. Many were his friends—some he had known since high school. In stark contrast to the few underperforming employees from the Mountain crowd, Joe saw Rudy as serious help. He hired him to work at the gas station, as a mechanic fixing vehicles, and to help with the business in general.

Ruth and Margit supported Robert in lobbying Joe for a dining room. They won out. Joe and Robert worked with the contractor to add on space at the west end of the building. They kept the walk-in box at the back of the kitchen but added a walk-in freezer, which they put outside. Margit got busy with interior design and creating uniforms for the servers—an apron with a Summit logo to go over their street clothes. At first some balked at wearing the uniforms. Ruth and Joe felt strongly that customers needed to be able to identify the servers as soon as they entered the café. They won out, and when the dining room opened in 1973, the aprons went on. Margit illustrated a new menu cover with a type of owl that mates for life, symbolic of the bond between Ruth and Joe. She titled the menu Papa Joe's Coffee Shop. Joe did not like the "Papa Joe" part, so eventually the new dining room was renamed Chiriaco Summit Coffee Shop. The original diner-like gathering place was now so much more than a little café.

*Photo 48: Coffee Shop Menu, 1975.*

In the '70s, Robert met Kenny Statler, who would become one of his best friends. Kenny ran the commercial operations at Eagle Mountain, including the café, store, gas station, and bowling alley. He went shopping in Indio and other large cities in the desert at least twice a week for supplies. He would usually stop at the Summit to have breakfast with Robert. They would share the gossip they heard about was going on at various desert communities, from who bought a new car to who was sleeping with whom. Most often, these two businessmen had serious conversations, including where to get the best deals on supplies they both needed. In one case they made a deal with each other. Kenny needed tires for his Cadillac. Robert needed an electric sewer snake for work at the Summit. They traded. Kenny became a mainstay during breakfast at the coffee shop. The trade may have been one of the more interesting things he did with Kenny. Robert did not consider him as exciting as some of his Eagle Mountain buddies, but he recognized the loyalty and sincerity of a good friend.

## Adding a few of the luxuries

Margit immersed herself in more projects that would appeal to the traveling customer, making more use of her art background. Back in the 1960s, Margit had started collecting antiques. A few came from the junkyard, but also from the Indio dump. Many dumps were open to the public in those days. Margit had no fear of foraging in these places. She also frequented more traditional haunts such as a store in the City of Coachella that sold old furniture. Rudy shared her interests, so together they collected items from travels, especially to Mexico. But where to put all these precious finds?

Ruth and Joe were now living in the double-wide. They had vacated the original home, pieced together in the early '40s. In 1973 Margit remodeled the old home as a combination display center and antique store with items for sale. Up went a sign with the old home's new name, Cholla House. Some of the first items on display were Ruth's collection of purple desert glass, which would have been made between 1870 and 1914 when manganese dioxide was used in the glass-making process. Glass that contains manganese dioxide tends to turn different shades of purple when exposed to the sun. Of course, there is a lot of sun in the desert; even so, it took years for Ruth's glass to turn color. It was not for sale. Items for sale included jewelry and antiques. Pauline sold her jewelry made from old transistors and feathers. She also sold earrings she made from exotic beads. Margit bought and then sold Indian jewelry made from turquoise and silver. The antiques of all sorts were displayed for sale throughout the store, items such as furniture, table-ware, quilts, toys, and period clothing. Travelers found Cholla House a nice respite. Many bought treasures to take home.

*Photo 49: Cholla House, established 1970s, this photo in the 1990s.*

Concurrent with the Cholla House project, Margit and Rudy salvaged several historic farm pieces and flatbed wagons from the junkyard. Some were so old that they had been horse drawn. With these pieces, they created Old West displays in public areas around the Summit. They set out an old mower they owned which years before had been used at the Hayfield Dry Lake near the old swimming haunt. Margit noticed that travelers not only stopped to look at them but also took pictures. The Chiriacos had created another reason for travelers to take their off-ramps, get back on, and show and tell all about it. Of course Heather and her friends (now about ten years old) did not just look. Several nights throughout the year, they crawled up on the flatbeds and gazed at the sparkling night sky, so clear out here far away from city lights. They counted some of the millions of stars and thrilled at comets and meteor showers. During the summer, they crawled up on these rustic relics to watch spectacular lightening shows, part of dry desert storms. Often, any precipitation evaporated before hitting the ground. No matter the season or the spectacle above them, they took the wonder of it all with them as they went in to bed.

Retired as she was, Ruth still got called into action—and not always as she might expect. It was a very busy weekend day in 1973 or 1974. A traveler approached Margit as she was waiting tables.

"I think the woman who was in the stall next to me is having a baby."

Margit's eyes widened in surprise, and then she went into action, getting a hold of Ruth. Sure enough, Ruth found a woman in labor in the bathroom. The birth was too far along to move the mother, so Ruth delivered the baby right there, which really affected her never-diminished sense of cleanliness. Fortunately, California Highway Patrol (CHP) officers were in the coffee shop. They called an ambulance, moved mother and baby to a cot outside, and handled everything once Ruth stepped aside. Ruth was almost seventy at the time of this incident, but she was still a nurse with the utmost professionalism. She handled the situation quietly; business in the coffee shop went on as usual.

*Photo 50: Antique flatbed with modern truck in the background, Chiriaco Summit.*

## A global crisis

The family was watching news on their TV and heard that due to US aid to Israel, OPEC raised the price of oil by 70 percent and decided to impose an oil embargo on the United States. In December of 1973, the US government, under President Nixon, reacted by raising gas prices and rationing gas. The Summit, like every other station at the time, had to abide by the new rules.

"Yes, the price has gone up," Joe's staff would have to tell customers who complained at the pump or in the coffee shop. Within weeks, the price climbed from twenty-nine to fifty-five cents a gallon.

"We can only sell you ten gallons, but that's more than your motorbike needs, right?" President Nixon had asked gas stations to limit sales per customer.

"I'm sorry, we can't serve you today," Summit attendants would tell drivers who came in on the wrong day. One strategy that California and other states employed for gas rationing involved alternating days at the pump, depending whether the vehicle had an even or odd license plate.

The Summit did run out of gas a few times, but not often. The Summit felt some pinch from reduced gasoline deliveries, but not as much as dealers in metropolitan areas. A bigger concern was the junkyard. The oleanders were no protection. Rudy took to guarding it with a shotgun to keep people from taking gasoline stored there or siphoning it from the six hundred or so vehicles in the yard. Joe had found crushing them very laborious, and so they mounted up for a while.

In 1973 the Environmental Protection Agency (EPA), established by President Nixon in 1970 before the crisis, increased its focus on fuel economy and safety. By the end of 1974 the gas crisis was over, but its effect on energy conservation lived on. The Maximum National Speed Law (NMSL) became part of the 1974 Emergency Highway Conservation Act prohibiting speeds more than fifty-five miles per hour (in effect until 1987 when Congress increased the limit to sixty-five and then totally repealed the mandatory speed limit in 1995). The speed limits hardly affected the Summit, but the EPA and its fuel regulations would have implications for the Summit in years to come.

## A family crisis bubbles up

In a short time, Rudy assumed more and more responsibility. Robert was more and more involved with the Eagle Mountain crowd and influenced by them. Joe hired a female friend of Rudy's to oversee the coffee shop. That was too much for Robert. To him, Rudy and his friend were usurping his role as second in command. In 1974, Robert took off for a few months without telling the family where he was going. Ruth became extremely worried about her "missing" son. Rumor had it that he was at Eagle Mountain.

"I am going up there," she told Joe.

"You treat him too much like a *poveretto*." For years Joe had been using that word. In Italian communities it was used to indicate overprotecting but literally means *poor little fellow*. This comment did not deter Ruth.

"I'm going. Margit will drive me," So mother and daughter drove an hour away to the mining community. Once there, they stopped at several places, rolled down the window, and asked about Robert. No one admitted he was there. In the process of conversation, they let it be known that Joe needed him and welcomed him back. Robert got that message. Not long after he returned, the coffee shop manager left. She did not understand or maybe no one told her that she needed to do actual work rather than just supervise—the wrong assumption around Joe. Dad reinstated Robert as second in command. Rudy continued to work with the cars and gas station. Margit managed the Cholla House. Robert focused more on the coffee shop, even though he kept carousing in nearby locations with friends he considered more fun than stalwart Kenny. The Summit business continued to expand.

## Two crises bubble over—for son and daughter

In January of 1978, Robert was racing off road through the desert with some of his Eagle Mountain friends in a jeep. They were not sober. The jeep flipped. When the rescue crew arrived, they found Robert motionless on the ground. They suspected a broken neck. Margit, Joe, and Ruth rushed to Indio Community Hospital. When they arrived, Robert was still unconscious, and the doctor was not hopeful. He was transferred to Eisenhower Medical Center (EMC) in Rancho Mirage, not too far from Palm Springs, where he underwent surgery. Then he was immediately outfitted with a "halo" to keep his neck still. It was touch and go for a while. Ruth and Joe were beside themselves until he started to improve. Robert stayed at EMC for several weeks and then spent another few months bed-ridden at his home. Friends and family cared for him. Two very able employees with connections to Eagle Mountain took over some of his duties in this crisis. Terry Raymond and Lawson Woody handled the ordering of supplies and the daily operations until Robert was able to come back to work in October. Terry had gone to Eagle Mountain High School from Hayfield Pump Station where his family lived. Woody lived at Eagle Mountain. These two made Joe better appreciate some of the Eagle Mountain crowd

Joe and Ruth had done a good job involving their family members in both strategic planning and day-to-day operations. Margit, especially, had her ear to the desert ground. She stepped up to help even though life had become unsettled for her. Another marriage had not worked out for her—for one thing, Margit never got over the fact that Rudy married her while still married to the mother of his children. Though they had remarried legally before Chris came along, the damage was done. At one point she started asking herself, *How stupid can I be?* In 1977, when Chris was about seven years old, she asked Rudy to leave and then legally divorced him. Margit stayed at the Summit with her two children. By this point, Joe and Ruth were angry at the whole situation, especially after learning about Rudy's former marriage. Margit now understood that she had been led by her heart and not her mind. Her attitude was that we all learn from mistakes and that other doors will open.

# 15

## *Sharing the Mind-set with Grandchildren, Third Generation, 1970s*

"Good job washing," Ruth complemented the small child who scrubbed the dish with a soapy washrag. "Now dip it in the soapy sink and try to get some of the suds off." Heather did just that.

"Sure, hop in." Joe smiled at ten-year-old Michael, Pauline's oldest son, who was itching to join Joe on a tow job.

Eventually, Joe and Ruth had nine grandchildren. As they got older, several worked at the Summit during the summers, making fond memories.

"I hope I can come next year."

"Me too."

"Me too."

### Bonding at work and play

Joe and Ruth involved all their grandchildren in the work and play there, whether they lived at the Summit or not. Back in the 1960s, Heather had been the only grandchild living at the Summit. Grandma Ruth and Grandpa Joe spent a lot of time with Baby Heather, who would not go to anyone but them and her mother. An inseparable bond formed between Heather and her grandparents. As an infant, on occasion she slept in a box under Joe's desk as he worked. Even as a toddler, Joe took her with him on late-night towing calls, never when there was a serious accident, just breakdowns. Heather watched and learned about the business from an early age.

For her, like everyone else, these lessons usually reinforced two rules: to do the job right, and—the cardinal rule—save water. In 1969 or 1970, when she was about six years old, Ruth stood her on a milk crate and started her washing dishes.

"Now use the other sink to rinse." Ruth pointed at the two sinks she had filled up and waited. Only adults at the Summit were allowed to turn on faucets.

In those days, restaurants had one sink for soapy water and the other for rinse water. (Today they have three for when washing dishes by hand is necessary: washing, rinsing, and disinfecting.)

Ruth coached Heather through a few more dishes. When they were done, she pointed to the rinse sink. "What do you think we will do with all that dirty water?"

"Oh, Grandma, I know that. You are going to pour it on that tree you are growing."

Ruth smiled. "We do not want to waste even a drop."

A few days later, Heather was outside playing. She wanted to see what it was like to pump water. She got the water running and pumped for a few more moments— a few moments too long. Ruth saw her and grabbed a switch. Heather felt it near her legs. She quickly let go of the pump. Using switches as a disciplinary method went way back to Great Grandma Paulina in Alabama. As Heather got older, she was not sure what she thought about it as a form of punishment. She did know that her grandma used it as an attention getter in emergency situations when stopping the action quickly mattered a lot. At the Summit, wasting water was always an emergency situation.

With Rudy gone, Margit went back to work. She worked in the coffee shop and wherever she was needed, especially while Robert was recovering from his accident. Ruth and Joe helped out almost daily with Heather and Chris. They took the children on picnics. Sometimes other family members and friends came along. When they were little, Joe played games and sang songs for the children on these outings. Grandpa Joe showed the children signs of animals and more than once caught horny toads for them. Chris held the toads in his small hands, looking at them in fascination. To him they looked like little rhinos. Joe took the family on these picnics in a comfortable car, which in the late 1970s was a Chrysler Newport. He had broken with his tradition of Fords to get a good deal. Although he was adamant about keeping the old Chevy for fixing the pipelines, he bought new family cars often. None were ever four-wheel drives; Joe was convinced he had no need of them. By the time she was a teenager at the end of the '70s, Heather noted her grandpa's skillful driving, no matter what challenging conditions the desert would throw at him.

Ruth maintained her tradition of sit-down family dinners with the grand-children. On special occasions she put out her best silver, china, and favorite red glasses. On Christmas Eve she served spaghetti dressed with hot olive oil and lemon. She also served fried oysters. When the grandchildren were little, they got to open one present after dinner, their new pajamas, which they wore to bed. After Rudy left, wanting to make sure that the holiday was merry, Joe started a tradition of going over to Margit's house on Christmas morning, pushing a wheelbarrow full of presents. In addition, he gave out a dozen roses: to Ruth eight roses with a piece of good jewelry attached to each one; to each child one rose with a small gift attached. One of the nicest gifts, showing his softer side.

Special occasion or not, there was no getting up and foraging for food elsewhere or leaving the table before dinner was over. This was, of course, before the days of iPads and cell phones. There were escape routes such as TVs, phones, and cars, but the Chiriaco dinner table was interesting, even to a teenager. As the decade ended, Heather was sixteen and Chris was a grade-school kid. All ages at the table participated in discussions about the world at large, the family and the business histories, dreams for the future, and stories that involved the Chiriaco work ethic. Bob Howe almost always joined the family for dinner. His stories about working at the Summit and about his long walks instructed and entertained. Sometimes the ranger family from Joshua Tree would come to dinner. Sometimes one of the tow-truck drivers and his wife would come. The very different guests brought wide-ranging topics to the ears of all at the table.

Once in a while an old friend would stop by. In the late 1970s, such a friend showed up.

"Well, look at you." Joe gave his old hitchhiking buddy a slap on the back. "So what's going on at the State? How many years have you been there now?"

"About fifteen now. I still remember hitchhiking out here for the Rose Bowl. How long ago was that?"

John "Bud" Collier had run for the State Assembly in District 54, which encompassed the west side of Los Angeles reaching to the ocean. He ran for the first time in 1965 and won with 71 percent of the vote. He came by and stayed for dinner now and then.

*Photo 51: Joe and Bud Collier, c. 1975.*

Some of the conversation at these dinners went back in time, reminiscing about the Rose Bowl in 1927 and the war years, which they both experienced differently. While Joe was serving troops or prisoners at Camp Young, Bud was in the army as a combat intelligence officer. Some talk was about legislation. For about fifteen years Bud worked on water concerns, always a topic of high interest at the Summit.

In this same time frame, someone suggested to Margit that she run for congress. She saw that as an opportunity to help make positive changes. In 1978 she entered the Republican primaries for the 37th District's congressional seat. Now she was busier than ever, moving about the desert communities. Heather and Chris spent more and more time with Ruth and Joe.

*Photo 52: Margit's ad for running for Congress. 1978.*

Margit didn't get elected, but another person recently married into the family did.

Bud Collier continued to stop by for dinner now and then. "Do you know Chuck Imbrecht?" Ruth asked Bud about a year after Margit's campaign for office. "He went to Occidental like you and was elected to the State Assembly. He just got married to my niece Alida."

Well, of course Bud knew him, since they were both members of the California State Assembly at the same time.

That same year, 1979, a new guest started joining the family at the dinner table. Jerry Rusche worked for Edison, supervising the building of power lines in the area. He came to Chiriaco to try to get a water deal with Joseph L. Chiriaco, Inc. for Edison. No deal, because, as he did not understand at first, the Summit did not have surplus water. Instead, he got it from Lake Tamarisk, near Desert Center, where Kaiser had created a lake with homes around it for the Eagle Mountain

Mine executives. However, in the process, he and Margit fell in love and became inseparable. Jerry had been married, but this time she knew it and saw him as honorable regarding his former wife. They started the process to get the annulments they needed from the Vatican. Jerry began helping Ruth and Joe on his visits to the Summit with small and big projects like enlarging the double-wide house without ever taking a dime. He became involved with the children at the Summit, never having had any of his own.

Learning was constant at the Summit. It happened on special occasions and in between. As she got older. Heather helped Ruth with all sorts of chores: cleaning the outdoor freezer, cleaning the kitchen and bathrooms, making beds and changing linens in the motel—sometimes with Bob Howe, who helped with everything. She also hung around Joe's office. As he was paying bills, he would say over and over, "Do not buy on credit. Pay immediately." Heather kept on learning about the business from the bottom up by being there.

Pauline's children were older. With them, Joe continued the tradition he had started with his brothers in the 1930s of employing family members. Pauline's children came as teenagers or college students in the summers from Visalia to work at the gas station or the coffee shop. The oldest, Michael, who had been at the Summit as a boy, came back as a college summer hire in 1977. He helped with the tow business and the pipes, thinking back to when he was ten and rode along with his grandpa. Whenever he got into a difficult situation, he asked himself what his grandpa would do. No matter how tough or hot the work, he could always draw on his days of suicide drinks and late-night ice creams to find fun and camaraderie. Over just a few summers, he earned enough to buy a Camaro.

His sisters, Jennie and Betsy, waitressed in 1978 and 1979. They were well liked by customers, and both girls loved the work. Pauline's youngest, Matthew, came summers from the end of the '70s to the beginning of the '80s. He was a natural mechanic, so Joe had him work in the gas station and at the garage. He took to calling him Little Joe, after himself but also as a reference to Little Joe Cartwright, played by Michael Landon, who was a very popular character on the TV western *Bonanza* in the early '70s.

## Junkyard profits

Joe kept finding abandoned vehicles on the old Highway 60 and the new Interstate 10. Sometimes people left vehicles at the Summit, not wanting to pay to fix them or haul them elsewhere. The ones on the highways Joe towed to the Summit if it made business sense to him. There he fixed them or crushed them for scrap. He also fixed or crushed those left at the Summit. Some he banked in the junkyard for further action that might involve restoration or selling parts. One of these was a

1931 Ford Model A two-door sedan. Like some other interesting vehicles, it was just waiting for some action from Joe.

The original junkyard became overcrowded, so he added a new junkyard with a chain-link fence.

The crushed vehicles, especially, became a problem. Joe's invention, the old K8 International Harvester truck with the heavy water-filled roller in front, smashed the junky vehicles into a load too wide for the highways. Joe had to trim the metal to transport them, which became so laborious that he hired a wrecking company to do the job, and then he waited for scrap to go up in price. Steel scrap prices were on the upswing throughout the 1970s and on, so early in the decade Joe started making trips to Los Angeles to sell his junkyard treasures. Some he kept for posterity, like the roller, which in time rusted, becoming picturesque in its own way.

*Photo 53: Robert with new Holmes-equipped tow truck, 1970s.*

Joe did buy a new Ford truck for towing about 1972. He equipped it with the Holmes tow apparatus—the best. Robert and the others all asked to drive it, but no. Joe kept it parked and shiny clean. With this new truck now twenty years after signing on with AAA, Joe had three tow trucks and one service vehicle in constant operation under the AAA contract. Yet anyone doing a tow had to use one of the old trucks until Joe felt the new Holmes Ford had aged enough to let it out on the road to do its job. Not Robert nor anyone else in the line of succession absorbed this tendency to delay the satisfaction of using something new.

## The gas crisis again

By June of 1978, Robert was vice president and general manager of the Chiriaco business. He reported to AAA's June issue of *Shop Talk* that the station was selling over 100,000 gallons of gas per month, sometimes exceeding 130,000. He also reported that the Summit used seven to eight hundred gallons of diesel per week to power its generators. By the very next year, bragging about fuel use would not be wise.

Ruth and Joe heard about decreased oil output resulting from the Iranian Revolution as they were listening to their TV in 1979. Not again! How would this affect their station? The decrease was actually very small, but the public, remembering the 1973 crisis, panicked. President Jimmy Carter's administration started deregulating oil prices by April. This meant that suppliers could raise prices every month, which of course was passed on to dealers. The Summit felt this pinch, but not as severely as the metropolitan dealers they knew. For one, thing, Joe and Robert kept their eyes on their gas supply—how much was left in the tank until their next delivery—and adjusted how many gallons they could sell to a customer. Customers got enough to last until at least the next stop on the map. In May, June, and July, long lines formed at gas stations early in the morning, with drivers thinking that the early bird would avoid those exact long queues. There was some backup at the Summit, but nothing like that in populated areas.

California reinstituted odd-even days. The fifty-five mph speed limit was still in effect, with the hopes of reducing the amount of gasoline consumed, but gas consumption was still a concern. Automobiles were still large in 1979. The average vehicle at that time consumed five to eight gallons of gasoline an hour just while idling. Some of this idling was when waiting in line for gas. Gasoline efficiency became a factor in the downsizing of US automobiles and the import of small cars from the likes of Toyota and Volkswagen. Joe continued buying full-size cars as the vehicles for his large family. He never warmed up to the Volkswagen Bugs or anything like them.

Business increased tremendously at the Summit with the off-ramps. By now in the late '70s, Joe had completely stopped relying on the mountain springs at Lost Palms Oasis, Munsen Canyon, and the cave-like tunnel that he had tapped into since the 1930s. The Summit's witched well was supplying all the water they needed—for now.

## Reflecting on the first five decades

By the end of the '70s, fifty years had passed since Joe first came to the Summit area as a surveyor and shortly thereafter met Ruth. With her he started an enduring business. With heavy competition, why was the Summit able to attract enough customers to keep it open? What sustained it to this point in its history? Desert Center actually had the lion's share of the business from the rural desert, even after Interstate 10 replaced Highway 60. They had the funds for highway ads, they had commercial electricity, their well water was easily drilled, they had lots of telephones, and they were closer to the Eagle Mountain mining population—advantages the Summit did not have.

So why? Location. Location. Location. But that was not enough. The answer goes back to the summer of 1928 to the swarthy young man who pushed his dark hair away from his forehead beaded with sweat and spotted with sand as he surveyed the Colorado Desert. It goes back to the pretty young nurse working in a sweltering hospital operating room.

Sweat, literally and figuratively, got the Summit off the ground. But Joe and Ruth's mindset involved more: the hard-work ethic, respect for scarce resources, pitching in as needed, perseverance in finding solutions, and their constant look to the future. Their children and grandchildren saw and lived these tenets.

A comment about future orientation: the Chiriacos knew that not every opportunity was worth chasing, but chase they did when they could see a good outcome. In those cases, Joe and Ruth did not just wait for the future to happen, they took action, as they did with water and with off-ramps. On the other hand, they were right not to move to Mr. Colby's triangle. The roads that formed it were abandoned and very lightly traveled after Interstate 10 opened. In fact, as the years went on, not Caltrans, not the county, nor anyone continued to maintain them. Many businesses along the section of the old US 60 near the Summit closed, since they were now off the new main highway.

Hard work and accomplishment sustained the Summit, but it flourished because Ruth and Joe built a community of people who were invested in doing whatever it took to make their mission a reality—*All of the necessities and some of the luxuries for the traveling public.*

Over the years, the Summit became a compound of residents living in cabins, mobile homes, and trailers. Ruth and Joe offered them homes at very little cost. The community had an effect on the children and grandchildren. Children could wander safely for fun or go purposefully to help from one house to another, to the coffee shop, the gas station, the Cholla House, and even the junkyards. They learned on the move.

The Summit collected actual wanderers, adults like Bob Howe, who for whatever reason had found—not lost—their way there. Why did they stop—and more importantly, stay? Joe and Ruth were accepting of different personalities. They offered fair opportunities, even giving some second chances. They were the type who never met a stranger. While they did expect a strong work ethic, it was hard to burn a bridge with them; yet they understood business well enough to know when someone should move on. Underneath it all, the Chiriacos were loyal, and the favor was almost always returned.

Almost fifty years into the business, Grandpa Joe was still in charge, with his son as his assistant. Robert had recovered and was back at work by the end of 1979, taking on more of a leadership role. Margit was using her diplomatic skills on behalf of the business. Heather was sixteen years old. By the end of the next decade, she and a whole new group with an even stronger, steadier work ethic would emerge in leadership roles at the Summit. This group would develop out of young love, and the community would grow and change again.

# Part Four

# Transitioning, 1980s, 1990s

*Fortitude*

And the county will require us to have more water if we expand;
you know, for things like fire suppression.

(Robert Chiriaco, early 1980s)

# 16

## *Immersed in Water, Early 1980s*

As the 1980s dawned, Joe, with Robert's increasing help, was still in charge. The skeleton-tank memorial was still all there was at the Summit for Joe's old friend. The witched well provided treated water, the Summit's only potable supply, to an increasing number of travelers. Some of the employees at the Summit continued to be the wandering type. The phone system remained less than adequate. By the end of the decade, all this would change.

### Water trickling

"Wine was free but not water—water—water." The words of Joe's immigrant father would echo in his head from time to time, especially when water was trickling as in this situation, pieced together from several memories.

"Robert!" Joe pounded on the door to Robert's house around lunchtime. Robert lived in a mobile home in line with the others in the little Chiriaco community.

He had not called by phone for reasons of privacy and expedience. Although it was no longer a crank phone, the system was still a party line in the early '80s. People could listen in on each other's calls even if by accident. Robert's house had no phone. There was a phone in the coffee shop and the office. There were pay phones outside the coffee shop and in front of the motel. There were no phones in the houses, except for Joe and Ruth's. Robert was connected to some of the phones by a buzzer system, but to Joe it was just more expedient to go get Robert.

Robert had been to Indio on errands. He had just come home and was about to head back to the coffee shop to help during lunch and then on to the gas station. "What's wrong, Dad?"

"Your mom says the water is not flowing right. She's been filling big barrels of water just in case."

"OK, then. Let's check it out." Robert started out the door. Joe was ready with a voltage/amp meter in hand. A switch at the top of the well connected to the pump a thousand feet down. Once the meter made contact with the wires on the switch, it would indicate if the pump needed replacement, although the real test was little or no water.

They got into Joe's old Chevy. They passed the junkyard.

"Look, there's Charlie Weyand," Robert said. "That was a good move, Dad, giving him a job at the junkyard."

"Yeah, it's good for me too." Joe no longer had the time or mobility to work in the junkyard. Charlie had delivered newspapers for years, dropping the Summit's bundle at 3:00 a.m. When he retired around 1980, he asked Joe if he could work the junkyard. His son, Laddie, was already working as a tow-truck driver. The two brought their own trailers, which they added to the Summit community. Charlie sold parts from the junkyard on commission.

"That was quite a trip for the tow guys the other day when the Capps got stranded," Robert commented.

"Yes, I know it was outside our tow area. But when Jimmy called from one of those highway phones to tell me he had broken down in that old ranch vehicle of theirs—and June was with him—well, I couldn't just leave them there. It was a really hot day. At least they weren't hauling any of their sheep."

"Or those 4-H pigs or chickens or rabbits their kids raise."

"See that old Model A there," Joe said, pointing to a rusty old car in the junkyard. "That guy who stops by here now and then asked me if he could buy it."

"Herb Whitmore? You said no?"

Joe nodded. He had not agreed to sell the old junker. Robert knew that would be the answer. Joe turned his mind back to the water problem. "I'll bet it's the pump. It's been a while since we replaced it."

"The generators sound normal, so it can't be power," Robert said with some cheer. Fixing the generators could be very uncomfortable in their stuffy shelter. They got out of the Chevy, walked over to the well, and tested its pump with the meter.

"But something's wrong. I don't think we are getting even three gallons a minute."

When working properly, the five-horsepower pump produced five gallons a minute. Five horsepower was all the generator could handle. The witched well had served them now for about ten years. Every two to three years, the pump wore out, and replacing it was not an easy task. The pump sat submersed in water down at the end of a thousand feet of pipe. So, of course, it had to be pulled up that far, replaced, and then the new pipe sent down. This was a tough and expensive job.

The bigger problem was that the restaurant seemed to be on the cusp of running out of water. The well supplied all the water, whether for drinking or not. Perfectly good water was being used in the bathrooms by more and more customers. Every once in a long while, the Summit would be down on water for a day or two.

"I can't see anything wrong. Can you hear the pump?" Joe tapped the cap of the well.

They could hear the pump, but the voltage/amp meter indicated a problem, which made sense with the slowed flow of water. Joe decided to call the company that serviced the well.

"Let's see if Mother was able to get lunch together." Joe was hungry as he started toward the truck.

Back at the coffee shop, Ruth had managed to keep the food coming out of the kitchen and onto the tables. This was partly because she had been banking water. Margit was helping Ruth. Heather, now seventeen, was also helping—and listening.

"It's time to do something about this water problem," Margit grumbled. She was helping out at the summit for a few days. She had driven about an hour from her home in Bloomington near Riverside, where she was involved with emerging technologies such as wind energy. There she could be close to Jerry Rusche, who was working for Southern California Edison as a project supervisor out of the Alhambra office near Bloomington.

Joe and Robert walked in on the conversation, tired and a little wet. It was summer, so at least they were not cold. Ruth was always ready for water shortages with prepared foods, full buckets outside for washing, and paper products in case they wanted to save wash water. They were always able to serve something. Ruth handed them each a hamburger on a paper plate and a soda as she responded to Margit. She was trying to save any water she had for travelers who asked for it.

"We need reliable water if for no other reason than all the people stopping here—seems like more every day."

Joe knew what they were discussing. He had heard it before. "It'll never happen. MWD won't provide water here—even though the aqueduct runs behind us." Joe sounded very tired, not just from his visit to the well but also from his long frustration with finding a way to get MWD water.

"We're damned if we do and damned if we don't," Joe grumbled on.

"You're right, Joe." Ruth agreed with his words, if not with his attitude. "We can't expand the business if we don't have water, and we can't afford the water unless we expand the business." They all knew the problem was more than immediate.

"I'm going to get the pump fixed." Joe went over to their phone, looked up the number he needed, and connected to the operator. The Summit's phone system still required calls, in or out, to go through the Toll Center in San Bernardino. Soon he was talking to the man who serviced their well.

Joe assumed that they would not get water from MWD for one main reason. At the time, water coming from the Colorado River through the MWD aqueduct could be delivered only to member cities on the Pacific Slope Side of the Coastal Range. Chiriaco was inland. Joe had his attorneys, Fred Woolpert and Wally Rouse, worked on securing Colorado River water back in the '50s and 60s, but they did not succeed. By the early 1980s, the Chiriacos were in a bind—the well water was no longer adequate. Not only did they need to be on the Slope, they needed to be a paying member, which was very expensive. On both counts they were out, unless they could find a way.

Robert picked up on Ruth's comment about the future. "And the county will require us to have more water if we expand—you know, for things like fire suppression."

Robert understood the special aspects of running this desert operation. "We could drill a second well," he suggested.

"I am going to make some contacts today." Margit stayed her course about MWD. She was determined.

"It'll never happen," Joe said again as he hung up the phone. "The pump will be replaced in a few days."

"Yes, it'll never happen," Margit echoed, "if we don't try. Water is our lifeline. We can make power, we can get gas, but we cannot make water."

Robert nodded in agreement. As with the gas station, the dining room, and the cars, he was ready to make the change.

"I'm going to make some contacts about getting commercial water here, Dad," Margit asserted with no hesitation.

Although Margit did not win the primary in 1978 for the 37th District's congressional seat, she had gained valuable contacts and experience in the process. She did not hesitate to use both.

## Going after reliable water

By 1982, Margit figured out that she needed an attorney who dealt with water issues. From her experience as a candidate and from living in the Riverside area, she learned about Redwine and Sherrill, an attorney group with water experts on staff. Mr. Maurice Sherrill on the other end of the phone was exactly that.

"Glad you called, Margit. Tell me what you're thinking."

"What are our chances for an agreement with MWD?" Margit asked, seeking advice.

"It's not just MWD. Caltrans is the key. They need MWD water, and you are a travel stop motorists count on. Start talking to officials. Find out their thinking on this, Margit, and how they can help."

They talked about who was who in the highway and water worlds. Mr. Sherrill armed her with a few names, some of which she already knew. They discussed strategy. He was realistic, encouraging her but letting her know she might have a long haul.

"Go ahead. See if there is a chance. Try to work out something. What do you have to lose?"

Margit thanked Mr. Sherrill. She hung up inspired by him, even more determined to get commercial water for the Summit. She started by inquiring with people she knew and some whom Mr. Sherrill had recommended. She wrote letters to MWD on behalf of Joe. She came to see why Mr. Sherrill considered Caltrans important, so she started to communicate with their decision makers. She discovered that Caltrans had a need the Summit could fulfill. At the time, Caltrans hauled water to roadside barrels, placed where people could get water for their radiators. Hauling water was costly, and there were other problems. The barrels were clearly marked *Emergency Radiator Water*. At least one newspaper reported abuses:

> ... the barrels have been spoiled with everything from household trash to dead pets.... [I]t is costing over $40,000 per year to keep the barrels cleaned out and filled.... Caltrans has a maintenance force of 45 people covering 450 miles of desert highway.... ("Emergency Highway Water May Soon Be Abandoned." *Kingman Daily Mirror*, August 15, 1975)

Ever since people started driving past the Summit (be it the old gravel road, the old Highway 60, or now the Interstate 10), radiators would overheat on the climb to the top, no matter whether they were coming from the east or west. Caltrans was still maintaining the barrels as Margit started her campaign, and now it was planning construction in the Summit area, which would require water for the work and for the workers, and not from contaminated barrels. Margit continued talking to representatives of congress, county supervisors, and others with influence.

There was another roadside concern: broken-down vehicles. Reliable water was a factor in making sure auto service continued. By 1982, Robert and tow drivers he hired were handling much of the towing on a long stretch of I-10.

"Come on, Little Robert," Robert would call out to a young child who had lived at the Summit off and on since his birth in 1978 and who related to Robert as a father figure. His mother had come from Eagle Mountain to waitress at the Summit. In fact, Robert brought her and her newborn baby boy home from the hospital to live at the Summit. The birth father was out of the picture by then. Little Robert, as almost everyone called him, sometimes went with Robert on roadside calls.

*Photo 54: Little Robert Lockhart in tow truck. 1982.*

## Loosening the reins

On a weekend in 1983, Joe and Ruth were taking Pauline back to Visalia, where she was living on the citrus ranch she and her husband had established.

"Let's stop to see Barbara in Bell," Pauline said. "I want to show her some family slides."

As soon as they arrived, Barbara sent her husband, Harry Clark (same first name as her father), to Kentucky Fried Chicken for a bucket of fixings. After they ate, he set up a slide projector and screen on their patio. It was a lovely, balmy summer night. They smiled and laughed and even shed a few happy tears as they made their way through a hundred or so slides of a family event. It was getting late. Everyone was feeling tired. Harry started taking down the equipment. Joe pulled himself up using his cane and hustled toward the breezeway that led to the kitchen door.

Suddenly he found himself face down on the ground; he had tripped over the edge of the patio. He had not even seen the small step down. Ruth rushed to his side. Joe could not move. She could tell he was seriously hurt and looked to Harry, who darted inside to call 911.

The emergency unit arrived in minutes. The paramedics suspected Joe had broken both legs; they were right. They transported him to the closest hospital, which was in nearby Downey. The doctors told him he would have to undergo surgery. He did not like being so far from home, so the next morning he called his trusted regular doctor, Dr. Wallace Wheeler, and got himself moved to Indio Community Hospital, shortly to become JFK Memorial Hospital through a series of mergers and acquisitions. Indio Community's lineage included Coachella Valley Hospital, where Joe had met Ruth. After surgery, Joe recuperated at home for months. Robert stepped in, taking more of a lead at the Summit. Margit and Ruth stepped up their involvement too, but Joe would not be left out of the action, even though he was incapacitated, and at seventy-eight he was well past retirement age.

"Have you got those papers for me to sign, Robert?"

"Look at these numbers. They don't match up. Figure out what's wrong."

"Go ahead. Get a new employee, but I want to meet him."

Robert, smiled, complied, but continued as he had been doing for a while, making more decisions on his own.

"Well, I did OK with Steve Tisdel," Robert said. Steve had come to work at the Summit in 1979 right out of high school.

"Yes, he knows his limits. I get along fine with him." Steve was one of the fellows who had lived at Eagle Mountain that Joe could tolerate. A year before Joe's accident, in 1982, Steve moved to the Summit when Robert promoted him to manage the Chevron.

"We can depend on him to hire—and fire if necessary. He can order and write out checks. He's a good backup man for me."

Joe nodded in agreement and then changed the subject to water. From the days of the oasis pipes, water was ever on his mind.

"Margit, how are we doing on getting MWD water? Be firm."

Margit did what was needed firmly but diplomatically.

Ruth, on the other hand, was just plain firm with Joe.

"I want a TV in this bedroom, Ruth."

"No one has a TV in the bedroom," she retorted, which was mostly true among people they knew in the 1980s.

But Ruth was also very kind. He had broken both legs and could not walk. She knew it would take some time for him to be mobile again.

"OK, we'll get you the TV."

"A big one; spare no expense," laughed Joe.

Robert and Margit kept Joe up to date on everything going on, even at his bedside, but they did not always agree.

"Dad," Robert said, starting to make a proposal, "I think we should go self-serve. Almost every state passed it in '81. Over 70 percent of gasoline sold is self-serve now."

"But not at convenience stores like ours," Margit said, stepping in. "I don't like that idea. We are here to serve the customer. They like us washing their windshields, checking their tires, and changing oil." As youngsters, Pauline, Margit, and Norma did all this as well as the guys.

"What about the equipment we need so people can pay at the pump? I read that device costs ten thousand dollars." Joe was always looking at financial implications.

"Self-serve can save us enough money to more than pay for any special equipment," Robert argued.

"Robert has a good point." Ruth was encouraging Robert to prod Joe.

"We could lose if people don't come in the store to buy things. Besides, who would want to pump their own gas? Or clean their own windshields?" Margit was emphatic about this.

She continued, "And ten thousand dollars for one device? What other costs are there?" She was echoing the sentiment of many convenience store owners.

Statistics gathered another ten years out in 1994 put the convenience store self-serve, even at that future date, at only 13 percent. Without knowing these future statistics but trusting her instincts, Margit won out—for a while. Robert kept his ear to the ground on this one. Robert and Margit were both risk takers, but not always on the same risks. The juxtaposition of these two, along with Joe's caution, kept the Summit on a path to innovation but all in good time.

Joe recovered well enough to resume most of his work using his cane. By the end of 1984, his legs were well on the mend, but the business was on the verge of trouble.

Right after the New Year, a young lady walked into the coffee shop looking for Robert. Everyone recognized her and wondered what she was doing at the Summit.

"Diana!" Robert saw her and showed his surprise. "Are you here on fire business? Everything here is in order?"

Diana was the volunteer fire chief for Station 49, which included one hundred miles along I-10. The Summit was in her jurisdiction.

"No, no, Robert. I just need a change."

Robert hesitated. Diana Ragsdale was the bookkeeper at the Summit's main competitor, Desert Center. She was part of the owner's family. Why was she at the Summit?

"I was hoping you might have some work for me here."

Robert couldn't believe what he was hearing. Who sent this angel? Ethel Bagshaw, the Summit's bookkeeper, had quit five months earlier due to a serious illness. Robert ushered Diana to Joe. He knew this was a rein Joe would want to wield. In fact, Joe had heard rumors that Diana might be available and put out some feelers. He hired Diana on the spot. On January 17, 1985, she started her over thirty-year career at the Summit. Ethel came in a few times to orient Diana, but she was really on her own. Within a few months she restored order to the books. The first computer at the Summit was installed for her use. It ran on DOS software that was designed for gas station accounting. She took to the computer immediately, creating templates that would serve the Summit for years.

## Just turn on the faucet

Margit continued her pursuit of MWD water. Finally, on September 10, 1986, Joseph L. Chiriaco Inc. signed a three-way agreement among themselves, Caltrans, and MWD. Caltrans was the purveyor, in a sense the broker of the water. MWD was the supplier. For years Joe had referred to their water system as the Chiriaco Summit Water Company. Finally, Chiriaco had authorized access to the water in Reservoir #4 with two new responsibilities. One was the responsibility added by the County Health Department for making and keeping water for human consumption potable by putting it through a treatment process. Over the years, the Summit had complied with every new county regulation on water treatment, whether for pipes or wells, so had experience with this requirement. To meet the new potable requirement, Chiriaco Water Company installed a water treatment plant for the reservoir. Their reservoir water went through the plant before it went anywhere on the site. The second responsibility was for making their water available to Caltrans and other public agencies that might need it for construction or emergency situations such as fires. This also was no problem.

One day Joe got a letter from the Joshua Tree National Monument superintendent. It made several important points: That Joe was no longer using the springs and he would lose his water rights to them if he did not use them, and that the NPS would like him to gift the springs to Joshua Tree National Monument. In fact, the Summit had not used spring water since the first days of their 1970s witched well.

On November 21, 1986, Joe signed a quitclaim deed to the Monument for the property known as Lost Palms Oasis. Little by little, Chiriaco Summit was coming into the modern world. No dial phones yet, but dependable water! Now, fifty-four years later, Joe the surveyor came full circle. He had started in the desert as an employee of MWD in the 1930s. In the 1980s, he was part of a three-way agreement with MWD, as his own boss. His last paycheck from his surveying job still hung on his office wall.

# 17

## *The Immigrant Impact, Later 1980s*

So many paths crossed in the late 1980s, making life and business better at the Summit. For some these were paths well-traveled. For others they were brand new.

### Love sprouts anew in the desert

Two love stories unfolded in the late 1980s. A third was on the verge. Margit and Jerry Rusche got their annulments and finally married on June 15, 1986. This was to be a long and happy marriage for her, finally. The second love story was also to be long and happy, but more complicated at the start and intertwined with another memorial for General Patton. The third would wait until the 1990s.

In November of 1986, President Reagan signed the Immigration Reform and Control Act, which granted amnesty to 3.2 million illegal immigrants. Backing up in time a bit to 1985, Leslie Cone, the manager of the Bureau of Land Management (BLM) office in Riverside, asked Margit if she would form a committee and start fund-raising for a repository of Desert Training Center (DTC) materials—in effect a museum. BLM administered the land that had been Patton's DTC. Earlier in 1985, *The L.A. Times* had published an article about the DTC that generated a huge response directed to BLM from more than seven hundred servicemen from across the country. Two desert locations, the City of Needles and Camp Young, vied for a memorial to those who had served at the DTC: Everett Hayes, the BLM area manager for Needles, suggested that a monument be placed there. Margit was lobbying for Camp Young right by the Summit. District Manager Gerry Hillier made the final decision—Camp Young. His reasoning was similar to that of Leslie's, who had researched DTC history, and Margit's, who had lived it. It had been the official DTC headquarters and the only DTC camp where Patton was ever stationed. BLM maintenance worker Ron Nordman designed and built a small pyramid-shaped stone memorial at the Camp Young entrance on Chiriaco property with Joe and Ruth's enthusiastic agreement. It was dedicated on May 8, 1985, the fortieth anniversary of the WW II victory in Europe (VE Day), with four hundred people in attendance, but it seemed not to be enough.

*Photo 55: BLM Memorial, established at Chiriaco Summit in 1985.*

The spot became a rallying point for veteran's groups, including the Super-Sixers, veterans from Patton's 6th Armored Division. The Chiriacos were part of the rallies. All Joe's brothers and many of Ruth's relatives served during World War II. For example, Ruth's twin nephews, John and Engel Bergseid, were part of the climb to the top of Mount Suribachi in Iwo Jima, although not the flag raisers in the famous photograph later made into a sculpture. The Super-Sixers, along with the Chiriacos and BLM, got actively involved with the growing support for a comprehensive Patton memorial.

By July of 1985, the California Desert District of BLM published the *Desert Training Center, Arizona-California Maneuver Area (DTC-CAMA) Interpretive Plan*. The plan added impetus for a repository museum. Margit and Leslie took this museum project on immediately. In the summer of 1986, their new committee formed a 501(c)(3) nonprofit with BLM under a memorandum of understanding. The development of the museum became a joint Museum Committee/BLM effort with enthusiastic support from veterans and the Chiriaco Family.

Donations were needed, and now the committee could legally accept donations and start fund-raising. One of the first donations: Joe and Ruth promised some of their land to the nonprofit for the museum, and later deeded it to them. This was land where Utopia once stood. After the aqueduct work was done, Utopia closed. Sometime after that, Joe and Ruth bought the land at and around it.

In 1986, Senator Robert Presley, a World War II veteran and California state senator representing the 36th senatorial district where the Summit was located, asked the Coachella office of the Department of Motor Vehicles (DMV) to donate to the museum four vacated modular buildings that were slated for storage. The DMV agreed, but it was not all that easy. They had to be disassembled and moved to the Summit—sweltering work in the very hot summer desert. How could the committee find anyone to do this work? Margit thought about her contacts and aha! She called someone she knew in Coachella Valley who supplied farm labor. He sent two young men, Santos Garcia and Jose Ordaz, and two older men, Tiburcio Sanchez and Felipe Lopez. All four had been picking grapes. As soon as possible, Margit and Heather volunteered at the immigration offices in Indio, Mecca, and other surrounding areas to help register those taking advantage of what some referred to as President Reagan's Amnesty Act. They registered these four.

The four men were extremely hard workers. They cleaned and dismantled the building in Coachella, readying all the pieces for shipping. This involved unbolting the four sections of the building from subflooring to roof beams. It meant working inside with no power or air-conditioning on these hot June days. When they were done, there was still no rest. They accompanied the moving contractor to the Summit.

Santos was ambitious as well as hard working. He was polite but not shy. He looked around and saw work just waiting for him. He asked the contractor to ask Margit if she had any jobs the men could do. Margit said she could use one person as a dishwasher. Santos jumped at the chance but did not forget his friends. The next morning the other three showed up for work at the Summit. They were desperate for work, a place to live, and a chance to make a good life. Santos asked Margit for work on their behalf.

Margit and Robert decided to hire them all. They gave them a cabin to share as their living quarters. Santos and Jose went to work in the coffee shop, at first as dishwashers. Santos took the night shift. The two older men started doing outdoor maintenance and cleaning. Robert was in charge of employees at this time. He was surprised that he suddenly had four new workers who spoke no English. Margit spoke some Spanish, but Robert spoke none. In fact, he had no experience with

Mexican workers. To communicate he pointed or demonstrated. Soon his surprise turned to delight. He and the rest of the family quickly saw the initiative and industriousness of these four.

The first night Santos came to work, Heather was in the coffee shop, filling in for a waitress who had the night off. She started to train him for dishwashing duties and for stocking and cleaning the minimart, which Joe had expanded from the original snack shelves of the 1930s and '40s, but it was still in the coffee shop.

One night Santos was trying to find the chemicals needed to clean the floor. He asked in Spanish. Heather looked up what he said in the dictionary she kept handy, since she spoke a limited amount of Spanish. Soon the dictionary was constantly near them both. Heather realized something was up one evening when Santos pointed to a word in the English section.

Heather looked at the print: *boyfriend*.

"Do you have ..." he said in English and pointed again.

"Oh, no," Heather answered.

Santos looked a little sad. Heather realized he had misinterpreted her answer.

"No," she repeated, "I do not have a boyfriend."

He smiled.

A night-shift waitress, Marian Geaslin from Eagle Mountain, showed him the ropes with customers, so in no time he was helping her serve tables. She encouraged him to ask Margit for a promotion. Santos wanted to move up officially from dishwashing and made that known to Margit, who did speak some Spanish. Her response was, "You'll have to learn to cook." Tears came to his eyes, but he didn't waste time letting them flow. He jumped in to learn by observing and enlisting anyone who would teach him about the Summit business. People immediately liked him. They saw him as a fast study. The cook, Russ Mills, who spent part of the year at the Summit and part at a fancy seasonal restaurant near Yosemite, taught him to make all the foods on the menu, which included the breakfast fare of toast, eggs, pancakes, and sausages; luncheon sandwiches and hamburgers; and chicken, roast beef, and fried steak for the dinner hours. In just a few months, Santos went from dishwasher to cook to cashier.

Santos started influencing other Mexican relatives and friends to come work at the Summit. They were all hard working, with no drinking, no smoking, and no carousing. Rudy Montoya came from a different connection. For a time in 1984–85, he worked for Sidney Ragsdale at the Desert Center Texaco station. Sidney was one of Stanley's sons. Stanley, still alive and in charge, continued to maintain the prohibition of alcohol on site. However, by the time Rudy got there, some of the residents and others associated with them were drinking at McGoo's and other places nearby.

Rudy engaged in wild partying and drinking that went on in these places. It got to be too much for him. He became unhappy and made his way over to Chiriaco Summit, where he started pumping gas at the Chevron. He also helped in the garage, fixing truck tires, replacing fan belts, changing batteries, and selling items such as propane. He'd pinch hit when needed with towing, usually bringing gas and equipment out to the emergency site. It seemed to him that there was always an accident out on the highway. In the Chiriaco spirit, he did whatever he needed to get the traveling customer safely back on the road. Rudy was quite capable. His father had taught him to do repair work, so he was ready to tackle most anything that showed up at the garage. It seemed that he would fit right in, even bantering with Joe.

One day at the Chevron, Joe looked at Rudy and pointed to his car parked under a tree nearby.

"What a mess!"

"Well, look at all the birds flying into that tree," Rudy replied.

"It's a good thing cows don't fly!"

Rudy laughed at Joe's response. He enjoyed Joe's sense of humor. The two bantered back and forth now and then, but something was wrong. Joe started noticing that Rudy had far too many unexplained absences and that he seemed to be having other problems. Like with his brother, Vincent, and others, Joe showed some patience for a while but eventually agreed when Robert, through Steve Tisdel, fired Rudy. Also like with Vincent, Joe and Robert would later give him another chance, making it possible for Rudy to fit in and for another love story to unfold. But first, the story of the secret lovers.

By June of 1987, Heather and Santos started dating, not letting anyone know. The family had expected the boss's granddaughter to go to college, become a nurse, and marry someone like them. She had started nursing school and had then come back to help at the Summit when her grandparents developed health problems. She was all set to resume college in the next few months. So naturally, she was hesitant to tell anyone of what was becoming a serious relationship. Later in June, Heather went on a seven-week RV trip across the country with her mother, Jerry, Chris, and her grandparents to visit relatives. They returned two weeks later than expected. When Heather opened the door to her bedroom, a teddy bear greeted her with a bouquet of red roses. The roses were dried up, but to her they still said *I love you*.

By the end of the summer, Santos asked Heather to marry him. Heather's family was shocked at first. Joe told Ruth, "Send him back to Mexico!" He complained that that his future grandson-in-law was not college educated, did not speak English, and had not been brought up in the same way. He had forgotten the comments about the dark Italian. Heather did not back down. Quickly, the family saw the good qualities in Santos. While there were cross-cultural differences, he was bright, hardworking, and very much like them in business mindset and work ethic. The family gave their full blessings.

*Photo 56: Heather and Santos, Wedding Day, January 24, 1988.*

On January 24, 1988, Heather and Santos got married in Bloomington at St. Charles Catholic Church, near her mother's home. At an employee meeting soon after the wedding, Robert announced to all that Heather and Santos would be trained as managers. Heather started scheduling the waitresses. Santos had learned enough to start managing the kitchen, including ordering supplies and staffing. Uncle Robert started talking about retirement, but Heather and Santos believed he would be just like Grandpa Joe, in charge until the end. Nevertheless, the newly married couple dove right in, working hard in the 24-7 business. Heather put aside plans for nursing school. She and Santos turned their attentions to the family business.

## Patton returns

Back in 1987 when Heather and Santos were secretly courting, Margit very openly started moving ahead with the museum. By then, the Patton Memorial Museum Committee had become the General Patton Memorial Museum, Inc.

Board of Directors. The board purchased five modules from PepsiCo in Riverside with a plan to knit them into a seven-thousand-square-foot facility. They put them aside on the Chiriaco property for a while. Leslie Cone remembers that Margit did an outstanding job getting volunteers. She would not take no for an answer. One of the first was registered local architect Robert Riccardi, who created the drawings for the museum using his concept of knitting together the DMV and PepsiCo modules. Other professionals, such as licensed engineers from Krieger and Stewart, Inc. in Riverside, got involved in planning the building, and they engineered the foundation.

By now Santos and his buddies were very involved in the day-to-day business at the Summit. The board hired contractors to knit together the PepsiCo buildings. But for much of the other work the community stepped in, almost like an old-fashioned barn raising. A group of skilled carpenters and electricians who were retirees from the Edison Construction Field Forces created the interior spaces as volunteers, led by Jerry Rusche, who had himself retired in 1986. They installed heating, air-conditioning, and new electrical wiring, and plastered the exterior.

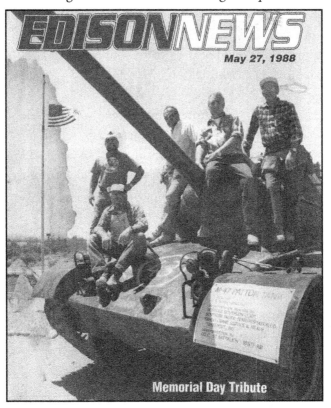

*Photo 57: M47 Tank, GPPM, Jerry Rusche, second from the left, Edison News, May 27, 1988.*

Soon another set of highly skilled volunteers arrived. Margit contacted a high school classmate, Rear Admiral Benjamin Montoya, chief of naval civil engineers. He arranged for a unit of Navy Seabees under his command to do the exterior rock work on the building. Some of these Seabees were World War II veterans. Their superior officers said they needed the practice, so they performed the work at no cost.

Donations started arriving: from Modern Alloy for the foundations, pro-bono legal advice from Joe Aklufi, and bricks from the Claus Family for a planned World War II Memorial Wall. Many others in the Coachella Valley, including Joseph L. Chiriaco, Inc., supported the effort with donations in cash or in kind. BLM assisted with costs for sealing, coating, and waterproofing the roof. They also funded the display panels inside the museum through challenge grants matched by the public.

One day when the board was meeting in the coffee shop, an MWD group a few tables away took notice of them. Bob Gomperz, the water district's public relations officer, surmised that Margit was the chair of the museum board. She was still talking as he made his way over to the board's table.

Margit was agreeing with everyone there: "November 11 would be a perfect opening day—not this year—we won't be ready, but in 1988."

"We have a map that would be perfect for your museum," Mr. Gomperz interrupted and then introduced himself.

"A map?"

"It's not just any map. It's a three-dimensional topographic map with local history. It was part of planning for the aqueduct."

The group looked interested, so he continued. "Los Angeles Water and Power commissioned it in 1927. It shows all the desert—to scale. Come to La Verne; we'll show it to you. It's in storage there."

"I think we should look at it," Margit replied.

The board included cofounders Margit Chiriaco and Leslie Cone. Also part of the original board were Stan Wolcott, Gina Wagner, Joanne Escher, Art Neff, Mary Jo Lewis, and Joe Aklufi. Some were there that day.

One of them spoke up. "What about Patton's training center?"

"It shows all the areas of the training camps. It covers California, Arizona, and Nevada to the smallest detail. You can see the mountains and valleys and the major waterways."

The board made the long trip to La Verne, about 128 miles toward Los Angeles—and yes, they wanted the enormous five-ton map. This was "The Big Map," transported to congressional hearings back in 1928. MWD refurbished it and brought it to the museum in the summer of 1988. Fortunately, it was still able to be taken apart. The museum staff readied interpretive signs explaining the map. But there was so much more to do before the opening.

*Photo 58: Section near Chiriaco Summit, 1927 LADWP Topographic Map of the Colorado River Aqueduct area, inside GPMM.*

The museum project was at the right time. People were feeling patriotic, having gotten over the distress of Vietnam. Ronald Reagan was president at the time. He saw in *Stars and Stripes*, a military paper, that the museum was trying to acquire a tank. He had one of his aides call Margit, telling her that President Reagan wanted to help. As a result, the museum got an M47 that came out of Anniston, Alabama, so now they had the start of what would become a large outdoor display of military equipment.

Also, the Summit got its first individual—not party line—phone number in June 1988, just in time for all the museum communication and pending business expansion. How did this happen? The Chiriacos always kept their eyes and ears open for the upgrades they needed and often had to struggle for them; in this case they lucked out.

California Public Utilities forced Pacific Telephone (PAC Bell) to offer service to the Summit even though they had no other customers in the area. The Summit was an island for PacBell in the middle of the General Telephone area. The Summit got its very own technician. PAC Bell assigned John Cote full time to the unusual system installed at the Summit. He explained to family members, "We only use it in extremely rural areas. You have one pair of wires coming into the Summit, which through a carrier splits into seven lines. But now you have a dial tone and a private line."

Explained more specifically, Pac Bell assigned one line for their technician's trouble-shooting, one for the museum, one for the towing business that was there at that time, one for a public pay phone that they maintained, and three other lines for the Summit as needed.

Robert then contracted for a PBX system to be installed, making the three other lines available to those living at the Summit. Little by little the Summit was modernizing.

The museum started accepting display items. Pauline donated the two Camp Young cots she used at UCLA. People started contributing uniforms, books, maps, equipment, and general memorabilia. Some had been scavenged from the camp-sites, and some came from the donors' own World War II experiences. Linda Beal, Ben Beal's daughter, found a desk just like the one Ben had used as a DTC clerk. She donated it to the museum. And, of course, there were all the items BLM had already collected from World War II veterans, the general public, and from the Chiriaco Family. All this meant more display signs.

The board had started selling World War II memorial bricks in 1986, well before the museum opened. The bricks, a major fund-raising effort, went into the first of several memorial walls to come.

*Photo 59: World War II Wall, GPMM.*

In early fall, the board sent out invitations and posted public announcements that the museum would open on November 11, 1988. Leslie Cone had taken a new BLM position in Washington, DC. She flew back for the opening ceremonies. Uncle Paul, Uncle Devio, Cousin Barbara, other family and friends made the trip for this special day. Paul and Devio helped place boulders as a perimeter to mark the road leading to the highway ramps from the museum parking lot. Alice Floberg came from Minnesota. She was Joe Bergseid's daughter and so Ruth's niece. (Joe Bergseid was Number Seven of the twelve Bergseids.) Alice and her husband helped sort thousands of letters announcing upcoming events.

Uncle Paul, especially, noticed similarities and contrasts with his 1940s days at the Summit. People were aging, of course, but with the same old habits. He saw Bob Howe walking with his oxygen tank and smoking on his way to the museum. Later he visited him in his lean-to. He was hooked up to his oxygen tank—and smoking.

"Aren't you afraid you are going to blow the place up?" Paul asked, quite concerned.

"Oh, nothin'll happen," Bob answered. Bob was considered a beloved member of the Chiriaco family. His health was failing, but no one could seem to stop his smoking.

It was also clear to Paul that while Joe was still his feisty self, he was unable to walk any distance. Paul saw him in a wheelchair. Ruth seemed to have slowed down some too.

On the other hand, Paul noticed many positive changes from his days working for Joe and from occasional visits since: the expanded coffee shop, the new gas station, and the historic displays all around. He saw the next generation stepping up, with different talents coalescing. Robert, with his knowledge of everything from the coffee shop to the tow business, had taken over the day-to-day operations. Margit, with her political sense, gave the business her strategic oversight. Her main home was about ninety miles away, but she had always kept a trailer home at the Summit so she could be there for extended periods as needed. Heather was using all that Joe had taught her about oversight and finances as a new member of the management team, and Santos seemed to be playing a large role, especially managing the coffee shop. But Paul missed the ceremonies. He had to leave suddenly for a family emergency.

November 11, 1988, dawned. The outdoor concrete area was barely dry in time. It was Armistice Day, Veterans Day, and General Patton's one hundredth birthday all at once. Right at 11:00 a.m., a huge crowd of about five thousand looked up to see a flyover by the air national guard. Bands played. A color guard unit preceded the talks from many dignitaries. Rear Admiral Benjamin Montoya gave the keynote speech and then cut the ribbon. Margit announced that President Gerald Ford agreed to be the honorary chairman of the museum's board. She recognized Corporal Ben Beal, the Camp Young clerk under General Patton, along with other WW II veterans who were in the audience that day. By the time Ben Beal was honorably discharged after the war, he had been promoted to corporal and went on to the 487th Engineering Water Supply Battalion of the 6th Army. Eventually, he went to work for the Coachella Valley Water District. Water was his lifelong career.

After recognizing the individual veterans, she stated the museum's simple mission at the time:

Preserving the peace through lessons of the past.

*Photo 60: Admiral Benjamin Montoya, General Patton Memorial Museum at opening, November 11, 1988.*

Later, the museum board voted on a new version with a more explicit focus on those who served. They integrated both versions on a display inside the museum and on its website:

To promote peace by honoring the service and sacrifice of America's veterans
while educating the public on modern US military history
through the preservation and interpretation of artifacts
from major conflicts of the 20th and 21st centuries

After the ceremony, some visitors walked up and down the memorial wall, looking at the bricks newly in place to honor those who had fought in World War II. Some of the crowd went over to the side of the museum to watch a USO show performed on an outdoor portable stage. Some took time to look at the tank President Reagan helped acquire. Inside, they went past the topographic map, a BLM display about the DTC, and toured the whole museum. Displays were sparse with room to grow, yet people were excited about what was already there. Some wandered outside all over the site, even among the Old West displays that Margit and Rudy had set up in the 1970s. The board, so well connected in the area, had an inkling that they would have a large crowd, so they brought in food vendors for the event. That was lucky, since the coffee shop was taxed to its brim. They also enlisted a large group of volunteers.

*Photo 61: Rudy Montoya (not related to the admiral) gassing up the M60 tank at the Chiriaco Chevron, November 11, 1988.*

The day of the opening, Rudy Montoya (no relation to the admiral) watched a soldier drive a huge M60 tank up to the Chevron. The soldier had been driving it on the grounds. There would be many stationary tanks parked near the museum in years to come, but this was a rare time the crowds could see a moving tank. Rudy filled it up and gave the soldier the bill. Joe and Robert had learned through their web of contacts in the desert area that Rudy had straightened out; they invited him back to work. He was back serving customers at the gas station and taking care of the generator.

In the time Rudy was gone, he had consciously set his life on a better course. He had been living at Desert Center with his brother. A Jehovah's Witness family there started talking to him, which reminded him of talks he had had with members of their church in years before. Now it made sense to him. He decided to live a clean, good life,

Rudy looked for an opportunity to show he was a changed man. He knew he had to prove himself. He tried to get work right there at Desert Center. Sidney would not hire him back. He did not give up. He asked David Ragsdale, who ran a place called the Drive-In, for work, and he got the job flipping burgers. People came by, mistaking the place for a movie theater but they quickly discovered the famous hamburgers made there. Rudy made burgers as fast as he could, especially on weekends and holidays when the place was hopping. He wanted to show what a good job he could do. He showed up for work no matter what. By some luck, a man from Chiriaco Summit stopped in at the Drive-In. He saw Rudy's good-looking truck and offered to trade his '67 Toyota Corolla for it, even though the truck did not run. Rudy jumped at the chance. As soon as he could, he took his Corolla twenty miles down the road to talk to a man he knew had hiring power there, Steve Tisdel. With Robert's approval, Steve rehired Rudy. In 1988 Rudy started working again at the Chevron. While he had been gone, the Summit business kept making changes. Robert remodeled the station to be self-serve, installed a cashier's station inside the café with a window to the outside, and with Margit's concurrence moved the post office into Cholla House. Self-serve or not, Rudy made it a point to do his best to give excellent service to customers. He was now a member of the Jehovah's Witness Church, which he credits for putting him on the right track and in the '90s leading him to the love of his life.

Patton was back, and this time no pipes to bust. The museum opened with water from the new system and a modern phone. Although their health was starting to fail, this was a happy, happy day for Joe and Ruth. They had finally made good on their promise to honor the general who had damaged and then fixed their water supply so many decades ago.

In a roundabout way they received a compliment from the general through

Robert Power, a World War II veteran and member of the National Restaurant Association. Less than a year later, in a letter to the museum dated October 3, 1989, he attached an article he submitted to *Nation's Restaurant News*. Relating to his experiences in the Battle of Bastogne and in the Battle of the Rhineland "under the command of those commanded" by General Patton, he wrote:

> It makes a difference who is boss.

And then in the very next sentence, he applied this observation to the restaurant business.

> I think this is exactly why some restaurants prosper and some wither. One owner or manager leads, inspires and directs with wisdom, giving proper times and places to do the task expected. And most of all he gives it his personal hand and caring attention.

With this short passage, Dr. Fisher described Joe and Ruth Chiriaco. Together over so many years they had directed the Chiriaco operation with a winning combination of explicit, sometimes hard-nosed direction and personal, caring, hands-on attention. The leadership style would change with the times, but the business would endure "under the command of those they commanded." The two pioneers had laid a strong foundation to build on in the next decades.

## Wanderers no more

Not only were Ruth and Joe aging, but so were some of the staff who had wandered in and out over the last few decades. Laddie Weyand and Charlie Weyand passed away by the end of the 1980s. The cook, Russ Mills, quit splitting time between the Summit and Yosemite, and spent his last working years at the Chiriaco Summit Coffee Shop. He passed away by the end of the '80s. Bob Howe was in his early nineties, with serious breathing problems. He continued to smoke anyway. Ruth nursed him for a period of time with Robert's help and Norma's when she was at the Summit. Ruth, in her eighties, hurt her back caring for him. so Margit made arrangements for him to come to her home to stay. She set up a special room with a separate bath for him.

He continued to smoke. Margit asked Jerry to ask him to smoke outside. One night his breathing became extremely labored. Margit and Jerry took him to the nearest veteran's hospital. There William Robert Howe quietly passed away in 1984, ending the era of wandering workers who found a place they loved and that loved them back.

Health was also an issue for the other Robert at the Summit. During the 1980s, Robert Chiriaco's health seriously deteriorated due in part to poor eating habits. To complicate matters, he had been drinking a lot with friends at McGoo's and other nearby hangouts. His friend Kenny Statler had left Eagle Mountain by this time and bought McGoo's. At McGoo's, although he sat with Robert, he did not encourage Robert's drinking. By 1982 Kaiser no longer saw Eagle Mountain as good business. Most of the Eagle Mountain mining operation and the facilities there shut down, leaving McGoo's with fewer customers. So Kenny moved to Desert Center and started working there. He continued his shopping trips and stops at the Summit for breakfast. This was one Eagle Mountain person Joe approved and liked.

By the mid-'80s Robert weighed about three hundred pounds. He started realizing he needed to make changes. His loyal friend, Kenny, may have played a part. In 1986 Robert joined Weight Watchers, with a goal to lose one hundred pounds by the time he and Steve Tisdel would board a plane for Hawaii to attend a Chevron Convention. As Ruth, Joe, Margit, Jerry, Heather, and Chris got ready to take off in their RV on a two-month cross-country trip, he told Margit, "I will reach my goal by the time you get back."

The travelers stopped in Minnesota and in Alabama to see family. This was to be Ruth and Joe's last time seeing their Eastern siblings. When the RV pulled back into the Summit, Heather's dried-up roses were not the only surprise. There was Robert, slimmer and trimmer. He still had some pounds to go, but he was on his way to his goal. "And I have quit drinking," he told them. He never picked up alcohol again. He made the Hawaii trip in tip-top shape.

The early '80s were marked by a serious water issue, family crises, and a need to get the financial records in order. The wandering type of employee was still in force. Some of these like Bob Howe were semipermanent, but others came for a short time as temporary workers. The wanderers and temps had served well, but as more and more travelers stopped at the Summit and Joe's leadership declined, the business needed a more stable force. By the end of the decade, new and different talents took a firm hold. Robert took charge, even though Joe was the titular head.

The very capable Diana Ragsdale came to stay as the bookkeeper. Steve Tisdel managed the Chevron, freeing Robert for broader management and more future-oriented tasks.

Heather had found Santos, who started a flood of workers who were thankful for their jobs and for the residences Joe and Ruth made available to them. They were first and foremost driven to achieve the American dream. They were also industrious, conscientious, polite, neat, and courteous. Rather than being wanderers, they stayed put, even moving family members to the Summit. And now there was a permanent tribute to General Patton, whose presence had helped the

Summit blossom. The Summit community, in the harsh desert where many would not want to live, was full of hardworking, loyal, grateful, and happy people. They were just the type needed for the growing business.

And the Summit finally had a dial tone.

# 18

## *Joe's City, Early 1990s*

The dream was threatened several times in the 1990s, with hard turns in the last years of the decade. Love made it all bearable—love that started the dream, blossomed among new arrivals, and made everything else possible at Joe's city on the hill.

### New love stories

From the days of Joe and Ruth's courtship, love and success intertwined at the Summit. Two couples from outside the immediate family followed that example. The common name, Sanchez, played in their two stories.

In the late '40s, Joe Chiriaco had a workman build a block laundry building, which he placed at the end of his line of cabins. It still existed, albeit without the old wringer washing machine. It had become a laundromat with modern machines for the growing number of people working and living near the premises. Rudy Montoya was one of those people. As he walked into the laundromat one day, he saw a young woman pulling her clothes out of the dryer. Rudy's good friend Albert Sanchez also worked at the Summit but lived in Indio. Albert told Rudy a lot about his family, even mentioning his sister, Beatriz Elena Lopez Sanchez. Santos also knew Albert, who was another of his Oaxaca piasanos. Back in early 1989, he made a call to Indio, where Albert was living, to ask if Beatriz might be available to babysit for his new son, Victor Joseph. Heather was needed back at work. Albert's sister accepted and moved to the Summit.

Beatriz looked up from pulling out the last of her clothes. Rudy caught her eye—or she caught his. In any event, at first they made an unspoken connection. After that, they ran into each other occasionally. One of those times Rudy said to himself, with a smile and a swagger, *She probably knows about my new, good reputation.*

So with confidence he started talking with her whenever he saw her coming or going among the buildings at the Summit. He thought to himself, *I have been cooking for myself for a long time so I can do it for two.*

The next time he saw Beatriz, he invited her to his trailer home, where he cooked dinner for her. He made his mother's rice recipe with chips on the side—a bachelor meal. No wine. He had given that up, and Beatriz did not drink either. But it was the conversation that mattered. Rudy started to tell Beatriz about his religious beliefs. He talked and talked, full of enthusiasm for his new-found faith and lifestyle. She listened with increasing interest. Whenever she had a break from work, she walked over to the Chevron to visit Rudy. Over a short while they could see that their value systems matched.

They married in 1991, starting long careers and a family at the Summit. Rudy's career picked up when in the mid-'90s Steve Tisdel left to work for MWD. Rudy became the main man at the Chevron, and proud of it. He took the day shift.

Rudy handled many issues, sometimes calling former employers at Desert Center. "We've run of out of gas here today; we're telling people to stop there." Sometimes he'd be the one to receive a reciprocating call.

"Just pumped the last gallon of gas we have. Don't expect a delivery for a while. We're sending people your way," a Stanco staffer would alert the Summit.

Stanco was Desert Center's brand of gas. Stanley had named the station after himself in 1990 after Texaco introduced the minimart system. Stanley told others, "I don't need a market; I've got a market right next door to my gas station. I don't want to sell groceries in my station." So he went independent, buying any gas he wanted, no longer tied to any supplier.

Beatriz took the night shift. Heather found a new babysitter so Beatriz, now a mother herself, could waitress at night and be home during the day. Rudy and Beatriz believed in caring for their children themselves. Between them they had that covered.

No relation to Beatriz, Hector Sanchez came to the Summit in 1991. He too was from Oaxaca and knew of Santos. His brother, Alberto (not to be confused with Beatriz's brother, Albert), already lived at the Summit.

Hector was very much his own man. In Mexico he was going to college for an engineering degree but could not afford to finish. He already had experience with electrical systems, plumbing, and construction when he called Santos to ask for a job. Santos said to come but told him he would be a dishwasher. That was OK with Hector. He started washing dishes but soon learned to cook. In the evenings, he wrote letters and made many calls home. He stayed for six months and then asked for a vacation to return to Mexico for three weeks.

Back in Mexico he reconnected with the bright young woman he had been calling and writing. Angelina Perez had been his girlfriend since his college days. He was so in love with her that exactly why was hard for him to put into words. Of course, he saw her as a nice person. But when he thought about it more, he realized that like himself, she had ambition. He admired her for finishing her secretarial studies. She was a match for his intelligence and work ethic.

Hector did not return immediately to the Summit. He married Angelina in 1992 in Mexico. By this time, he was working with his brother and sister in their Oaxaca business. He realized he liked working. School dropped out of his sights, at least for himself. He told Angelina that he had seen the American dream and wanted for them to be a part of it. He started to save the money for the trip back.

In 1995 he returned to the Summit with Angelina. Angelina became a caregiver for Ruth and Joe. Hector came back as the official cook. He noticed tiles that needed repair in the kitchen. He fixed them. He saw leaks. He fixed them. When a small electrical issue popped up, he took care of it. He helped Rudy Montoya service the generators. He heard talk of remodeling the motel; he did it all. Margit noticed his artistry and exactness. Robert noted that he was dependable. In 1997 Robert offered him a job doing electrical, plumbing, and construction work. He also took over servicing the generators. A year or two later, Curly Ulhorn, who had helped maintain the air-conditioning system, retired. Hector had proved himself to be the person to take his place with the AC and a myriad other maintenance tasks, from dealing with the sewer system to the electrical system to carpentry. By the year 2000, Hector was the full-time maintenance lead.

Both these couples started new lives at Chiriaco Summit, working toward their own success and that of the community of which they were now a part. They were different in terms of religion, education, and earlier lifestyle, but they were examples of the immigrant work ethic at the Summit based on dedication and gratitude: dedication to doing the best possible job on the quest to a better future, gratitude for what they had been given.

## A special worker

The tradition of grandchildren working at the Summit continued. Norma's two older daughters, Winnie and Vicki, spent time working there for a few weeks during their family's summer vacations. Like all the grandchildren, they took their turns cleaning the cabins and newly remodeled motel rooms. As Joe and Ruth got older, Norma came to the Summit several times a year. When she did, she spent at least a week there helping her parents with whatever they needed to maintain their home. Jackie, Norma's youngest daughter, came along.

She had been coming since she was born in 1968. Now, in the '90s, she was in her twenties. She loved domestic work. Her school had arranged some actual experience for her at the Phoenix Veteran's Hospital washing dishes, cutting up fruit, and folding clothes. When at the Summit she did a small chore here and there, often spontaneously and well. Robert and the waitresses at the Summit noticed. They gave her a chance to do dishwashing. She jumped at the chance. She handled the big machine expertly. No more hand washing like her mom, aunts, uncle, and Heather had done. One of the waitresses showed Jackie the routine: rinse, load the dishes correctly in the dishwasher, run the dishwasher, and then remove and put them away.

The waitress and Robert came into the kitchen to inspect during her first shift. They found all in order. Best of all, Jackie seemed to be enjoying the work. They returned when she was done.

"Here you are." One of the waitresses shared her tips for the shift. The next day it was a different waitress who shared, and so it went. Jackie's regular reaction was to smile and say thank you.

Whenever she was at the Summit, Jackie reached out to help, shared tips or not. One day she saw a pile of laundry. She started folding. She did it so perfectly she could have been working for the clothing section of a department store or a fancy laundry. She found that she loved folding. She could fold and fold, always making the right crease. Before she knew it, she was helping Heather, whose growing family produced piles of laundry. Heather paid her for this, but again Jackie's main reward was the enjoyment she got out of doing it. As Heather's four children grew, they wanted Jackie to play with them. She did. Jackie has Down syndrome, but that did not stop her or anyone around her. She was part of the team. The Summit folks put smiles on her face, and she put smiles right back on theirs.

## Joe's city, not a mirage

"Chris," Joe said from his hospital bed, "you know what I see?"

Chris, home from a college break, was visiting his grandpa when he was hospitalized with an ailment at the beginning of the '90s.

"What do you see, Grandpa?" Chris asked, knowing his grandpa was envisioning something in his mind's eye.

"A city. A city to keep the family close and to keep our family business from generation to generation."

Chris knew exactly what his grandpa meant. He'd seen it start to play out as a child and firm up over his years going back and forth from college to the Summit.

Joe and Ruth had consciously created what Joe referred to as *their city,* although it was, in fact, an unincorporated community in the Coachella Valley. They built not just a place but a sense of community by being supportive of everyday life events and by offering opportunities for advancement through working right with employees providing hands-on experiences, family or not. Ruth had already handed over the reins. She trusted the next generation—and good thing. In 1987 she had back surgery, which slowed her down.

By 1990 Joe and Ruth had realized they needed help with their day-to-day living. Margarita Tapia was already a caregiver for the Chiriacos by then, but more help was now needed. They hired help from a professional caregiver agency. Margit noticed evidence of doing drugs in the caregiver bedroom. The family dismissed the agency and their workers, kept Margarita, and turned to Santos to find additional dependable help. From her experience with them so far, Margit, in particular, believed that the Mexicans Santos knew would be kind to the elderly and would not be into anything illegal.

One of his first recommendations for caregiving was Leticia Sanchez. Her husband, Alberto, Hector's brother, had come to the US about the same time as Santos. Alberto and Leticia were working and living at Desert Center when Santos contacted them. He knew Leticia had been a nurse in Mexico. Leticia took the morning shift, from 6:00 a.m. to 2:00 p.m. She was a little hesitant because she spoke no English, and Joe and Ruth did not speak Spanish. Margarita was bilingual but either on her way out or gone when Leticia arrived in the morning. Joe wanted Leticia to help him shelve books and maps. He decided to teach her.

"Bring me the magazine."

Leticia looked confused.

"He pointed. "Magazine." Leticia picked it up. "Bring it to me." He motioned for to her to come toward him. She did.

He took the magazine in his hands and again said, "Magazine." He waited for Leticia to mimic his speech.

"Magazine," he said another time.

"Magazine, magazine" Leticia repeated. He realized he was teaching English, not just shelving.

He started to use this technique with everything in the house: table, chair, plate, bowl, and so on.

Ruth used a similar technique. She loved to go into her garden.

"Rose," she said and pointed to the flower. Leticia repeated.

Back inside, "Vase," Ruth said and pointed to the vase. Leticia repeated.

By 1991, at the age of eighty-six, Ruth was bedridden. Nurse Ruth started to teach Nurse Leticia how to be a caregiver the Bergseid way. She used English words along with gestures to indicate techniques for lifting and moving a patient. Leticia understood. She took on the Bergseid way.

By 1992, when he was eighty-seven years old, Joe was in a wheelchair off and on. Never one to be slowed down, he also used a mechanized scooter to get about the Summit. He kept to a daily routine: staying up late watching TV, getting up late, eating cereal and dry toast and prunes for breakfast, and then going to his office, where he worked much of the day. He wanted to see all the numbers, and, as Robert and Diana experienced, he wanted them to be to the penny. He still held on to the reins, but Robert was making a lot of important decisions by this time, some with Joe's knowledge. In many cases he made them more quickly than his father would have; that was due to Ruth's example and influence.

That year Santos brought both his parents, his father, Rogelio, and his mother, Belen, to the Summit from Mexico. Santos, like Joe, had a penchant for raising stock animals. No turkeys for him, though. He decided to raise goats. He bought two females and bred them one weekend. They started multiplying. Newly arrived Grandpa Rogelio cared for the increasing flock. Little six-year-old Victor helped feed them. Grandma Belen was thinking about another project.

In 1993, Ruth lost consciousness due to congestive heart failure. The highway patrol happened to be at the Summit. They revived her and called the ambulance, which took her to the hospital. Joe wrote to her from the Summit. His letter of April 2 is reminiscent of the passion they had for each other back in the 1930s. For some time, Joe had been adding a special signature to his letters to Ruth.

I'm sitting on the edge of the bed writing. I couldn't find a piece of paper so I tore apart my Kleenex box for stationery. It's awful lonely being here all alone. I looked up on the wall and saw the picture of our four children and realized more than ever how great it is that I love you.

So I opened my album and found the prettiest picture of you and gave it a big kiss. [Around the oval Kleenex box hole] I won't tell you what I wrote in this hole so you will make up something I'm sure, but keep it nice. So now I'll go back to bed and dream about you with all my love and please come home tomorrow.

Soon Ruth and Joe needed round-the-clock care. The two caregivers needed a third person.

Margarita called her sister in Mexico to come join the staff. In 1994, Elfega Tapia arrived at the Summit. When she first met Ruth, Ruth reached up from her bed to hug Nina, as she wanted to be called. A wonderful new feeling came over the young woman. She felt liked. In Mexico she had been ill treated by a boss who constantly told her she was a good-for-nothing secretary. Nina spoke no English. Margarita translated, but Joe soon told her, "No one knows how to speak Spanish in this house. You must learn English." He embarked on his pointing technique with Nina. Margit and Heather started helping Nina study for her citizenship test.

In 1995, when Angelina Sanchez, Hector's wife, joined the caregiving staff, she started by taking the night shift, 10:00 p.m. to 6:00 a.m., but eventually the caregivers traded off shifts. Also now since there were four they could cover for each other on days off. The family had been doing the covering. Angelina spoke some English, which, of course, Ruth and Joe encouraged her to use. Ruth had a morning routine, which they all supported. Ever the lady, she wanted to first shower and then put on makeup and lipstick. For breakfast she had hot tea, oatmeal, and a piece of toast.

When she could, she sat in a wheelchair on the porch, watching all the Summit activity. Sedentary as their health had made them, Joe and Ruth remained engaged, especially with family but also with the business.

Little Victor, now seven, joined them after school to watch cartoons on their TV for an hour or so. This became routine for him in his great-grandparents' last years. It was where he wanted to be, and not because of the cartoons. They made him feel like he belonged there—in their little city.

While comfortable in their small town, they were also comfortable in the greater desert community. With all their focus on overcoming their challenges, the Chiriacos still found time to support the Patton Museum as it was expanding and to rejoice with their Joshua Tree neighbors as they grew their spectacular outdoor horizons.

# 19

## Old Alliances Anew,
## Still the Early 1990s

While work consumed the Chiriacos, they found time to build on their desert friendships from Joe's old friend, the general, and then with the nearby rangers, who more than anyone else understood their survival challenges.

### Patton's tanks and critters

A lot happened at the new General Patton Memorial Museum right at the start of the 1990s. The museum acquired sixteen M60s from the Defense Reutilization and Marketing Organization near Barstow. Acquired is not exactly right. The military continues to own its equipment, even though in this case the museum got the tanks on permanent loan, exhibiting them in a huge outdoor area by the entrance to Camp Young.

At Easter, people came from all around to attend the first Sunrise Service on the grounds not too far from the tanks. At their Veteran's Day outdoor ceremony, General Curtis LeMay, the father of strategic air command, received the museum's second Patton Award. The museum had started the annual General Patton Award the year before, in 1989, presenting it to General James Doolittle, who had served heroically as a pilot in World War II. All the awardees to the present day are listed on a wall in the museum.

Inside, the board oversaw a new exhibit of animal life indigenous to the Mojave, Sonoran, and Colorado deserts. In a note to members known as Friends of the Museum, the board wrote:

Along with their training the men who served at the Desert Training Center during World War II had to contend with hard environmental conditions, as well as occasional visits from some of nature's creepy crawlers.

This was reminiscent of General Patton's encounter with rattlers while scouting the desert with John Hilton in the early 1940s. The museum leadership also added exhibits of desert minerals, gemstones, and fossils to their growing collections of military weapons and gear.

All this activity led the board to hire a professional in April of 1993. They selected Steven R. Nelson as the first executive director of the General Patton Memorial Museum. Soon after, the museum added Pershing, Sherman, and Patton tanks to the outdoor display. As the years went on, the museum board acquired and displayed more and more vehicles as part of the nation's military history.

## Joshua Tree National Park

On October 31, 1994, President Clinton signed the California Desert Protection Act, which redesignated Joshua Tree National Monument as a national park. The new park was the size of Rhode Island, over 790,000 acres. Part of the new acreage was old acreage; land that had been mined in the 1950s was returned to the new park. Portions of Eagle Mountain are an example.

The rangers, who lived at Cottonwood, still picked up mail at the Summit Post Office, so the Chiriacos heard firsthand about the monument being elevated to a national park.

The Chiriacos had been all for re-designating their neighboring park. In addition to looking forward to more travelers in the area, they saw beauty where others saw wasteland. Because of their health, Joe and Ruth could not attend the opening-day program at the Twentynine Palms headquarters. Norma and Robert went on their behalf, excited to be there. They were some of the many community members who came out that day. The program included ceremonies conducted by local indigenous peoples: the Cahuilla, Serrano, and Chemehuevi Indians. The newly named superintendent, Ernie Quintana, talked about the importance of the unique geology of the park and surrounding desert areas.

"Our new park spreads across two distinct ecosystems, the Mojave and Colorado Deserts," Superintendent Quintana said. "You can see the divide between the higher Mojave and lower Colorado clearly. This is a great escape from Los Angeles, which is about three hours' drive away. Here you can sit in peace with clean air and under clear skies. If you want adventure, you can climb the boulder formations in some parts of the park. In other parts you can climb to bubbling springs. Some years you can see a blast of color from millions of wildflowers."

*Photo 62: Geology, Palm Oasis Hiking Trail, Joshua Tree National Park, Camp Hosts, Dick and Phyllis Clawson.*

He went on to explain that the gnarled, knotty-looking Joshua trees grow in the higher desert, the Mohave. Ironwood and palo verde trees grow in the lower desert, the Colorado. In contrast, spectacular wildflower shows erupt over the desert expanse in wet years, starting at lower elevations in February and moving up to the highest elevations as late as June. Regardless of elevation, water could be scarce depending on precipitation, which could affect the Joshua trees' blooms and the number of wildflowers.

While Ernie was speaking, Jeff Ohlfs, a law-enforcement ranger at the time, walked the premises. His mind was on security, first aid, and protection of desert animal and plant life. This crowd probably knew, but on other days he reminded people to make sure no tortoises were lodged in one of their favorite places, under tires. It didn't happen often, but occasionally the endangered animal became a crushed chock block. And then there were the people taking some of the rare desert plants, but not this group today. As Jeff continued to make his rounds, Ernie finished his talk.

"Now this land will be protected in perpetuity. It will be there for the grand-kids of our grandkids."

Not only would the park, as did the monument, preserve rare plants like the very unique Joshua tree, but it would preserve history—especially the ancient history of the fifteen cultural tribal affiliations who made these two deserts home. Although not its mandate, it would preserve more recent history: the history surrounding General Patton's Desert Training Center and histories of places like Chiriaco Summit. The park's story was intertwined with that of the Chiriacos.

The Cottonwood rangers and the Summit residents had long shared some of the same challenges of isolated desert living. Jeff Ohlfs, as an example, experienced these challenges daily. He had come to what was the monument in 1990 as a law-enforcement field ranger. He came from an eastern post to be near his ailing father, and lived at Cottonwood. This was the same place Ruth and Joe had taken their family many times, only then not a soul lived there, at least not officially. There were always the few wanderers and miners, but they were mostly gone now. By 1991 ranger families with children, a college research team, and volunteers lived there in houses and trailers in a community of about between thirty to forty people, all living with few amenities. They had washing machines, but no two families could use them at the same time. Their power came from a generator.

In at least one way, the Summit was better off. There were no phones at Cottonwood; the rangers used radios to communicate. When Jeff needed to use a phone for park business or to call family, he drove to the Summit to use the pay phone there. One day in 1991, Jeff received a radio call from park dispatch.

"You need to get over to Chiriaco and call home."

Jeff drove right over. He made the call to his mother, sat quietly for a few moments, and left immediately for home. One of the great influences on his life, his dad, had passed away.

Now on this cool, fall day of the opening celebration, Jeff was a key member of a national park staff because of the influence of his parents. His dad had been an outdoorsman, his mom a parks and recreation worker. He continued making his rounds at the northern entrance to the park, the Twentynine Palms headquarters. He saw Norma and Robert in the distance. "Next time I get a chance, I am going to tell them they ruined carne asada for me. I can't eat it anywhere else. The Summit has the best."

Like others who worked for the park, Jeff felt a part of the Summit community. The rangers and their superintendent attended Summit events, especially at the Patton Museum. Superintendent Quintana was a Vietnam War army veteran, and like many others who came, he got a tremendous sense of pride when attending the Veterans Day ceremonies. Over the years he noted that the Chiriacos acted quickly to resolve matters in their sphere of responsibility. He shared a relationship with the Summit that was always businesslike and cordial, both looking out for their own water interests as would be natural in the desert.

At one point in 1994, Jeff told Robert, "You aren't using those pipes from the springs. They are in terrible shape. I have volunteers who are willing to take them out. We'll bring them here to you once we have them all dismantled."

*Photo 63: A remaining pipe coming down from the springs.*

Robert agreed. Jeff enlisted his two volunteers in the winter of 1994–95, John Evans and David Smith, who removed the pipes from Lost Palms Oasis to Chiriaco Summit. They started at Chiriaco Summit and moved up the wash. They removed about ten feet at a time. The pipes were brittle, so they could snap them at the joints. As Joe did, they drove a truck up as far as possible, about two miles, loading it as they went. They reduced the tire PSI about 40 percent so they could drive on through the sandy, rocky wash—but once they reached the falls coming from the oasis, they had to hike. That meant miles carrying the pipes down to the truck. The two volunteers removed 90 percent of the pipes. Since their mission was to remove visible scars, they left those under sand or rocks. They did not remove those on Chiriaco land.

Jeff arranged for the pipes to be delivered to the Summit, where they were added to the scrap metal in the junkyard.

At Christmastime, David and John started attending the yearly posada at the

Summit. The posada is a Mexican tradition. At the Summit it involved going from trailer to trailer enacting Mary and Joseph's search for a room at the inn, praying the rosary, and singing—accompanied by the generators. Children and goats ran around freely. The men carried the nativity scene on an ottoman. The women wore colorful shawls. Afterward, everyone went to Margit's house for a big feast (Mexican, Italian, and other foods). David and John were newcomers. They felt welcome and fully accepted even though they were not residents there.

# 20

## Hard Turns on the Road to Expansion, Later 1990s

Fast food and fancy hotels. Vapors and tortoises. Still struggling for power and water, always water. But a cell tower.

For a good part of the 1990s, the Chiriacos navigated turns on their road to expansion. Some were the hard turns of business struggles. For many travelers, luxuries had become necessities that would take more than the Summit's generator power and limited supply of water. To complicate matters, environmental regulations started to affect the business, almost taking over the focus on water. The frustrating drama at the end of the twentieth century would have discouraged the less hearty, but not the Chiriacos.

### A fancy hotel or fast food

Travelers along Interstate 10, from its beginning, would find state-run rest areas where they could stop, use the bathrooms, and rest in the parking lot from driving. Over time, state highway agencies added information kiosks and picnic areas but not much else, and for good reason. Several states including California had laws on the books prohibiting commercial development at state-run rest areas. A federal statute also prohibited such stops along interstates. These laws were meant to protect small businesses, but they made it so that when travelers wanted a room, hot food, or a convenience store along interstates, they needed to take an off-ramp and drive a little way into a town or community, such as at Chiriaco Summit. However, across the country on the Pennsylvania Turnpike, there was and is a very different scenario. The Turnpike Commission leases the rest areas to commercial businesses such as Chevron (Sonoco in Pennsylvania) where travelers can access commercially operated service garages, restaurants, and convenience stores on a quick turnoff and then easily get back on their way.

In the mid-1990s, Caltrans started considering a turnpike-type stop near Chiriaco Summit. They knew they could not legally operate it. They had had good experience with Chiriaco Summit over the years, so it made sense to contact Joe about a commercial venture. After the initial contact, a Caltrans official in charge of rest stops met with Margit and Robert to discuss the concept. "What do you think about a rest stop across the highway from you?" she asked the Chiriacos and then added, "It would be commercially operated, but not by us."

"You mean across the highway where we own the land," the Chiriacos replied, thinking about the possibilities. Joe and Ruth had started in 1933 with forty acres; by now they owned over six hundred. Whenever property in the area came up for sale, Ruth, Margit, and Robert encouraged Joe to buy it. Usually he hesitated. Almost always his family won out.

Caltrans agreed that Chiriaco Inc. would be the operator. Robert and Margit met many times with Caltrans representatives at their San Diego headquarters and at the Summit. Since the plans called for several fast food outlets, a truck stop, a motel, and a rest area—a big commercial operation—they also made trips to meet with possible vendors such as Marriott, Dairy Queen, McDonald's, Carl's Junior, and others. Joe and Ruth were especially excited about the Marriott. Chiriaco Inc. would own and operate part of this large buildout. Marriott would operate some parts, in particular the lodging. Chiriaco would operate the gas and diesel station, a fast food and coffee shop, and would contract with Caltrans for the parking lot rest area. Chiriaco would own the land with long-term leases to vendors. They were getting their feet wet thinking about a new business model. But then ...

After Joseph L. Chiriaco Inc. entered into serious negotiations with Marriott, a set of issues started to arise. As the Chiriacos understood the situation, one issue centered on a rest stop at Cactus City, an unincorporated area in Riverside County about fifteen miles east of Indio. Caltrans planned to close that rest stop and move the facility onto Summit land across the highway. This would be in addition to the current location. Caltrans would contract with the Chiriaco operation to run it. But Cactus City presented a problem. Caltrans used a firm that employed handicapped people to keep the Cactus City rest stop clean. The firm had concerns about losing their contract thus the work for their employees. Yet another issue had to do with the realities of commercial entities. The Marriott expressed interest in more rest stops along Interstate 10, but Caltrans could not promise that. No other hotel chain was jumping at the chance for the one guaranteed stop across from the Summit. And, of course, there was the water issue.

"Well, let's downscale our plans," was a course-correction comment made among the Chiriaco siblings after the Marriott pulled out.

Margit was specific. "We need to keep our core tight and build here on our original site."

With Margit and Robert leading the charge, the Chiriacos abandoned the idea of the rest stop across the highway and focused on expanding the site they currently occupied and operated. The core of their plan became a McDonald's inside a convenience store close to a planned new Chevron with updated pumps. Chevron would finance the building of the new complex. This pleased Ruth and Joe, who had long thought the Summit should be developing a bigger gas-station complex.

Some years went by.

## Not so fast: tortoises and vapors

Desert life, including the desert tortoise, had fascinated the Chiriaco four as children. This species of tortoise was out and about in the springtime, moving slowly so anyone near could watch them—and catch them. Much of the rest of the year they lived in burrows. These animals were hardy creatures able to survive ground temperatures over 140 degrees Fahrenheit. These tortoises could live to eighty years, but in 1990 the US Fish and Wildlife ruled that desert tortoises north of the Colorado River were dying off and threatened. This tortoise was on both the California (1989) and Federal (1990) endangered species lists.

*Photo 64: Desert Tortoise near Chiriaco Summit in Joshua Tree National Park.*

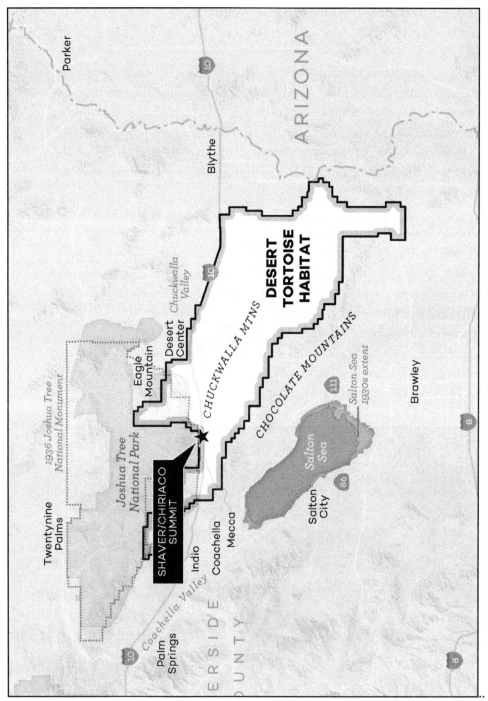

*Map 8: Chiriaco Summit in relation to Joshua Tree National Park and the Desert Tortoise Habitat.*

The Chiriaco Four had known enough to leave the desert tortoises alone. But now, for decades desert visitors had taken them home as pets and then released them back into the desert with diseases. Cars ran over them as they lumbered across the increasingly traveled highway. Roadkill brought ravens. Ravens ate tortoise hatchlings. The diseases and the very roads that the Summit depended upon for business were causes of the dwindling desert tortoise population. On February 8, 1994 the *Federal Register* recorded that the US Fish and Wildlife Service designated approximately 6.4 million acres as desert tortoise habitat. Mandates for the recovery of the desert tortoise followed. The *Register* included maps. One of them showed Chiriaco Summit in the designated habitat. Since it was in desert tortoise habitat, it would be affected in time by the mandates—but not just yet.

A more immediate problem to the business was a set of three interrelated environmental regulations affecting gas stations. These regulations had to do with a gasoline additive, contaminated groundwater, and regulation tanks. These regulations affected the Chiriacos in the midst of signing on with Chevron for the loan for the new buildout—the complex to include the Chevron and a McDonald's inside a convenience store. The Chiriacos had already prepared the land for the new facilities, having demolished the motel and tow shop when the set of regulations started to affect them. Plans for a new motel went on hold. The tow business was over.

For some time, Joseph L. Chiriaco Inc. (Chiriaco Inc.) had been renting the old tin mechanic's garage shop to Chavez Tire and Mechanical. One windy day in early April of 1996, while Chavez towing was still on the premises, a driver towed in a wreck full of office paper. The paper started flying all around. Some got into the radiator of the big generator and ruined it.

While this could have been a time to get rid of the generators, that was still impossible. With other expenses mounting and their hopes for expansion, Robert rented a replacement generator. Joe concurred with the rental. This incident added to how tired Robert was becoming of the tow business. Besides, the tow shop stood on what was to be the Super Chevron. When Chavez moved to another location, Chiriaco, Inc. had the tin building demolished, thus ending the Chiriacos' many years with AAA. This was the end of tire changes, oil changes, and other vehicle services as part of the Joseph L. Chiriaco business. But Robert, always concerned about motorists, kept a list of mechanics and tow businesses for them at the coffee shop and at the Chevron. The old Chevron still stood near the coffee shop. Soon it would have to be closed, but attention first turned to the ailing founders of the Summit, Ruth and Joe.

## Passing the legacy

Late at night on April 12, 1996, a new caregiver on duty, Patty, called Robert to tell him that Ruth was asking for him. She wanted to go for a walk outside. Robert arrived moments later at about 2:00 a.m.

"I want to see the stars," she told him.

Robert wheeled her around the Summit. She wanted to look at everyone's house in their little city. The moon had reached its fullness on April 4, about a week before. It was waning but still produced enough light for Ruth to see all around her.

"What a nice house Heather has," she said. "And Margit's, how pretty with the flowers; and Robert I like your house, too." She commented on how lovely it was outside. She looked up at the moon and stars. After about thirty minutes, Robert took her back to her bed. She died very shortly after at the age of ninety-one, with Robert holding her hand. Within minutes she was surrounded on all sides of her bed by family and the workers to whom she had been so kind. At her burial in Indio, Chris watched his grandpa as he stood for a very long time by the gravesite of his best friend and the love of his life.

A few months later, during the morning of June 21, 1996, Robert was chatting with his dad about a business issue. As was sometimes the case, they expressed different opinions. Joe still saw himself as the boss even though he was steadily declining.

Earlier, Margit had called Dr. Wheeler, who had saved Joe on several occasions in the past, but was now sad to say there was nothing anyone could do for Joe; it was only a matter of time. Robert felt his dad might pass away that day, but not immediately, since his dad was still feisty. It was Victor's birthday. Jerry Rusche, who loved having the family he never had, was taking him and anyone who wanted to come along fishing. Since so much family was there, Robert felt he could go outside to talk to a tow truck driver. Norma, Jerry, and Margit stayed with Joe. Within ten minutes Norma came out to tell Robert that Dad had just died. He was ninety years old.

The family was grieving, of course. Joe and Ruth were strong powerful influences in both matters of business and matters of the heart. Their family felt their loss profoundly, but they knew their parents would encourage them to keep the business moving while considering the lot of others affected. So they did keep the Summit open and quickly made sure the caregivers had places to work. Margit arranged for Nina to work for a doctor in Westwood, near UCLA. Robert brought on Angelina and Leticia as waitresses in the coffee shop. Beatriz was already waitressing there.

At first, some family members wanted to sell. Those who did not prevailed. There was no dispute about succession. While Joe had kept the financial responsibilities and stayed on as president of the board and CEO, he had given day-to-day responsibility and management to his son. For over thirty years, since he had come to the Summit after graduating from NAU in 1962, Robert was Joe's number one assistant. Ruth and Joe had written Robert's succession into their will. Shortly after Joe passed away, the board passed a resolution confirming Robert as the new CEO of Joseph L. Chiriaco, Inc. and as chairman of the board. Margit, as board secretary, recorded the resolution in the minutes.

## A new water problem

In 1998 the California Water Resources Control Board called for soil vapor recovery from leaking gasoline tanks. This vapor-recovery regulation was to counteract the earlier Air Resources Board regulation that called for methyl tertiary butyl ether (MTBE) to be added to gasoline to reduce air pollution. Air was one thing; ground was another. It was not long before MTBE was found in groundwater. MTBE comes already in the gasoline delivered to underground storage tanks. It corrodes the tanks, leaks its vapor into groundwater, and affects drinking-water quality. To solve this leakage problem, the government mandated double-walled fiberglass tanks, which the Chiriacos were preparing to install at their new station site across from the old one, planned for shutdown. But what about the old tanks? What if they were leaking, shut down or not—and how would anyone other than an inspector know?

Robert or someone else took measurements at the same time daily and made comparisons, which indicated whether or not there were leaks. One day, a reading caused Robert to suspect a leak. If there were a leak, it would prevent the old station staying open while the Super Chevron was being built. This meant Chiriaco Inc. had to have the tanks installed at the new station by September 1998. The MTBE situation at the old station would not allow it to function as a backup past that government-mandated deadline.

Robert, Margit, and Heather worked together to make sure that the regulation tanks got installed at the new site on time. They knew that there were a limited number of workers qualified to install the regulation tanks and that owners who hesitated to hire them would not make the deadline. Jerry Rusche started looking for these experts.

At one point in the process inspectors found an MTBE leak in one of the old tanks, just what Robert feared. It had to be remediated immediately with a vapor recovery system. When used for remediation, these systems usually operated for a year.

To complicate matters, the very day the County of Riverside approved the McDonald's, in September 1998, the famous fast food chain sent a letter pulling out. The reasoning: water, always water. The McDonald's decision makers did not believe that Chiriaco, Inc. would be able to supply water for some years into the future. Since McDonald's pulled out, Chevron did not come through with the financing for the convenience store and new gas station.

Soil vapor recovery was costly for gas station businesses. Fortunately, the Chiriaco business had paid a per-gallon fee into the California Underground Storage Tank Cleanup Fund (UST Fund), which helped with those costs. Even so, with the money put into the plans for the rest stop and then McDonald's and Chevron backing out, along with the costs related to complying with EPA regulations, the Chiriaco business almost didn't make it this time.

As September approached, Chiriaco, Inc. was still trying to contract and schedule construction workers qualified to install the regulation tanks at the new site. The Summit missed the deadline. The old gas station closed due to the leakage, but the new one was not yet ready. Chiriaco Inc. had to wait it out. The business was on the verge of financial collapse. Without blinking an eye, Eileen Heimark Fariester, who had been associated with the Summit since the days her father delivered beer there, and her husband came to the rescue with a loan that Chiriaco Inc. paid off within two years.

The last years of the '90s was a tough financial period for the Summit, but the business there was better off than where gas station owners sat on the double-walled and MTBE requirements. By the time some owners decided to install the regulation tanks, the workers they needed were booked up with a long backlog. Some also had not paid into the UST Fund so were on their own with soil vapor recovery costs. Many small gas stations couldn't weather the long downtime and went out of business.

The new Chevron did open across from the coffee shop. It opened in February 1999 with new tanks, new pumps, and an ATM kiosk lent by Chevron for people who wanted to pay without walking across to the coffee shop. When Riverside County approved the kiosk, Rudy Montoya went to work in it immediately. Typical of these kiosks, it was small and cramped, but Rudy's gratitude for his job and Summit life outweighed any inconvenience.

All the Summit staff breathed a sigh of relief as customers came down the off-ramp and gassed up at the Chevron pumps. Their ranger friends pulled up. They were new customers. They had been coming for food and to use phones, but not for gas. The park had its own pumps until the MTBE issue. Its leaders decided it made more sense to gas up at facilities like Chiriaco rather than go through the expense of installing glass-walled tanks, so they closed their on-site gas stations.

On May 29, 1999, Robert wrote a letter saying that Heather and Santos would assume full responsibility of the Summit business as of June 15; but as Heather and Santos earlier suspected, Robert, like Grandpa Joe, could not let go that easily—not yet. In another way, he was different from his dad. He was not as hesitant—so on with the expansion.

## New facilities but on our terms

Now with time and some resources to resume planning, Robert and Margit started meeting again with many fast food businesses. They found that most wanted Chiriaco to carry all the costs. They did not want to help build or help with infrastructure. They wanted everything in place—ready to move in. Over time Robert, Margit, Heather, and Santos voiced their frustrations and ideas to each other.

"If we do this, I say we own it," Margit said, speaking like her father.

Robert warned against making a similar deal. "McDonald's was going to pay us a very low rent and that was it. We carried all the liability."

"We won't make the same mistake," they all agreed.

"We need to get a franchise we ourselves own and control, like Foster Freeze. Ice cream is like water in the desert." Heather, with Santos backing her, up was thinking like a heat-exhausted traveler. The Chiriacos investigated and found that with Foster Freeze they could buy the franchise. They liked the idea.

Margit especially made comments like, "With them, you are not tripping on a bible full of rules."

Again, she sounded like Joe—this time reminiscent of the 1950s when he said about Mr. Colby's triangle, "Even if it is a good deal, I do not want to take orders from anyone."

They also believed that routine practices should be in place. "Let's look for a contract that provides ready vendors—ones where the process is there for us to buy from them. And a contract where they set up their menu, and we just follow it."

But there were more kinks in the road.

## A cell tower but still fighting for water and power

It was clear as the '90s came to a close that the Chiriaco business was straining its infrastructure again, especially water and power. Well, at least they had their cell phones. During the '90s, L.A. Cellular Company (later sold to Verizon) put up a cell tower in the Chiriaco Summit area. They gave the Summit one cellular phone. Just one, but they were thrilled.

"Wow, now we are getting into the new millennium," they exclaimed.

The family bought more phones for personal use and for tow drivers when they still had that business. Since the 1970s, the drivers had used a Motorola radio system. Joe maintained an FCC license for it. The radio signal was not always good. By the end of the '90s, the tow business was gone, but cells were proliferating among the Chiriacos—in some ways as they were in developing countries with few or poor landlines. The cell tower was a sign of things to come, but at this point they still had to use the old phone system with the PBX for everyday use. Even so, they were better off than their ranger neighbors at Cottonwood, where cell reception was minimal and they still used two-way radios. Jeff and others had to drive down to the interstate to park on a nearby roadside to get any reception.

The operation that started with two gasoline pumps and a diner-type café had grown over the years to include a full gas station, sit-down coffee shop, post office, airstrip, antique shop, and junkyards. For a while it also involved a six-unit motel and a tow service in a vehicle-maintenance garage. About seventy-five permanent residents lived on or near the premises. For over sixty-five years the generators had powered the residences and the business structures. The Summit had just enough water but not enough for any expansion. As the new millennium came onto the horizon, Chiriaco Summit was one of the last communities without commercial power or water in San Bernardino and Riverside counties.

The Chiriaco Summit Water Company had been supplying the community since the 1986 agreement among themselves, Caltrans, and MWD, but this was a workaround that provided reliable but limited water. Caltrans and others were concerned that in the event of a catastrophe such as a highway fire, that water would not suffice. Riverside County deemed that an upgraded water system was necessary for any business expansion at the Summit. The county wanted the Summit to add a diesel pump that firefighters could use to tap into the Summit reservoir. In addition, some county officials recognized that the Summit water was important for the everyday traveling public, especially since it was still one of the few stops on the I-10 through desert terrain between Indio and Blythe.

The Chiriaco leadership knew, as Joe had known, that the best option was water directly from MWD rather than through Caltrans. The law made that difficult, if not impossible, legislating that water coming from the Colorado River through the MWD aqueduct could only be delivered to member cities or to a state or federal agency.

"Why not become a member?" Robert, Margit, and Heather asked themselves, but this was more of an answer than a question.

"We'll never get it," they could hear their father saying. According to law, member cities had to be on the Pacific Slope Side of the Coastal Range. Chiriaco was not. Joe knew that law and had put his attorneys on this issue years ago—to no avail. But now it was decades later, and maybe some restrictions had changed.

The leadership talked among themselves. They retained engineering consultant Krieger and Stewart, Incorporated. With their advice and the vote of the Chiriaco Inc. Board, Robert and Margit decided to petition the Riverside County Local Agency Formation Commission (LAFCO) to form a water district at the Summit. But why? What good would this do? Chiriaco Summit already had its own water company. Margit and Heather were ready with answers when they went in front of the County Supervisors in late 1999.

"We need to improve the system so we can be of service no matter what the catastrophe in the area. You have to be a water district, not a water company, to get grants to improve the system."

"It will assure continuation of water not only for those who live at the Summit, but more importantly for those who travel and stop there. As you know it is the only stop for many miles."

"More travelers are stopping and are asking for more services. We need more water to grow the business. We have to be a district—a district, not a company—to get more water."

"There is no advantage to being *Chiriaco Summit Water Company* as privately held any longer. It needs to be a state and county agency."

"We want to be a community that has services like most of the county, services like modern phone lines, reliable electricity, and sufficient water."

How tiring all this back and forth was, but the Chiriacos hung in there. They still did not have phones for every home at the Summit They did not have commercial power—but commercial water was finally coming their way. On October 28, 1999, the Local Agency Formation Commission (LAFCO), County of Riverside, approved the formation of the Chiriaco Summit County Water District. Since existing facilities would be replaced or reconstructed right where they were rather than in new places, the new district would not be subject to environmental regulations. But before the changeover could be complete, registered voters in the proposed district had to vote, hopefully for creating the district, in a regular election. Then, if the vote was favorable, the Water Company had to officially transfer its assets to the new district. Since there were few registered voters in the proposed district area, mostly living at the Summit, a favorable vote was likely. The Chiriaco Summit Water District would become operational—early in the new millennium.

The power line was a tougher sell. It depended on federal approval for a new eight-mile line through rugged terrain and through the desert tortoise habitat. In this case, since new facilities and structures would be involved, environmental regulations applied. If they could get it, the new line would triple the amount of electricity the generators provided. So why not go after the lines?

The cost of installing them was prohibitive, more than the county or Summit could bear unless an offset were found. The Chiriacos got busy anyway, going after commercial power. They had no time to grumble, but they would make comments about the situation among themselves.

"New lines will be so expensive. Do you know that we have to buy a little over three acres as part of the Desert Tortoise Management Plan for every one we disturb?"

"On the other hand, with the air quality penalties our generators are becoming costlier. We need to do something so we can shut them down."

The Summit was in the Southcoast Air Quality Management District, a very stringent district serving Los Angeles as well as areas out to the Summit. Sometime in the '90s, Air Quality had informed Chiriaco Inc. that the generators violated their regulations and to get rid of them. When the generators kept on whirring, Air Quality fined the business for emissions.

Some sentiments expressed among those at the Summit during the late '90s showed some disappointment at the way things were going.

"Everyone else gets get new stuff before us. We are too far out, so we always have to create our own utilities."

"No one wants to run a line all the way out here."

"I'm not giving up." It was Margit again. Robert agreed. So did Heather and Santos, but what to do?

In the midst of all the drama at the end of the '90s, the Chiriacos kept their heads clear. Wisely, they let Margit lead the move to obtain the water and power needed to keep up with Joe's slogan, *All the necessities and some of the luxuries*. Of course, in earlier days the traveling public was happy to find water-filled radiator bags and a bologna sandwich. Now they were looking for an air-conditioned place, a choice of fast food, some home cooking, and modern restrooms.

Margit made several statements to the local *Press-Enterprise* in its June 21, 1998, edition. Her statements were part of the article that summarized the Summit expansion plans and possibilities for acquiring commercial utilities.

> Quaint is cute and we're going to keep some of that. But we also know we have to upgrade in the 20th Century, because we want to be there for the millennium.

> The Summit survives by serving the traveling public on I-10 from L.A. to Phoenix. To do that we must expand and keep up with customer demand for quick service, clean and enlarged restrooms, and easy access.

The Chiriacos would not disappoint. As the world was worrying about Y2K—the idea that major problems would erupt on January 1, 2000, maybe even ending the world, the Summit leadership concentrated on keeping its head above water, literally and figuratively. They had no time for other worries. They used every minute preparing for a new era that would require they overcome their core challenges—always water, almost solved, and now power.

Part Five

# The Twenty-First Century Comes to the Summit

*Foresight*

Why build an itty bitty thing that you are going to have to
turn around and make bigger later?'

(Margit Chiriaco, Early 2000s)

Map 9: The Chiriaco Summit Site as of 2017.

# 21

## *Updating the Basics, 2000–2002*

Tremendous expansion came with the first years of the new millennium. That "damned Italian" had passed on, but his business was still very much alive, with the third and even fourth generations becoming active. The year 2000 started with the usual noise and bustle. It never quieted down—except in one case.

### Silence

Margit and Heather looked over to Robert and then to Heather's son, twelve-year-old Victor. They all held their breath. IID electricians stood by. The generators whirred loudly in their tin shed. Robert had nursed those generators back to life many times. He made a move.

Not a sound. It was strangely quiet. Nothing. Nothing. And then a sigh of relief followed by clapping, loud and joyous. It was Friday, June 16, 2000. Robert had just flipped a switch turning off the generators. They could see a light was still on in the shed. Right before the gathering in the shed, the electricians had finished installing the new system and turned on a steady, even flow of power into the Summit. No longer would light bulbs pop. The air-conditioning might even work better. No longer did anyone have to worry about having enough diesel to run the Caterpillars or worry about them breaking down. Robert would not have to get up in the middle of the night to fix the big Caterpillars.

The sigh of relief was for what could have happened—not just if the switchover wouldn't work, but what would have been the consequences. Because of the fines, without commercial power Chiriaco Inc. would have had to scale down if not go out of business. With the flip of the switch, the generators and the fines stopped.

Victor had been born into the noisy generator environment. Now and then in the months following, when it was especially quiet, he would wonder if he should go help Uncle Robert fix the generators. These were fleeting moments broken by something like a bleating goat nearby. That was the new noise. There were about sixty of them.

*Photo 65: Chris Baldivid and youngest of Heather's children,*
*Heather April Garcia, goats at Chiriaco Summit.*

## What it took to flip that switch

That simple flip of a switch, a spit-second act, was made possible by several years of negotiations. Margit and Robert made many trips about one hundred miles south to IID headquarters in El Centro to meet with their board of directors, starting when Joe and Ruth were still alive. IID did and does supply part of Riverside County with power.

At one point, the family gave Margit the lead for pursuing commercial power. She had the interest, the energy, and the political know-how. She was up on the Desert and Summit issues because of connections she had made when she lived closer to the City of Riverside, because of her community involvement such as her role on the Desert Advisory Committee for BLM, and because no matter where she lived, she maintained a presence at the Summit. She had kept a small trailer on site since her return from Alaska in the early 1970s. After her parents passed away, Margit and Jerry maintained two homes, one in Bloomington, and Joe and Ruth's home at the Summit. All the while, Margit kept an unbroken connection with the business. So in the year 2000 when the air-quality fine on the generators made power an urgent issue, she concentrated on solving that problem.

First, she held a meeting at the Summit to enlist support for commercial power at Chiriaco Summit. She encouraged supporters to write letters to IID. She contacted and worked with the BLM and US Fish and Wildlife to get their support.

With some support behind her, she went before the IID board with a request that they consider electrical power for Chiriaco Summit. The board members agreed to look into it. Look into it they did by commissioning a team of experts to study what it would take. In the meantime, they received letters in favor. Some came from local business leaders, such as Jerry Bench of Hadley's Dates. Some came from government officials. The Riverside county supervisor at the time, Roy Wilson, sent a letter of support. Many elected officials in the area let IID know the value of Chiriaco Summit to Riverside County, especially to sheriffs and fire and emergency personnel.

Finally, at a meeting in late 1999, the IID board heard the results of the study. Margit and some of her supporters were in attendance. After listening to Margit present justifications for commercial power, to letters being read, and to some supporters speaking, the board called for the experts to give their report. They summarized their findings. It would take miles of new lines. The old lines that would connect with the new had to be checked and reinforced. There would be environmental issues along with their added costs. IID had the funds, but was it worth spending them for this cause? The experts said yes. The numbers indicated that since the area would grow, IID could recoup their investment in the future from additional paying customers.

Margit and Heather listened and hoped that all the presentations they had heard would add up in their favor. After some discussion, the IID board agreed with the analysis. At the end of the meeting, board members shook Margit's hand and with that told her Chiriaco Summit would get commercial power.

"I am used to operating on handshakes. I know you will honor your word," she said, having had experience with many of the board members; many were farmers she had known for years. They were do-as-you-say, say-as-you-do folks. The IID board made good on its promise—eventually.

Joseph L. Chiriaco, Inc. would have to pay for the line extensions. Oh, were it that simple! First of all, 8.5 miles of 119 new wood poles were involved. All the poles were to be erected in protected desert tortoise territory. In addition, IID followed the US Fish and Wildlife environmental assessment titled *Biological Opinion of the Chiriaco Summit Electrical Transmission Line Project*. This document listed thirty-one mitigation measures. The first: biological monitors were to oversee sound construction practices throughout the entire project, to assure avoidance of the tortoise, and to rescue tortoises. Some other measures: construction crews could not drive in areas where there might be tortoises, which meant almost everywhere they would be working. Fortunately, there were dirt maintenance roads running next to the existing towers. Mitigation measures allowed dirt roads to be constructed where new poles had to be raised. The measures required special precautions such as checking for any tortoises that might be in harm's way and using boom trucks to avoid disturbing some areas. Margit observed all this in action and could not help but think, *Part of what makes business hard out here are things like this. People in town don't have tortoises to worry about.*

Another tortoise factor: because the electrical substation built near the airport was a new structure in the Desert Tortoise Management Area, IID had to erect a special tortoise fence around it, adhering to Fish and Wildlife specifications. The main expense, though, was that for every acre of tortoise habitat disturbed, IID had to buy 3.42 acres of desert tortoise habitat or pay California Department of Fish and Game (renamed Fish and Wildlife in 2012) $2,002.54, to be used for replacement habitat. Chiriaco, Inc. paid these expenses back to IID through line charges.

The implementation played out a little differently from what was stated in the opinion document. IID paid for the construction up front but recouped some of it through the regular charge on kilowatt hours. IID rolled costs due to environmental mandates such as the acreage and tortoise fence into the electric bill—but just for a period of time. The Chiriacos felt the charges doable and worthwhile for business reasons—but also from childhood they had understood the tortoise and so now supported its preservation.

With the generators silent, Margit, Heather, Robert, and others tested everything they could, as soon as they could—kitchen appliances, mixers, hair dryers, power tools. They were delighted with each success.

"I have toast!"

"I'm using the hairdryer!"

"I hear your power drill."

"It all works!"

On June 21, 2000, Chiriaco Summit sponsored a big party with an invitation to the public on the cover of the June 2000 edition of the local *Chuckwalla Valley Buzz*. It read in part:

Chiriaco Summit

Power-Up 2000

Good-bye Generator

Welcome IID

The Chiriaco Family invites you to celebrate
The arrival of commercial power
To our little town.

IID board members and many of those who supported the effort came out. They gathered on the patio outside the coffee shop. Symbolically, Supervisor Roy Wilson flipped a switch on an old electrical box. There were speeches. There was food. The generators were not invited.

*Photo 66: Supervisor Roy Wilson flipping a symbolic switch to turn on electrical power at Chiriaco Summit. He stands with Margit and Robert.*

## Now for water like everyone else

On July 11, 2000, the Riverside Board of Supervisors, in resolution 2000-01, approved the Chiriaco Summit Water District as long as a majority of the twelve registered voters in the proposed district voted for it. The supervisors prepared the question for the ballot:

> Shall the proposition to form the Chiriaco Summit County
> Water District Under the County Water District law be accepted?

The ballot also had the names of candidates for the five positions on the water district's board: Heather Garcia, Virginia Vanderhoef, Diane Ragsdale, Margit Chiriaco Rusche, and Joseph R. Chiriaco. Joseph R. was Robert. Diane was listed as Diane and not Diana. Virginia was a longtime employee and resident at the Summit.

Election Day, May 9, 2000, came and went. A few days later, the registrar of voters reported to the supervisors that the vote was unanimous in favor and that all five candidates were elected. The new district board elected Margit as chair of the new water district. They waited for official papers.

"Yes, Mr. Krieger. Is it good news?" Margit held onto the phone with hope.

It was late summer in the year 2000. Robert Krieger of the engineering consulting firm was on the other end of the phone.

"The county officially recorded the formation of the district a few days ago."

"When? I haven't see anything official." Margit knew this document would be an important one to file.

"On August third. I'll send you the written notification. Thanks to you, the community has a water district!" Mr. Krieger could sense Margit's excitement. He continued.

"Now, we still have some work to do. You have to transfer your Chiriaco Water Company assets to the new district—actually, you have to sell them and then close the company."

A few months passed while the consultants and the Chiriacos made sure all the assets were in order and properly listed. On Feb 17, 2001, Robert signed the bill of sale. Even the old, now inoperative, witched well was on the list. There was still one step—actually getting water from the MWD aqueduct.

## Can't fly, let's drive

In the fall of 2001, the Summit witnessed the quiet resilience of Americans in a way only someone who lived at a highway stop could. Cars were piling up at the Summit, coming from airports, mostly from Los Angeles (LAX) or Phoenix. Some were motorists on business trips. Some were families. Some were sharing rides with strangers. The coffee shop bustled to serve these unexpected customers. The gas station staff directed people looking for food, restrooms, or just a bench to sit on for a while.

Very quickly, the Chiriaco Summit staff knew what had happened. No planes were flying. Some motorists who stopped at the Summit had landed at LAX in time for a connecting flight to Phoenix, but no such flight took off. Many just rented a car and drove as soon as they discovered that their flights had been cancelled. Others never got on any plane, just drove if they had to travel. No one was going anywhere by air.

It was September 11, 2001. There were four thousand planes in the air that day when the FAA ordered a nationwide grounding of flights at 9:45 a.m. Many travelers had to land far from their original destinations, adding to motorists on highways everywhere. Aviation in the United States took weeks to return to normalcy, even though the FAA started allowing flights to resume within a few days of the attack.

"Well, at least I am here. My cousin is stuck in Greenland."

"I wonder how long before we can fly again."

"I am still trying to contact my sister in New York City."

These were the types of comments people at any stop might have heard in the aftermath of the terrorist attack on the twin towers in New York and the Pentagon in Washington, DC—and at a crash site at what is now the 9/11 Flight 93 Memorial on a field near Shanksville, Pennsylvania. At the Summit, all the way on the other side of the country, travelers were saddened, shocked, tired, and inconvenienced, yet they were polite and kind. It was a terrible way to start the new millennium, but at least in this time of nationwide mourning, Joe's city could provide some of the basics and even some luxuries. However, this tragedy highlighted how much they still needed commercial water. A few steps remained so that they could serve even bigger unexpected crowds or for when emergencies would erupt on the highway.

On August 1, 2002, almost a year after 9/11, MWD and Caltrans executed the contract to sell water to the new Chiriaco Summit County Water District, which soon became officially CSWD, leaving out *C* for *county* in order to avoid confusion with and calls to county agencies.

The previous private company went defunct. The State of California created the Chiriaco Summit County Water District as a public entity subject to all the rules applied to the biggest water districts—a few rules were tailored for smaller districts. Heather, as secretary of the district, was on top of all of that. The CSWD appointed Santos as the operations manager. There was no fanfare, just relief knowing they had enough water for emergencies and expansion, and that travelers finally had a true oasis at Chiriaco Summit.

# 22

## *And Some of the Luxuries, 1998–2005*

In 1998, before the promise of adequate water with the formation of the Chiriaco Summit Water District, the old service garage and motel had been demolished to make space for a six-thousand-square-foot convenience food store.

"Why so big?" some asked.

"Why build an itty bitty thing that you are going to have to turn around and make bigger later?' Margit would reply.

### Contrasts at opposite ends of the highway

In 2002, Robert had a surprising phone call. Suzanne Ragsdale did not expect Robert to know her when she called, because while the Chiriacos and Ragsdales interacted as children, they did not as adults. Her grandfather, Desert Steve, who had passed away in 1971, set a practice, still in effect, of ignoring the Summit. He saw it as far down the highway and not part of his community. It was also true that Joe concentrated on his business and did not engage much with the people at Desert Center.

But circumstances had changed. The twenty-mile distance was nothing in this twenty-first-century era of multiple-lane highways and fast cars. And Shaver, now Chiriaco Summit, had grown tremendously. Suzanne began to see two business powers in the area: Desert Center, which she worried was declining, and Chiriaco Summit, which she recognized was growing. She followed up her phone call with a visit to Robert. She knew that the relationship even to the present, while civil, had not been collegial; but Suzanne had developed courage and a mind of her own. Her mother was a factor.

When she was eighteen years old, her mother said to her, "You are a girl. You won't have the advantages here in Desperate Center that the boys do." Yes, she said *desperate*. She went on to say, "You need to get out—and education is the only thing that will get you somewhere. Otherwise your job will be just to cook, clean, and make babies." Crystal Ragsdale had primed her daughter for college her whole life. She suggested to her that that she become a nurse. Suzanne bested her mother's suggestion. She became a nurse practitioner in family practice for Kaiser Permanente, the same groundbreaking HMO started by Dr. Garfield near her home in the 1930s. She moved away but came back and forth once in a while.

Desert Center had not budged much since she had first left. Even in 1999, the year he died, her father, Stanley, was still refusing to have a computer in his office. He had been kind to family and employees, but controlling, strict, and specific with instructions. As said at his funeral, "He would tell you exactly where to dig the trench—and where to place your foot on the shovel." Yet he left his succession vague. While Joe at the Summit had a temper and was also controlling, he and Ruth raised independent thinkers, exactly what Suzanne had become. So here she was, right at the Summit, only one of five living heirs, trying to learn what she saw as critical information and to possibly influence some change.

"Robert, I am hoping you can give me some information about ATM cash machines."

Desert Center still had attendants serving gas and taking money. She had no experience with the ATM system in a business like hers, but she had a business head, so she asked pointed questions.

"What kind of machine do you use?"

"Is it better to lease or buy?

"What distributors do you use?"

Robert explained to her everything he knew about an ATM system in a gas station. She went back to Desert Center with this information. She tried to influence some change, but that was it. She would be back with a proposal later, though. Like Margit, she was not one to give up easily.

The Summit kept moving ahead with concepts for a modern travel stop. Finally, five years after the garage and motel had been demolished, in 2003 construction workers started that six-thousand-square-foot building. Like Foster's Freeze, the Chiriacos would own the Food Mart. This time the contracts were secure, no repeat of the Marriot and MacDonald's fiascos. Robert and Margit were both heavily involved in the contracting. Her involvement freed up Robert to manage the day-to-day business, which helped keep the existing services open through what turned out to be another lengthy process.

In a letter to customers in 2003, Margit wrote, "Why so long?" She answered that question in the same letter.

> The Chiriaco Family wants to thank you for your patience during this extremely long period of construction. The mini mart is nearing completion and along with the mini mart is also a new water system and filtration system for the Chiriaco Summit Water District. The new building could not have been completed or open for business without the new water system in place for the business and the community. Together the two projects took additional time and of course money, and we know many of you have been curious as to the "why so long?" This is the simple explanation and we must thank you for your continued loyalty to our businesses and for your patience during the dust, the rough roads and some confusion from time to time.

When Margit wrote this letter, the water filtration system and a diesel pump needed for the fire system were yet to be installed. The County of Riverside would need to inspect the new facilities and issue a permit. People tended to refer to the new area as the Chevron. Margit made clear in her letter that the new facilities, while they were near and associated with the Chevron, were Chiriaco owned and operated.

> We value your support and continued loyalty to the Chiriaco Travel Center and we look forward to providing you with even better service in the months and years to come.

By the term *Chiriaco Travel Center*, Margit meant the whole Chiriaco Summit business area, including the Information Center and the coffee shop across from the Chevron.

Margit and Heather managed the process, from funding to contracts to opening day. They applied for and received a grant from the Desert Alliance for Community Empowerment (DACE) to help with the cost for the diesel pump needed at the old reservoir. This reservoir could hold one acre-foot of water or 330,000 gallons. Riverside County would not sign the permits needed for the expansion without a diesel pump that could deliver 1,500 gallons a minute from the reservoir in the event of a fire on site or nearby. Such a pump was expensive. They arranged for other financing. Then they contracted for construction and started to choose suppliers. Santos and Heather went to Chevron University in San Ramon, California, to learn the new systems that came with the Food Mart and to Lemoore, California, to learn the Foster Freeze systems. As the building neared competition, Heather and Santos conducted the employee training. Santos had hired about twenty new people to cover the three Food Mart and two Foster Freeze shifts. He recruited them from places that were downsizing like Desert Center. Some came knowing him from Mexican communities in places like Mecca and La Quinta.

The Summit did not go dormant as it did in the late 1960s due to highway construction. Customers stayed loyal to the gas station and to the coffee shop even though for almost a year, the area was a dusty, noisy construction zone.

Finally, in early 2004, construction workers finished their job. Chiriaco, Inc. took out the kiosk. Now customers could pay at the gas pumps or in the Food Mart. All systems, including those for the water system, passed inspection, so the county issued the permits needed. The Food Mart opened for the July Fourth weekend. Inside, customers enjoyed the air-conditioning as they waited in line to buy refrigerated and open-shelved fare. Some bought freshly made sandwiches. Some left with a Foster Freeze cone. Others browsed through the gift items and bought them along with food.

The employees operated computerized registers. This was new for them, but they were trained and ready when the new facility opened. Heather and Santos had taught them to use their new technology. Both management and staff were glad to have the inventory and business control that the new computers allowed. Diana Ragsdale had been the bookkeeper for almost twenty years. She efficiently ported the templates she had created with some changes over to the new system. Now not only could she more easily find those pennies Joe had always looked for, she could also see trends and provide management the information for more informed business decisions. Diana kept doing what she had always done best—keeping track of the money, just with more tools. The expanded business needed expanded office space so the antiques in Cholla House moved into the coffee shop. Cholla House became the Joseph L. Chiriaco, Inc. headquarters and the Chiriaco Summit Rural Branch of the Indio Post Office. The Cholla House name retired—for a while.

The Summit put off the celebration to the fall when it would be cooler and closer to Veterans Day. Right before November 11, Margit and DACE CEO Jeff Hayes cut the ribbon. So many had helped on the long road to this day. They were there: members from the chamber of commerce; elected officials at the national and state levels; officials from IID, MWD, sheriffs, Caltrans; suppliers such as Chevron, Shamrock Farms, Frito Lay, Hadley; and customers old and new. Most left the store with a hot dog or corn dog from the Foster Freeze, given away to all who came by that day.

Everyone was excited. In later years, Rudy Montoya, remembering the changeover, may have expressed what other employees were feeling in 2004. "How has it changed? Look around! We have a huge store. We work inside, not just outside all the time. We still go out to help when someone needs us. The handicapped can call into the store and we go right out."

*Photo 67: Rudy Montoya taking a break, Coffee Shop patio.*

Two newly trained employees from different sides of the family were named Victor Garcia.

Victor Joseph, Heather and Santos's son, started working part time, mostly summers, at the Chevron in 2003 and continued for years while he was in school. Once the Food Mart was opened, he worked as a clerk and a cashier. He stocked the open shelves and the refrigerator. He cleaned bathrooms. He still worked outside cleaning the pumps and washing down the pavement. He was learning the new business.

Another Victor, Victor Manuel, Rogelio Jr.'s son, eight years older than Victor Joseph, quickly became Santos's full-time right-hand man at the Chevron area, including the Food Mart and Foster Freeze. (Rogelio, Jr. was Santos's brother, who now lived with his family at the Summit.) Both Victors had to maintain their knowledge of the older way of doing things, though—for when they were called to help at the coffee shop.

The coffee shop and the gift and antique sections inside it stayed on the old cash register system. Heather and Robert wondered why they needed the coffee shop at all and suggested closing it.

"No, no way in hell are we closing that restaurant! Self-serve gas is fine, but we have to have other amenities for people like sit-down food. The heart of Chiriaco is in the coffee shop." Margit wanted to continue with traditions set by Joe and Ruth. She sounded and acted like the boss.

## A desert woman takes the lead

Robert wanted to step down once the Food Mart was opened. After he hit his target weight in 1987, he maintained it for a while, but as the business became more demanding, he put some of it back on. His health and his weariness with his 24-7 schedule were two reasons he submitted his resignation to the Chiriaco, Inc. board at their meeting on March 2, 2004. The board of directors appointed Margit as the new CEO and Heather as the CFO of the corporation. Robert had kept the business going through some very hard times. His expertise was welcomed on the board. They re-elected him as board chairman and elected Heather as secretary and treasurer. The board did not elect a vice president.

Shortly after he stepped down, Robert did something he had been thinking about for a long time. Newspaper reporters interviewed Margit regularly about the Summit. She took a few of these opportunities to say that her brother was still available. That got printed but did not help. Robert never married. Little Robert, now an adult, had been like a son to him, so he made it official; he adopted him.

Ruth and Joe had worked with an attorney to make sure that transitions to successors were smooth. They named their son, Robert, as their first successor. That attorney came into play again as Margit was about to take over. The transition was almost as easy this time as when the parents passed away. The difference was Robert stayed on as board chairman and continued living at the Summit. He stayed involved even though he was officially retired. He was Joe's son, after all, and Joe held on until the day he died. For Robert, holding on was because others held on. Employees loved him, so sought him out. It was just plain natural for him to respond with advice and direction.

Margit and others kept reminding Robert that he was retired. It took him a while to relax and back off. By the time he did, Margit was solidly in her new role. It was a natural sequence for her to step into that position. Over the years she gained experience in many of the functions at the Summit. And she had the will for and excitement about the role. She readily admitted that she had always wanted to be CEO; however, she saw the role somewhat differently from her predecessors. She comfortably delegated authority. The new growth demanded this.

Chiriaco Summit started as a garage business—the gas station type, not the Silicon Valley type—but it was going through similar growth challenges, especially in regard to distributed but well-defined roles and in regard to enlisting newly needed talent. Margit came to the lead just in time.

She officially enlisted the third generation as active decision makers. She had already involved Heather and Santos in the process of developing the Super Chevron, Food Mart, and Foster Freeze as part of the new Chiriaco Summit Travel Center. Now she gave Heather and Santos roles as co-general managers along with authority to make decisions. Santos took over as the operations manager. Heather oversaw all office functions. She made the crucial day-to-day business decisions. She had been in training for this from the time she sat under Grandpa Joe's desk as a baby. She had worked under Grandma Ruth's tutelage from the proverbial bottom rung, washing dishes. She had earned her place as an up and coming woman in charge.

Margit gave a critical role to a person outside the family. Hector was a fast study. He quickly learned how to monitor and maintain the water treatment system. Seeing this, Margit made him chief of maintenance—all maintenance. He and the assistants he hired moved from task to task at the Summit doing preventive work and solving problems, whether they required plumbing, electrical knowledge, and/or construction. Margit encouraged him to get other credentials, particularly for water treatment, which he did. She relied on his knowledge and his ability to express it so much so that she began taking him and then sending him on his own to power and water meetings.

Margit got help from her husband, Jerry, at the business and museum sites, but she was clearly in charge. The Summit started as a man's vision, Joe's. Ruth believed in his vision and stepped up to finance it—and she spoke up. Of course, that was not enough. With her realistic encouragement of Joe and her relentless hard work, the vision became a reality with staying power. While her role was different, Margit had the same indomitable character as Ruth. Hector said of Margit when he talked about the growth of the Summit a few years later, "She never stops."

*Photo 68: CEO Margit Chiriaco Rusche on Summit Grounds.*

## Stranded for gas

While the Summit was starting new ventures, progress was still not going on down the highway, although Suzanne kept trying to convince her brothers. Heather, a third-generation Chiriaco, picked up the phone late one night. The voice on the other end sounded frustrated.

"I passed you up and went on to Desert Center. I always stop there for gas. Do you know the Stanco is closed?

Heather started to answer. The caller continued without stopping.

"You should. I have small children in this car."

Heather tried to get a word in, but the woman continued. She was becoming irate. "Stanco is closed. Closed. I drove on to Blythe. What else could I do? But I ran out of gas before I got there."

Heather continued to listen.

"I had to pay for a service truck to deliver fuel. I had to wait a long time—late at night—along a busy highway—with children in the car. Why didn't you change that sign that says twenty miles to the next gas station?"

According to government records, the Stanco Station stopped selling gas in 2005 because it was out of compliance with an environmental regulation regarding hazardous waste, an issue causing many gas stations to close. Now instead of about twenty miles between gas stations on the interstate going east, it was about sixty. Heather kept getting calls either blaming her for the inaccurate signage or asking her to please get Caltrans to change it. Heather was not the only one getting calls. CHP was responding to a bevy of similar calls from drivers with empty tanks. Finally, Caltrans changed the fuel sign to read correctly. Of course, the Summit profited.

*Photo 69: Chiriaco Summit ramp sign going east, indicating distance to next services.*

## Our Lady of Interstate 10

"She never stops," said Hector. But Margit did stop now and then to reflect, especially by the Guadalupe Shrine at the Summit. By the time the new facilities opened, the shrine had been near her house for a few years. One of the ways Ruth kept the soul in what could have become a hard-core business family was her devotion to her faith. Margit had that same devotion.

In the early days of their marriage, Joe and Ruth traveled to a parish in Indio on some Sundays. Joe started staying back. Someone had to be there when work at the Summit became 24-7. Not to be deterred, Ruth encouraged the priests she knew to come to the Summit. Since most were too busy on Sundays, she asked them to come to say Mass at her house on Saturday evening. They came; never mind that most Catholic churches at the time did not recognize a Saturday Mass as satisfying the Sunday requirement for going to church. If no priest could come, a brother or deacon from the Indio parish would come and at least recite the readings for that week's Mass and give communion. After Ruth and Joe passed away, Margit kept up the tradition of Sunday on-Saturday church at the house.

Santos's mother missed some of the Mexican religious traditions, especially those around Our Lady of Guadalupe. According to official Catholic accounts, the Virgin Mary appeared to Juan Diego, a poor Christian Aztec, starting on December 9, 1531, in an area that would eventually become Guadalupe, a suburb of Mexico City. Native roses growing out of season convinced the Archbishop of Mexico City that the apparitions were real. By the late nineteenth century, Mexicans saw the story as one of Mexican origin. It became a factor in uniting them against Spain and a factor in their eventual independence. This story is not without controversy, but Our Lady of Guadalupe is absolutely a part of Mexican religious devotion. So it made sense that Mrs. Garcia talked to her sons, now several at the Summit, about building a shrine. They mentioned it to Hector who discussed it with Margit.

"Do you think we could make a shrine?" Margit knew the story and why it would matter to most of the Mexican families living at the Summit.

Hector added, "We had a shrine like that in Oaxaca. Señora Garcia wishes for one here." He went on to explain that many in the community would like to have the shrine.

"Sure, there's a good space at the front near the coffee shop, but who is going to build it?" Margit asked.

Hector already knew that the Garcia brothers, Santos, Rogelio and Max, would be part of the team. They were all living at the Summit by the turn of the century. By the evening of Wednesday, December 12, 2001, the date that Mexicans celebrate the festival of Nuestra Senora de Guadalupe (Our Lady of Guadalupe) the base and glass encasement were ready for the small statue that Sra. Garcia arranged to get from Oaxaca. After some prayers in front of the statue, the Mexican families shared a traditional Guadalupe feast with the Chiriacos: tacos, black beans, spicy chicken with mole sauce, rice, guacamole, and flan. They drank one of Mexico's national drinks, tequila or mescal. Starting the following Saturday, each day a priest came to say Mass at the shrine at 5:00 p.m., with those attending seated in a semi-circle on folding chairs. If the weather was inclement (meaning rain or too hot), a sign on the door of the Information Center announced the indoor location of the Mass, which was Margit's home or the Information Center. Some travelers saw the sign and joined the service wherever it was, but especially when it was at the shrine.

*Photo 70: Rogelio and Juventina Garcia, Santos's parents, Shrine at Chiriaco Summit.*

Residents and travelers started adding more statues and rosaries, as is done in Mexico. Margit started calling the shrine Our Lady of Interstate 10.

Even if Joe did not, Ruth and then Margit took Father Lee's 1936 words to heart: "It's hard in your position to keep up with the duties of religion." His words referred not only to the 24-7 nonstop work week, but also to being far from a church. The solution: if the people can't get to the church, bring the church to the people.

Why did any of this matter? Certainly a business does not have to provide religious services. It mattered because the Chiriacos understood that they needed a pause in their 24-7 business. It also mattered because it meant a lot to many of their employees. Of course, Saturdays and Sundays were big business days for a travel stop, a time when employees needed to be on site. Given all these reasons, the Chiriaco women did what they could to make church services possible in what some would call the "godforsaken desert." Not so godforsaken. As Margit stood at the shrine after the Food Mart's opening day, the Summit had just opened the door to a new era, serving travelers in new or upgraded facilities, still with the basics but now with more comforts—which Joe would have called luxuries.

# 23

# *Seizing the Future, 2006 to 2015*

Work and change. It never stopped. The opening of the Travel Center was only the beginning of modernizing at the Summit. In the next few years, Chiriaco Inc. with Margit at the helm would be involved in remodeling everything on the coffee shop side of the Summit, upgrading the pumps across the street at the Chevron with the newest technology, and securing water for the decades to come. In the midst of all this, Margit, now firmly CEO, found time to smell the roses, only they weren't roses.

## Wildflowers across generations

"It's God's paintbrush out there. This is a bounty of blooms," Margit was quoted in the *Press Enterprise* in its March 1, 2008, edition. She was talking about Joshua Tree National Park's annual wildflower show. The show was especially spectacular that year due to soaking rains followed by warm weather. The display matched the one in 2005 when Margit had recently taken over as CEO. Busy as she was, she took time almost every year to get out among the bursts of wild color. In fact, some of the best color was close by, on the old Camp Young site, where the flowers benefited from the southern exposure and from drainage to the fan-shaped sandy flats, known as *bajadas*.

"With these flowers it's a rebirth of everything," she said. "You go through here in the summer and it's so brown and gray and dry and hot." Recently Margit herself had gone through a gray time.

Back in 2007, the Patton Museum Board had erected a small memorial near the museum. It read in part:

> The most loving, kind and generous man who is deeply missed by family, friends, and the Board and Staff of the General Patton Museum.

Jerry Rusche, Margit's love, confidant, and business partner, died suddenly on November 17, 2006. Jerry had been involved with the museum since he supervised the building of its first structures. He was an integral part of the family, so much so that Victor had considered him a grandfatherly figure. He had spent time teaching this fourth-generation Chiriaco to be hardy. He taught him hunting, fishing, and camping skills. Margit, supported by family and caring employees, found the strength to carry on without him. Jerry, her husband of twenty years, would always be in her mind, but within a year she was thinking about next steps with the coffee shop, the gift and antique shops, the gas station, the Food Mart, and the Foster Freeze.

She elaborated about the wildflowers to the *Press Enterprise*. "It's just a brief time for them and they're gone. A snap of your fingers in the grand scheme of things."

But these wildflower shows would be back for the *grandchildren of grandchildren*, as Ernie Quintana had said. Unlike wildflowers, if the next generations were to be successful, they had to be cultivated. That was through family example, through on-the-job learning with mentorship—not always from family—and through some formal classes.

From the surveying days, the Chiriacos understood that they had to be lifelong learners. Regulations changed, infrastructure changed, equipment changed, and so did operating procedures. For example, Chevron made improvements regularly. Many Chevron sites included convenience stores such as the Summit's Food Mart. In February of 2007, Chevron University offered a business-management course for convenience store operators in San Ramon, California. Heather and Santos both attended. There they learned the Chevron way of management, including providing the best customer experience, creating and maintaining the Chevron image, and personnel management. The course instructors presented information about the Americans with Disabilities Act (ADA), age-restricted sales, robbery deterrence, store economics, card processing, workplace safety, and regulatory information. While Joseph L. Chiriaco, Inc. owned and operated the gas station and the convenience store, their contract to sell Chevron products included their agreement to abide by the Chevron philosophy, which they embraced, especially since it was, like their own philosophy, customer and particularly traveler focused.

### Fly-by hamburgers

Not everyone drove to the Summit. Some flew into the airport. The Summit was an ideal lunch stop from other Southwestern airports, as long as the planes were fueled up. No more taxiing over to the gas station. The pilots approached the 4,660-foot runway in anything from light aircraft to business jets. After they landed where Patton's own plane had touched down, they walked over to the coffee shop for a top-rated hamburger—the same place where soldiers in the 1940s clamored for pickled pig's feet. In 2007, the *Hundred Dollar Hamburger,* a pilot's online guide, gave the Chiriaco hamburger a five, its highest rating. Only six out of 110 California airport restaurants scored so highly. Interviewed in the March 2007 *Pacific Flyer,* Margit made sure that the pilots would know, "we're also noted for our chili, pot roast, ham dinner at Easter and turkey at Thanksgiving." Always sensitive to customer tastes over the years, no pickled pig's feet!

David Smith and John Evans had moved on from Joshua Tree. Before they left they spent much time at the coffee shop talking with Robert about airplanes. Like John, Robert had a pilot's license. The two NPS employees took posts at the Grand Canyon National Park and then separate posts for a while. They bought an airplane together, which they landed at the Summit from time to time.

Of course the *Hundred Dollar Hamburger* was regular price, about $4.75 at the time, but even that would become a stretch for some travelers by the end of 2008.

## The effect of the 2008 recession

"People have changed buying habits. They grab something quickly in the Food Mart or at the Foster's rather than ordering a hamburger or meatloaf dinner at the coffee shop." Margit was making a point at a board meeting in early 2009.

The United States sank into a serious recession in 2008, some say the greatest in eighty years. Financial experts blame soft credit and the housing bubble. They suggest that the American consumer did not save and took unreasonable financial risks. Some of the effects of a recession are a downturn in consumer spending, unemployment, and business closures. The Summit was affected mostly by changes in consumer spending. What about downsizing and closure? Well, the second-generation Chiriacos inherited Joe and Ruth's aversion to debt. They paid off any loans quickly. Joe and Ruth balanced each other's tolerance for risk. Margit took a calculated approach to risk with cost/benefit analyses. She also moved quickly to adjust when needed, especially with compliance to regulations.

At board meetings during the recession years from 2008 to about 2014, part of the conversation was about spending trends and adjustments.

"We are very responsive to price changes, especially with fuel. Let's keep that up—make sure we lower the price as soon as others do."

"We are seeing the effects mostly where we sell gifts. We have been careful not to overstock gift items at the Food Mart, or souvenirs and antiques in the coffee shop."

"There seems to be little effect on food sales at the Food Mart or the coffee shop. It's a bit more grab and go, but people still need to eat."

"And gas up. Little or no effect there either."

"What about staffing? So many others have had to lay off employees."

"Attrition has taken care of that for us. We're OK."

"Thank goodness we operate a lean business. That keeps our margin where we can weather a storm. Let's keep that cushion."

About 2008 or 2009, Suzanne Ragsdale again visited the Summit. "Robert, we got this whole valley to ourselves," she started and then went on to talk about a possible joint venture.

Robert referred Suzanne to Margit. Margit was now CEO; but, more importantly, this sounded like a project right up her alley.

Sure enough, Margit took this on in full force, investing the necessary time and money to conduct the careful research needed for a business plan. With the plan together, she and Suzanne met with her brothers. Like their grandfather and father before them, they did not see the Summit as part of their community. Suzanne's idea stalled, but she had planted a seed.

The Chiriaco business held steady, with planning for upgrades started in the recession years. In fact, Department of Transportation (DOT) records indicated that by 2008 over a thousand vehicles were coming though the Summit every day. (The last record of Summit ramp data was 2008 according to a 2015 DOT report.) By 2011, the Joseph L. Chiriaco Inc. Board decided they could afford to move ahead with their plans. Suzanne Ragsdale was flying back and forth from her home and job up north, trying to keep one of last vestiges of Desert Center business open, the café.

## Remodels

Over the years, many regulations became more stringent.

"We are going to have to get rid of that outdoor walk-in freezer," Margit was telling Robert, Heather, and Santos at an impromptu meeting. Quietly, she was laughing to herself about the times in the 1950s she had locked Pauline in a similar walk-in with her boyfriend.

Robert added, "Yeah, I get it. The health department is concerned because we store meat there. Well, it's not really the meat; it's because we have to go outside to get the meat and bring it into the coffee shop."

Heather and Santos weighed in. "And there's the issue of opening the freezer door outside in the open to put things in and take things out. We could just install a new freezer in the kitchen."

"Of course, we'd have to make room for it, which will cause a domino effect. That freezer is only one of the items we need to deal with to bring the whole facility up to specs and make it more comfortable for our customers. A total remodel is in order." Margit was thinking ahead.

The Chiriaco Inc. Board agreed that it made business sense to make the changes all at once rather than piecemeal. Margit took charge of the project. She started with an overall plan and a sequence.

First, the coffee shop, which needed more seating. That meant moving the antiques section, which took up quite a bit of floor space. Where to?

The Information Center next door? That would mean a redesign of that building too.

What about the fact that church services were held there sometimes? Well, enough residents lived at the Summit to warrant a community center. Margit had been thinking about building one. Now was the time to start the game of dominos. The first domino was the coffee shop; the community center would be one of the last.

Regulations required some changes to bring the operation into compliance with new codes, but many were cosmetic. Chiriaco Inc. worked with Riverside County throughout the process to make sure all requirements were met. Margit drew the design for the coffee shop. As with a home, she drafted the general layout, then as a team the Chiriacos chose new flooring, new tables and chairs, and new appliances. Only the oven and grill, recently purchased, were to remain in the kitchen. Margit put Hector in charge of all the construction. She closed one-half of the coffee shop at a time during the renovation process. Soon Hector told Margit it was time for the cook to vacate the kitchen.

"How will you cook while I'm in the kitchen?" Hector asked Margit.

Margit had watched Ruth still manage to serve food when water or power failed over the years.

Margit knew the answer: "We'll close the kitchen for two weeks and only offer cold sandwiches. We'll print a temporary menu."

With the kitchen done and the full menu back in effect, Hector moved over to the information center. He turned the front part into the antique shop. The section in the back became the new and improved information center. Hector put up two new signs: Cholla House 2, and another sign directing people to a side entrance for the Southwest Information Center. There travelers could find AAA maps, BLM maps, and other tourist information—some of it free

The reality was that travelers wandered through the antiques even when their destination was maps in the back. Many people bought small items like old plates, dishes, and utensils. Some bought large items like old cash registers, old scales, and old furniture. This was the beauty of having an antique store at a travel stop. Some people had vehicles with them with room for hauling big things. A few items were not for sale. Ruth's purple glass was still for show only.

*Photo 71: Cholla House 2, Southwest Information Center.*

The Cholla House and new Information Center garnered enough activity to warrant a staff. Martha Stewart, one of Santos's nieces, had been ordering and managing inventory for the gift sections in the coffee shop and Food Mart. Margit gave her the added responsibility of managing items in the antique shop. Heather's daughter, Teresa, started working at the Foster Freeze. Teresa and Cecilia, another of Heather's four children, rotated with other waitresses at the Information Center.

The new coffee shop got a lot of business during the day, but nights were slow by 2012. Truck plazas where drivers could plug into electric outlets, get Internet service, and take showers became popular. Chevron had no plans for such a plaza at the Summit. Margit and the board decided to close the coffee shop at 11:00 p.m. Still, trucks filled many of the spaces set aside for them near the gas station, be it late at night or in early-morning hours. They stopped at the Food Mart, which remained a 24-7 operation.

The truck plazas had an even bigger effect on Desert Center. With its gas station shut down and nothing like a Food Mart, the restaurant there closed in 2012.

Nevertheless, the Summit business remained steady with a bustling onsite community ready to serve. By Thanksgiving of 2014, Margit made good on her last domino, her plan to open a community center on site. Hector managed the placement and interior configurations of a single-wide trailer that would serve the purpose. It had a large room that soon housed meetings and parties of all sorts in air-conditioned comfort. The two smaller rooms accommodated a few people for small meetings. Sometimes an individual came by to sit in the comfy chairs just to read or think. Margit had an additional purpose in mind for all three rooms.

## Holy Water

Back in 2007, Father John Keefe, from Our Lady of Soledad in Coachella, learned that the Summit needed a regular priest. He started coming once a month and then weekly. Father Jack, as he was commonly called, was a congenial bilingual priest who had lived in Mexico. Like priests before him, he said Mass at the shrine if the weather allowed. He was strongly devoted to the Summit community no matter what the language or circumstances of its people. Somewhat unusually, he said some parts of the Mass in English and others in Spanish, going back and forth, so that no one would get bored.

*Photo 72: Father Jack Keefe, Heather April Garcia, Mass at Chiriaco Summit Our Lady of Guadalupe Shrine.*

In 2009, Father Jack was reassigned to Phoenix and then to Notre Dame University in Indiana. Seven years later in an e-mail of March 22, 2016, he summarized his experience at the Chiriaco Summit shrine.

Mass was usually at sunset. People driving in for gas would notice our celebration and some would join us at Mass. I remember some truckers would stop because it was their only way to get to Mass they said. A portable sound system would show up from somewhere. It was much appreciated because of the noise of the traffic to and from the gas station/rest stop area could be loud especially from big trucks. The singing was good or bad depending on who was available to lead. It was better with the snowbirds because some were gifted to lead [singing] or [with] playing the guitar.

One of the great things at Chiriaco was the gathering after the religious service. There was always sharing after service. We ate together, laughed together and listened to the events in the lives of each other. As was said, sometimes it had to be in Margit's house because of weather. But most often it was on the spot right after Mass. Everyone shared no matter in English or Spanish. For me personally, this was real "Church."

After Father Jack left, priests from Coachella and other nearby areas kept coming. The largely Mexican Catholic population came to the shrine or to Margit's office for Mass, no longer to Margit's house. The church crowds kept getting bigger, especially after another bilingual priest, Father Guy Wilson, started coming on a regular basis.

*Photo 73: Father Guy Wilson, Easter Mass at Chiriaco Summit*
*Our Lady of Guadalupe Shrine.*

Eventually, Margit's office could no longer house Saturday Mass. Too many people came. She had Hector place about twenty-five folding chairs in the large room of the community structure. Next she had him move in an old, ornate chest that could serve as an altar. She had him arrange one room so that a priest could also use it to vest for Mass or for meeting with individuals. The other room stored religious items. Catholics at the Summit and nearby communities came together for Mass in the big room. When no priest was available, a deacon or other church official led a Sunday celebration that included most parts of the Mass. In either case, the faithful followed tradition from the moment they came through the door. They dipped their fingers into a small Holy Water font, which Hector had installed at the entrance. Sometimes there was an overflow crowd.

In addition to religious purposes, the church provided a place for people from different desert communities to socialize, such as from the ranger homes at Cottonwood Springs in Joshua Tree National Park and from Lake Tamarisk near Desert Center. After the mine closed, Lake Tamarisk became a retirement community. People came to church services from there with the same spirit Father Jack described.

Paul and Elsie Williams, snowbirds from Medford, Oregon, would come when they were in town. Paul was one of the musically gifted Father Jack referred to. He would play his guitar to accompany the hymns. Dan and Diane Roberts, snowbirds from Kalama, Washington, would enjoy the potlucks after services, which reminded them of church gatherings from long ago. Sometimes they would eat in the coffee shop and pick up some diesel or propane before their drive back. Jerry and Veronica Grey, who called themselves *rainbirds* from San Francisco, would come to church and then stay around to visit. The Summit folk made them feel at home.

While the community center also served as a Catholic Church, the few residents of other faiths were welcome to conduct their services there. By the end of 2014, they probably all prayed for water, since they knew by then that the Summit was again in a precarious position.

## Water, water, forever on the lookout for water

What a struggle water had been. First there was the arduous task of maintaining the pipes, then periodic replacement of the well's pump, and then the complicated negotiations for the three-way agreement. Caltrans and MWD renewed that agreement several times over the years. Then on January 18, 2011, Caltrans sent a letter addressed to Robert, who was still the board chairman, informing Joseph L. Chiriaco, Inc. that it would be terminating its three-way water contract. The Chiriaco Summit Water District had about eight months to figure out what to do. Margit, as CEO responsible for the business, made some contacts who set up a meeting to deal with the situation. Feedback through the grapevine told Margit that "it did not look good." In fact, neither she nor Robert nor anyone from CSWD was invited to the meeting

Margit and Robert felt tremendous angst over what they knew was a make-or-break situation. The convenience and safety of travelers was at stake. The Chiriaco family and employees could lose their livelihoods in an instant. For once, the Summit leaders were unsure how to resolve the problem but not inclined to just wait for something favorable to happen. They considered drilling a well, but soon realized that would take too long. They explored the possibility of buying water shares from surrounding areas, but no shares were available at an affordable price. They kept contacting people who might have information or influence. One was John Benoit, a former CHP commander, state senator, and now county supervisor. Another was State Assemblyman Manuel Perez. Both knew the critical nature of the water issue to travelers as well as to the Summit. They were also wise regarding ways to resolve it. Together the Summit leaders and their supporters started making some headway, but they still needed a Caltrans signature. Although the Chiriacos never relied on luck, once in a while a little luck did help. The eight months were almost up when a change in leadership at Caltrans created an opening. The new official at the Caltrans district office signed for a few more years.

Whew! Summit leadership and management breathed a sigh of relief. Then in January 2015, MWD and Caltrans extended their contact with Chiriaco Water District to January 1, 2034. Yet the Water District Board stayed on the lookout for alternate sources of water, just in case.

Others were on the lookout for a way to honor the Summit pioneers who had fought so many battles to create a desert oasis for the safety and enjoyment of others.

"You know, Margit, it's time your parents get recognized for what they started and what this place has become," said David Miller, a supplier to the Chiriaco Food Mart and Coffee Shop, who had stopped by with his wife, Suzy.

"We are volunteers for the Walk of Stars in Palm Springs. You'll be hearing from us," Suzy added.

# 24

# *Preserving History, 2005–2015*

At the same time that the Chiriacos were modernizing, they were preserving history through their support of the expansion of the Patton Museum, the start of a classic car collection, the replacement of an historic plaque, and an honor paid to Joe and Ruth, which placed their names near eminent public servants and glitzy movie stars.

## The museum expands its scope

Since the mid-1980s when she cofounded the museum with Leslie Cone of BLM, Margit continued to volunteer her time as a board member. The museum was not part of the business, but a separate nonprofit established through a memorandum of understanding with BLM. In the 2000s, the museum board took on some new projects.

"Let's angle it like this."

"Good idea, but make it a little longer."

Margit and two other board members, Jan Roberts, the current president, and Gina Wagner, were drawing with sticks in the sand out in front of the museum. Jacque Schindewolf, the museum conservator since 2002, was watching. In 2005 contractors hired by the board erected the West Coast Vietnam Memorial where the sand line indicated. Its black granite tiles acted like a mirror. They reflected the desert and the visitors. Sometimes a living buddy's name was etched in white next to that of his friend who had made the ultimate sacrifice.

Inside the museum, visitors still passed the topographic map at the entrance. Then they walked though exhibits of weapons, uniforms, letters, and so many artifacts that even after several hours, a visitor would have more to see. A few displays were about World War I, such as the trench art in several glass cases. Some were from conflicts post World War II such as the Vietnam War although its biggest exhibit was outside.

*Photo 74: From Two Who Returned on West Coast Vietnam Wall.*

Inside or out visitors would not see a fine-art exhibit until November 11, 2009, when the first ever soldier-artist show at the Patton Museum opened. The soldier had served in the Pacific, not Patton's jurisdiction, but the museum board agreed that the exhibit was within its mission. The exhibit's program read:

> Victor Bruno Contini, a young Italian immigrant, was fascinated with his new home and painted scenery whenever he could before he was drafted to serve in World War II. His captain noticed his talent and arranged for the home front to send what art materials they could. Fortunately, he sent some of his sketches and paintings home, before he was killed on Saipan in 1944. Victor's known work includes sketches of fellow soldiers, prewar scenery in Ohio, Army barracks in Texas, and the beauty of Hawaii where he was stationed right before being sent into combat.

The exhibit, which also included excerpts from his letters, stayed up until the fall of 2010. Periodically, the museum loops a slide show of his over sixty works, especially on military holidays. Since PFC Contini's exhibit, a standing display of the work by Pulitzer Prize–winning editorial cartoonist Bill Mauldin graces the same museum walls. Permanent indoor exhibits, including the Medal of Honor

and Holocaust Rooms, honor those who fought or gave their lives in twentieth-
and twenty-first-century conflicts.

Jacque Schindewolf had come to the museum in 1996 and grew into the role of
conservator by 2002. Many years before, during the Vietnam War, she had been an
air controller in the navy. Part of her responsibilities had to do with the wounded
and dead soldiers who came through Jacksonville, Florida, where she was stationed. So she had great empathy for soldiers who had made great sacrifices and for
their families. As conservator her job was primarily managing the ever-increasing
artifacts, but she took on some creative projects too. She had noticed that many
Vietnam veterans visited the museum. They often asked where to find displays
related to their service. There was one, and only one at first. Jacque thought this not
enough and worked with the board to add more. The Vietnam wall was her idea.
She worked with Margit and others to make it a reality. In 2009, she had been the
first contact for the soldier-artist exhibit, bringing the idea to the board—helping
that fallen soldier realize a dream cut short.

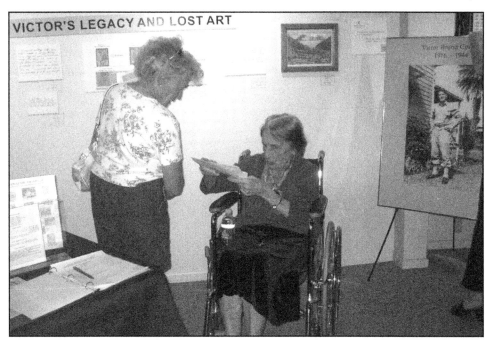

*Photo 75: Rosaria Contini, Victor Contini's sister-in-law who saved his art, Victor Contini
Exhibit, General Patton Museum.*

Early in 2011, she began to think about a Defenders of Freedom Wall honoring
those who served in the Iraq and Afghanistan conflicts. Margit had the same idea.
The general consensus of the board, now chaired by Richard Ramirez, was in favor.
By the tenth anniversary of 9/11, the wall was up.

By 2014, Jacque was ready to retire. Before she left, the board ratified the appointment of Michael Pierson as general manager. Michael had been a staff sergeant in the army, a Vietnam veteran, and a Green Beret. He and the board saw his role as managing the artifacts, but also as strategic leadership. He immediately started to promote the museum and make significant improvements. In the promotion arena, he successfully applied for grant money, spoke at community meetings and schools, and represented the museum on several veterans' committees. In the area of improvements, he coordinated the designs of three of the four memorials. By 2013 when he helped build the Korean Wall, he also updated the Vietnam Wall and the Defenders of Freedom Wall so all three had matching black granite tiles. The World War II Wall stayed with its original brick.

The museum added an exhibit that reached back many centuries. Duane Shockey, a pilot who often flew into the Chiriaco Airport, noted the outdoor exhibits by the museum. He suggested to the Patton board that the Leonardo da Vinci Weapons of War and Inventions from the San Diego Air and Space Museum be displayed there. The museum could no longer store them. An advantage at the Patton besides being a relevant display—the desert dryness would help preserve the full-size models of weaponry based on the master's sketches.

*Photo 76: Da Vinci Exhibit, Patton Museum.*

Inside and outside, Director Pierson oversaw the addition of many military vehicles but saw the simulated tank frames mounted on Jeep beds as the most valuable and rare. Joe had used one of these back in the 1950s as the first desert memorial to his friend General Patton.

*Photo 77: Indoor display at the Patton Museum.*

Father Jack regularly gave the invocation at the Veteran's Day ceremony while he was in the area. After he left, other priests and ministers from other faiths gave the opening prayer. The 2015 ceremony focused on the clergy. The General Patton Award that year honored four US Army chaplains (Lt. Rabbi Alexander D. Goode; Lt. Rev. George L. Fox, Methodist; Lt. Rev. Clarke Poling, Dutch Reformed; and Lt. Father John P. Washington, Roman Catholic). These four men gave their lives to save others as the SS Dorchester sank after it was torpedoed by a German submarine in 1943. This ceremony, as did the ones in past years, recognized any World War II veterans in attendance. As the years went on, there were fewer and fewer of these veterans at the ceremony. Ben Beal, in his nineties, kept coming, and Margit proudly introduced him.

## Junkyard to classic cars with the fourth generation

Victor loved to explore the junkyard. Maybe it was in the blood going all the way back to another junkyard in Alabama, the one that belonged to Joe's maternal grandfather, Fred Fago.

*These are cool cars. Maybe I could fix them*, Victor would say to himself as he wound through all sorts of discarded vehicles. Several of Joe's old tow trucks had come to rest here. He daydreamed of restoring them too, but did not know how to start.

In December of 2007, his soon-to-be mentor stopped in at the coffee shop.

"I'd like to see Joe," he told a waitress.

"Oh, I'm sorry to tell you he passed away some years ago. His daughter is here, though—sitting over there." The waitress walked Herb Whitmore over to Margit.

He gave her his condolences and talked about the old days. Then he asked. "Do you still have that 1931 Ford Model A? I tried to buy it from your dad years ago." Margit knew just where it was. She called Victor on her cell phone, and he came right over. He too knew where it was, the exact spot in the junkyard.

"It's a piece of junk," Victor said as he stood with Herb by the old heap. This was not one of the cool cars Victor liked.

"Oh, we can fix it. I know how and so does my son."

"But, but—" Victor started to object.

"It'll take some work, but we can get the parts." Herb's confidence lit a fire under Victor.

Herb brought his son, Herb Junior, to the Summit. He was a mechanic and a fabricator capable of making modern and obsolete parts. Chiriaco Inc. contracted with him to work with Victor on classic car projects. Victor and Herb Jr. renovated the old Model A. They had it in classic shape by the Summit's seventy-fifth anniversary in 2009. Once done with the Model A, Victor asked his grandmother, "What are we going to do with it?"

"It's not a toy," she responded as CEO. "The car and the garage are part of our business. This car is the first in our classic car collection—which we will show to the public eventually."

Margit encouraged Victor to make his classic car interest a business interest. "Join the Model A Club," she urged him, and he did.

Margit had bought the first few cars to be renovated. As more were acquired, she bought and owned them all, except for a few she gave to Victor. She maintained her roles as advisor to and funder of the operation.

Since 2009 Victor had been going to college off and on, until he became seriously ill in the 2011–2012 scholastic year. The family almost lost him. When he recovered, he stayed at the Summit.

In between working at the Chevron or elsewhere on the premises, he worked on cars with Herb Jr. Curious travelers came over to talk with them. The old gas-topped pumps and the nostalgic cars started conversations that sometimes gave Victor or Herb hints of where they might locate parts they could not find in the junkyard or easily make themselves.

Victor started taking his truck with a trailer to small towns in the west to haul the parts, but sometimes he would come back with a car. He made it a point to look in the local classifieds or to strike up conversations, eventually leading to a classic on the market. Luck? Maybe. But like his great-grandpa Joe, he was willing to go the distance to haul what he needed. Once there, he watched and listened for opportunities. Once in a while a great find just came to him.

One day in early 2015, Jimmy and June Capp stopped Robert in the coffee shop. They had come for their usual weekend breakfast.

"Why those old cars out there? What's going on?" Jimmy asked.

"We're starting a collection to display to the public," Robert explained.

"You know that 1965 Malibu station wagon?" June said, thinking out loud. "We don't know what to do with it. It served us well when we were raising the kids."

"We don't want it to get chopped up or be hot-rodded," Jimmy said. "Could we donate it to the collection? It needs some work, but it is fixable."

General Motors started marketing the Malibu Station Wagon Chevelle in 1964. So the Capps' '65 was an early Malibu, fifty years old in 2015. Some enthusiasts would list it as past the classic car category and into the previntage group. Victor gladly put the car in queue to be restored.

By summer 2015, Victor and Herb had restored six cars and gotten them running. Five more were in progress. In addition, Victor delivered a 1939 Cadillac that he had been storing to its owner, the Patton Museum. It was the same year but not the exact model Patton had driven when he was at the DTC. Michael Pierson took over its restoration and planned to display it at the museum as soon as it was ready. Then back to the workshop where they had a line-up of work.

*Photo 78: Inset - Victor Joseph Garcia, a 1928 Ford Sport Coupe hot rod at the Chiriaco Workshop*

Vehicles, like the Malibu and a 1931 Woody station wagon, were waiting for restoration. The junked tow trucks (the 1930s K8 International, the 1950s Ford, the 1950s Chevy) were also slated to be brought back to original and running condition. Victor had plans to restore the gas station garage to what it had been in the 1950s, with period-correct pumps. In the meantime, he rotated some of the dilapidated vehicles in front of the 1930s pumps there. Even in their poor state, these vehicles garnered interest.

Victor and Herb were very capable of not only restoring but also modifying cars for customers. Herb Sr. came by once in a while to provide some strategic insights. Victor realized that he had the kernel of a business with the garage. He also saw that his future at the Summit could include taking on the leadership role that his great-grandparents, his Uncle Robert, his Grandma Margit, and his mother and father had taken or were currently in. At one point Margit, acting as CEO and grandmother, told him that he needed to learn all the facets at the Summit—Chevron, Food Mart, coffee shop, Information Center, not just the garage—before he could step into any lead management role. He did both: kept the garage going and helped at the other facilities as needed. He started thinking about finishing his business degree. It was now relevant to him.

*Photo 79: 1967 Volkswagon Bug, 1917 Model TT, Flatbed Truck awaiting restoration.*

## Kaiser at the Summit

Contractor's Hospital had been abandoned in the late 1930s and then forgotten. That was until Steve Gilford, a senior history consultant to Kaiser, got involved. In the 1960s, Desert Steve's son and successor, Stanley, had stumbled over the outline of a foundation when out hunting. In the 1980s, while making a film near Desert Center, Steve Gilford met Stanley Ragsdale. They talked about the old hospital. Years later, around 1990, Stanley took the Kaiser historian to see what he had found. It was the Contractor's site, all that was left of it. Mr. Gilford informed Kaiser and then on the company's behalf succeeded in having the site declared a California State Historic Landmark. Now where to put the plaque? The isolated site made anything of value ripe for the taking. So in 1992 Stanley agreed to have the plaque placed at Desert Center. To discourage theft, he had it attached to a boulder.

Joe and Ruth Chiriaco were two of the guests at the dedication ceremony. Steve Gilford recognized them. In 1987 he had interviewed Ruth and Joe as part of a local history project. In that interview Joe reminisced about his aqueduct days, telling Steve how he felt about tunnel work, "I told them I'd spend enough time underground eventually and I wasn't going to start now."

In 2013, the boulder remained, but the plaque went missing, presumed stolen. Steve Gilford again approached Kaiser Permanente. The Southern California Permanente Medical Group agreed to replace it and conduct a celebration as part of its sixtieth anniversary in 2014, which also would be Contractor's eightieth. Mr. Gilford set out to find a new and safer spot for the plaque. The restaurant, gas station, general store, and ice cream stand at Desert Center were closed. The area was basically abandoned, making any replacement another easy target for thieves. Suzanne Ragsdale was very disappointed but could not justify to her family the cost of the added security needed to keep the plaque there.

Since Steve Gilford had interviewed Joe and Ruth Chiriaco some years before, he knew that the Summit had some history with Contractor's and with Dr. Garfield. On a one-hundred-degree day, he stopped there. He noted people everywhere at the stop. He sought out Margit.

"Oh my," she said, smiling broadly. "My parents knew the hospital and Dr. Garfield well. Mother worked at a hospital in Indio with Betty Runyen. Then Betty became Dr. Garfield's first nurse and went to Contractor's." Margit went on to talk about Dr. Morris and his relationship with Dr. Garfield. Mr. Gilford was convinced that the connection was real, but he had another concern.

"We're looking for a place with historic context for this plaque. I know you have that. But will it be safe here?"

"It should be. It's lit up all the time, and people are out and about twenty-four-seven."

Margit showed Mr. Gilford a few places for the plaque. He settled on one along Chiriaco Road between the coffee shop and the museum. Hector got involved, readying the location. Margit orchestrated some of her staff to prepare for the celebration.

On May 14, 2014, Dr. Garfield's grand-nephews and Susan, one of Betty's daughters, an employee of Kaiser Permanente in Hawaii, participated in the unveiling of the new plaque. Suzanne Ragsdale was invited to the unveiling, but had to work that day. At the bottom, in small print, the plaque still identifies the abandoned site as California Registered Landmark 992 near Desert Center. In large bronze capital letters, the plaque reads:

In 1933 Dr. Sidney Garfield opened Contractor's Hospital thirteen miles east of here. This facility successfully delivered high quality health care to Colorado River aqueduct workers through an innovative prepaid insurance plan. Later in association with industrialist Henry J. Kaiser, Dr. Garfield applied the lessons he first learned at this hospital to create their enduring legacy: Kaiser Permanent, the nation's largest nonprofit prepaid health care program.

Today, the plaque stands at the Summit, where many pass it on a daily basis. Before a year was up, Dr. Garfield's friends who had founded the Summit in the 1930s would have an inscription of their own—on another walkway in a nearby town.

## Walk of Stars

Michael Leedom, Pauline's son who as a ten-year-old had accompanied Joe on tow calls and pipeline maintenance, was standing in front of the See's Candy shop at 144 South Palm Drive in Palm Springs, California, talking to relatives and friends as more and more people gathered around a cordoned-off section of sidewalk. Chris and his wife, Jen, were there with their seven children. They had come from Northern California, where Chris was now in real estate. Jackie was sitting in one of the seats of honor that had been set up around the perimeter created by the gold cords. She was calling and texting on her cell phone. Uncle Paul, now in his nineties, was at his home in Maryland, but he sent his regards. Cousin Barbara Bergseid Clark, Uncle Harry's daughter now in her eighties and ailing, sent flowers. Alida Bergseid Imbrecht Rodebush, Uncle Ted's daughter, was there in person, walking around and talking with people—as friendly as her Aunt Ruth. Heather was directing guests to light refreshments set out on the sidewalk.

Chris's older girls were joyously passing out See's candy. Margit was handing out mementos and going over last-minute items with dignitaries. She made sure to thank the Millers for getting the process started to honor Ruth and Joe.

*Photo 80: Avila, Hope, and Lila, Chris and Jen Baldivid's oldest daughters handing out See's Candy, Walk of Stars, Palm Springs.*

David Smith, the new superintendent of Joshua Tree National Park as of September 2014, was talking to people. Margit said hello and handed him a keychain memento. David represented the park, a continuous neighbor going back to the 1930s. Since then, visitors to the south side of the park had relied on the Summit for gas, water, and for many years, even phones. In 2015, the park rangers still got mail at the Summit. They still frequented the coffee shop and now could access e-mail there. Back at Cottonwood, they still relied on well water. They had traded their generators for solar power, but not landline power, so they still struggled with shortages.

David and those who had had lived at Cottonwood had a deep understanding of the survival lifestyle the Chiriacos had weathered. Better than most outside the family, he understood the challenge of Joe's 1930s water system. He had been one of the young volunteers Jeff Ohlfs directed to remove the old pipes in the '94–'95 winter. Jeff was not here today. He was busy back at the park in his new role as chief ranger. Michael Leedom had recently sent an e-mail that mentioned what was left of those old pipes. It read:

> Several years ago [c. 2011] I was backpacking with friends. We hiked from Cottonwood in Joshua Tree to Chiriaco Summit. We came upon the old pipeline and several repairs that were made either by Grandpa Joe or Bob Howe. I brought a piece of a repair to my Uncle Robert. He and my Aunt Mag fed all of us the best bacon cheeseburgers, fries, and homemade cookies. My backpacking friends still talk about the hospitality we were shown, something my aunt and uncle inherited from my grandparents.... It was a memorable time made possible by the hard work and generosity of my grandparents.

Michael and other guests could see a podium and red tarp-like carpet in a cordoned-off area with a speaker podium. Besides Superintendent Smith as the park representative, sheriffs, county and state representatives, MWD officials, Caltrans officials, and others from alliances over the years started to sit down.

The Chiriaco Four, Pauline, Margit, Robert, and Norma, took their places right in front. Robert, by the way, was back to his slimmer self. He sat down with his longtime friend, Freda Lockhart Tisdel.

After Father Guy's opening prayer, followed by some Hollywood entertainment, a number of speeches summarized the inspiring story of a couple who by the strength of their love for each other and for those in their lives turned a desolate, inhospitable area into a welcoming, comfortable, enduring oasis for millions of travelers. Riverside County Supervisor John Benoit was one who so eloquently captured the importance of these two desert pioneers.

When the speeches were over, Margit leaned over on this March 3 of 2015 to help pull back the carpet to reveal a new star on the Palm Springs Walk of Stars. It stated simply:

Ruth and Joe Chiriaco

Pioneers

Chiriaco Summit, EST. 1933

Then many of the guests drove about thirty miles east to share in the down-home desert hospitality still so much a part of the coffee shop and all of the Summit. The Chiriaco history was secure, the future full of possibilities.

*Photo 81: Chiriaco Star, Walk of Stars, Palm Springs, California.*

# 25

# *The Dream Realized, Eastbound, 2015 and On*

I had come by in June 2014 with my daughter. This April of 2015 I was alone. I had arranged with Margit to live on site for about a week to work on the Chiriaco story.

I was determined to make some observations and talk to customers and employees. I got out early every day before the sun was up to walk around. My last day pulled all the pieces together—the visible ones—and the always underlying water. Water came into play after a busy day, breaking the nighttime quiet—as a solution instead of a problem this time.

## The usual busy day

The place was bustling before dawn this Saturday morning. It seemed full. People were going in and out of the Food Mart. Some truckers, parked in the large spaces between the airport and the gas station, were starting their engines. The sun was coming up over the mountains. I walked along the fenced runway as far as I could. There were no planes on the tarmac yet this morning, but I had seen some on other trips.

I passed through the big rigs on my way to the Food Mart. In I went. People were checking out at the cash register as I wandered around. It was bustling in there already. I was tempted to get coffee, but no, I decided to wait until the coffee shop opened in about an hour. Back outside, I noticed a hefty driver making her way with her Food Mart coffee to her truck. She was one of the few women truckers I had seen this week. I caught up to her just as she was about to open the door to her cab. I told her who I was and what I was about.

*Photo 82: Chiriaco Summit Airport with plane on tarmac.*

"Why do you stop here?" I asked.

"I come for the coffee," she replied. "It's the only place for a long while."

"But it's so hot here for months," I whined a bit.

"Yes, but that's the desert and the breeze is cooler here even in summer than other places. And there's plenty of good truck parking."

I thanked her as she climbed into her rig and watched her pull away.

I noticed a large flatbed parked toward the airport loaded with more bales of hay than I had ever seen. These were the rectangular, not the round bales, stacked very, very high. I wondered to myself, *Where is all that hay going—where did it came from?* I didn't see a driver, so I continued walking around. The sun was not bright yet, but dawn had broken.

It was a crisp, cool April day. A thin old man wearing a straw hat was sweeping the sidewalks on the coffee shop side of the street. I had seen him out here before. I later asked Margit who he was. "That's Santos's father, Rogelio. He's almost ninety years old, but wants to work. As long as he wants to and can do it, he's our groundskeeper."

I wandered over to the antique shop and looked in the windows. I could see blankets, dinnerware, furniture, and so much more. I walked over to the dry camp. I could see you have to have your own water there. I saw the camp manager's tent. I had met her once at the post office. I had heard that she knew all things about desert wilderness. She was gone, or I would have struck up a conversation. I walked around the outside of the Patton Museum, stopped at all the walls, and said a prayer at each one for the families of the brave souls who were memorialized there. I checked out the Da Vinci exhibit. My watch said it was almost time for the coffee shop to open, so I went back that direction.

A group of high school students and their teacher were standing not too far from the Guadalupe Shrine, close to the coffee shop patio. They were on a field trip. This was their breakfast stop.

"What a pretty place this is," one said, noting a flower garden and two saguaros. Ruth had planted the two large cacti so many years ago. One was a skeleton. The other was doing fine. Neither should have made it; neither Joshua trees nor saguaros grow here naturally. Joshua trees need the higher elevations of the Mohave; the saguaros need the wetter Sonoran.

One small group of the students was stooped over. "Look, there are so many," said a girl, pointing here and there.

"They're so cute. They're so cute. Look at that one." The students kept exclaiming about the big cats, small cats, brown cats, gray cats, and a few mottled kittens swarming around the area.

*Photo 83: Trucks at Chiriaco Summit parked at dawn.*

The cats consumed their conversation. I did not interrupt them to tell the long story I knew about how Ruth rescued a few cats in her early days at the Summit. The few became a swarm. This current generation knows to show up in the morning from wherever they outwitted the desert coyotes. Margit took over feeding them years ago.

Santos opened the coffee shop about 6:00 a.m. I was the first in and asked him if I could get breakfast quickly, just the basic eggs and toast. I was in a hurry to get a lot done today and truthfully wanted to beat the field trip crowd, still out with the cats. Santos took my order and gave it to the cook. Santos, Angelina, the morning waitress, and the cook were it for a while. I watched Santos do any job needed. I could see he was a hands-on manager.

*Photo 84: Hector Sanchez at work near a temporary building, 1930 Ford Coupe in background.*

Later in the day I sat down to talk to several employees. I heard over and over the words *like* and *love*. They all, yes all, told me how grateful they were for their jobs. Many of them lived at the Summit and told me how thankful they were for that too.

I asked each employee who talked with me, "Why do you stay?"

They all smiled as they gave me their answers, which made me smile.

"I love the community. The people are so nice."

"I like my job. I like this place."

"I like helping people when they are lost. They are so grateful. The people here watch out for each other."

"I just like it! I get to work close to home. I like the job."

"I like living in the desert. It's peaceful like a Mexican small town. My family is happy here. It feels like family here. I feel appreciated. I return the favors by doing the best job I can."

"It was my first job. I love it."

"I love the place. I love helping Margit. It's like family."

"There's always something new to do, so much room for improvement. It's dynamic. I just like it!"

I learned that some of these employees had children in college, one even in premed. The Chiriacos encouraged education, giving each son or daughter of an employee a small scholarship when they graduated from high school. If they did well, the scholarship could be renewed.

After breakfast I walked over to shelves in a corner of the coffee shop stocked with Chiriaco Summit preserves. I bought a few to take home as gifts. Then I took a few steps across the patio and into the office. Heather, Diana, and other staff were busily packing things. Margit had ordered a large trailer as a temporary office. In the late '40s and early '50s, the current building sufficed as business office, post office, and home for Joe and Ruth and their children. Right now it was just a business and post office, but even that was too much for the twenty-first-century activity. Hector had the temporary trailer ready for the office. The post office was in the process of moving to the Information Center. He was anxious to get busy remodeling and reconfiguring the old structure.

In preparation, Eduardo Guevara was boxing files to be moved to the trailer. On August 15, 2012, seventy-nine years to the day that Joe and Ruth opened their business, Margit hired him as a clerk and office assistant for the business. She had found Eduardo through the Coachella Valley Center for Employment Training (CET), an organization she enthusiastically supported. He rose quickly in the Chiriaco business to become the regulatory expert, to help with accounts payable and receivable, to take on some of the water district responsibilities, to handle some human resources tasks, and to help Margit with her volunteer projects throughout the local area. By 2014, she made him the administrative assistant for the business and her personal assistant. In Mexico he had held an information technology (IT) position for fifteen years. Margit soon found that he was talented with computers and IT. She started shifting his other duties to another person hired from CET, Yasselen Saucedo, a talented graphics designer who also had administrative abilities. Margit was aware of twenty-first-century skills needed and was hiring accordingly. Eduardo was moving more and more into a full-time IT role, and good thing since the Summit had computers everywhere now, but today he needed to ready the paper files. The office staff was moving out in the next few days. This was my last chance to experience the old structure. Ruth's wallpaper still graced some of the walls.

Margit, Heather, and Santos were busy all day. Robert came in and out of the coffee shop and office with information people needed. He was retired but definitely still engaged. I saw Hector out fixing a drain and then a little later with his two employees moving some boxes into the new office structure. This may all seem rather mundane until you realize how much goes on simultaneously in this small business, what a well-oiled wheel it is, and how much depends on everyone taking initiative from the time they wake up.

## A quiet evening but noisy night

In the evening, Margit asked if I wanted to go into Coachella City with her, her daughter Heather, and granddaughter Heather April, the youngest Garcia. I was tired from the day, but they were still full of energy. "OK," I said, and off we went.

This turned out to be a trip to take Heather April to meet some of her high school friends at a restaurant. It was senior year for this group. Heather April had already received college acceptances and even a scholarship to study art—a talent she inherited from her Grandma Margit and Margit's sister Pauline. This visit to town gave me a glimpse of the life Summit residents experience on weekends.

After leaving Heather off, we shopped at a few big box stores and some smaller ones. Before going back, we ate at a famous desert spot, the Café at Shields Date Garden. It was right on a path winding through a seventeen-acre date farm with two distinctions of interest to travelers: many varieties of introduced date palms (different from indigenous fan palms in the mountain oases Joe tapped for water), and stunning scenes with statues that depict the life of Christ. I could tell from their interactions with people we met, Margit and Heather were well connected in their desert community.

"How is Heather April getting back?" I asked.

"One of her friends is taking her and spending the night," was the answer—reminiscent of many overnights so many years ago. But what a night to be at the Summit!

About 1:00 a.m. I woke up to a noise I did not recognize. It continued off and on throughout the night. The next morning Hector told me what happened.

"There was hay on fire flying all over the freeway. I got a call about 1:00 a.m. to get ready. Fire trucks started coming from the Mecca and Desert Center fire stations to get their water here—at our water district." Hector's pride masked how tired he was. Mecca Station 40 and Desert Center 49 kept sending trucks all night.

"Could that have been the hay truck I saw yesterday morning over by the gas station?"

"Probably one like it."

"Were you up all night?"

"Yes, they kept coming. One of the firemen left the water pump on so it overheated. I fixed it."

"Did the hillsides burn?"

"No, the trucks got there in time. Besides we've had so little rain for so long—it's been about four years of this drought. There wasn't much to burn."

So that's what woke me up, the pump. I couldn't help but think to myself, all the supporters for CSWD were right about having the pump and enough water for firefighting."

Later I asked Diana if she had anything to do with the firefighters coming from Desert Center.

"No," she said. "I retired from the volunteer fire department years ago."

I went over to the coffee shop for breakfast before heading back to Tucson. It was Sunday. The Capps were there. They told me about Joe rescuing them and their Malibu. When I asked why they come here, Jimmy answered, "There's no competition for this place," meaning that for him there was no better breakfast food around. "I usually order the traveler's special. It's pancakes, eggs, and sausage."

June said her orders vary. She summed up their Chiriaco experience by saying, "Most of all we like being here with friends."

The coffee shop after all these years still remains a gathering place: In its earlier days for truckers, travelers, soldiers, and prisoners of war. In the twenty-first century for all sorts of visitors including recreational groups such as Broads on Quads, retired women who explore the desert on their specialized vehicles. Their quads were among the many different types of vehicles coming in and out all day and into the night.

*Photo 85: Modern Coffee Shop Complex, Inset L-R of Cook Max Garcia and waitresses Angelina Sanchez. Leticia Sanchez (not related).*

## What's next?

After breakfast, I got into my car. I made the turn onto the ramp going east, back home to Tucson. I wondered what I would find the next time I came. The office would be done. What else?

"Margit never stops," Hector had said to me a day or so before. He meant that in a good way.

I certainly saw what he meant. In talking with Margit, I found that she planned to rebuild the motel one day. That's not all. She also planned to add an RV park, a mobile park, and expand the coffee shop to make it more of a restaurant. And she is still involved with the ever-expanding Patton Museum. What started there as a two-year commitment for her has become a thirty-year work of heart. Her other plans were more futuristic. Not only is she supportive of the Classic Car Garage, but she sees it as a green fuel station with biodiesel for trucks and business fleets. She is watching for the right conditions to install chargers for electric cars and to offer compressed natural gas for big trucks. She explained that the technology is not there yet, not enough people are clamoring for environmentally better vehicles, but the Summit has a temporary charger and will be completely ready when the time is right.

On the other hand, some things will not change.

"We are surrounded by about eight hundred acres that belong to the family. We have only developed about seven. The family has an interest in leaving much of the rest as pristine desert," Heather told me when I first talked to her months ago.

Margit is determined that the coffee shop will still be there as the heart of the operation. Pilots will still find the best $100 hamburger around.

I started thinking as I was driving that the Chiriaco Story is a business story and a love story; but what did love have to do with the successful business I saw today or with the whole history of the place for that matter? I passed signs on the I-10: Hayfield, Eagle Mountain, Desert Center, all familiar to me now.

I was just one of those several thousand vehicles who had stopped at Chiriaco Summit in the last twenty-four hours. I kept driving and thinking.

*Photos 86: Sampling Chiriaco Summit Traffic, Broads on Quads and clockwise, dirt bikes, camper, tanker, ATV, hay load, 2014–2016, and ATV Experience outing, 2017.*
*ATVs are not allowed in Joshua Tree National Park, but are allowed in designated areas of Chiriaco and BLM properties.*

# 26

## *What Does Love Have to Do with It?*

"Darlin', I am awfully happy to think we will be together for always—to work and build together—and we'll make the wall so strong that it may never crumble or fall." Ruth wrote this to Joe before they were married in her letter of December 13, 1933.

On June 9, 1934, shortly before their wedding, she wrote, "Just a few more days now darling and we will be together for always.... [We] must build together and make it such a strong bond that nothing can tear it apart."

Time and again the wall was tested.

It was happening again on Sunday, June 19, 2015. It was dinner hour as more and more people were winding off the ramp to the Summit. The coffee shop and the Food Mart were getting crowded. Norma's granddaughter, Maddie Meyer, was working at the Foster Freeze when a customer told her that there had been a big accident on the highway near Desert Center. She told Heather.

"It'll clear up soon and we'll be back to normal," Heather responded, taking this in stride. It was after 6:00 p.m. on that Sunday. Employees on earlier shifts had left the Summit to go to places like Coachella City or Indio for the evening. Beatriz and a newer waitress, Itzel Moreno, worked as fast as possible in the coffee shop. They suspected no backup was coming.

It had rained very hard down the road the day before. The area around Desert Center had flooded, but not the Summit. It rained again on Sunday. The large-screen TV in the Chiriaco coffee shop warned of flash flood watches. Prior to the twentieth century, excessive rainfall was not a problem. Then as the desert became populated, the rainfall could become threatening.

Suddenly the Summit was swamped with people and their vehicles. Heather learned the truth.

The Tex Wash Bridge on the I-10 near Desert Center had collapsed an hour or so earlier, about 4:45 p.m. The tremendous rain and its flash floods had undermined its foundation. Caltrans had closed the interstate between Blythe and Indio. CHP turned around those going west before they reached the collapsed bridge and sent them back in the direction of Blythe or Phoenix. They did not reach the Summit.

Going east was another matter. So they would not reach the failed bridge, CHP was U-turning those people at the Summit, sending them back in the direction of Indio or Los Angeles. About eight thousand trucks (never mind cars) travel this section of highway every day. The Phoenix to Los Angeles route is critical to the trucking business, especially because of the deliveries and pickups to and from ports along the coast. Since it was Sunday evening, there were few trucks but many, many cars. As the hours went on, the traffic backup got worse and worse. Many motorists got off at the Summit for gas or just to wait it out.

All the Summit facilities were flooded with travelers in no time. Margit and Robert had just left for a short trip to Portland, Oregon. Heather was in charge.

She called Margit and asked her to make a series of calls for help. Heather was too occupied to make any calls. Besides, she knew Margit would have the contact information at her fingertips. First Margit called Riverside county supervisor John Benoit to find out what was really going on so she could assess the full impact to the Summit. Next she called Sheriff Stan Sniff, knowing that the crowds Heather reported would not be dissipating any time soon. Sheriff Sniff responded quickly. He sent out deputies to handle crowd control, but actually most people made the best of an uncomfortable situation. Margit also called the CHP, who stationed officers at the Summit for the full five days of the closure, making sure no one who got through to that point, unless authorized, went on to the area of the collapsed bridge.

Sunday night into the wee hours of Monday morning, people waited in line for gas, reminiscent of the '70s gas crises. Some ran out of gas waiting and had to be pushed forward. The Summit itself ran out of gas about 10:30 p.m. The delivery tanker was stuck in the eastbound traffic backup. Heather made another call to Margit, who made another call to CHP. The tanker showed up a few hours later.

Heather decided to keep the coffee shop open for a while, but those on duty became exhausted. Since backup was gone with no way to get to the Summit, about 2:00 a.m. she asked Victor to lock the doors. Then she made an announcement to those in the coffee shop.

"We will serve those of you here, but for others the coffee shop is now closed. We do not have the resources to serve the thousands of people coming through here. The Food Mart and gas station will stay open." She noticed how nice people were. They understood the predicament they all shared.

On Monday the remaining stranded motorists left the Summit. Until the highway reopened on Friday, the only visitors to the Summit were the maintenance workers who lived at the Hayfield Pump site, the rangers at Cottonwood, elected officials, some repair workers, and the media. No one else was allowed on the closed stretch of highway.

"It's so quiet," Rudy Montoya told reporters as he cleaned up some litter left by stranded motorists at the gas station and at the museum site. "We don't even hear the traffic noise like we always do."

Riverside Supervisor John Benoit and other elected officials came by almost daily to make sure that the Summit residents were OK and the Summit could continue to serve the emergency responders. In addition to Rudy, Heather and Victor spoke to radio, TV, and newspaper reporters. Santos spoke to Spanish stations. This was a role Margit would have played, but she was not there. The third and fourth generations showed the world their grace under fire.

On Monday, Hector, Santos, and Heather discussed plans for managing over the next few days, but first Hector talked about his unusual experience driving home from church in Mecca the night before.

"I showed CHP my identification. They saw I lived here and let me though. It was so dark on the interstate except for the lights at the Cactus City Rest Stop. I could never see those before. Usually, all you see is red tail lights."

Then Hector volunteered, "Looks like we will shut down for a few days. This is a good time for me and my crew to do repairs and maintenance." His bosses agreed.

Those who could prove to CHP that they were residents, like Hector, were allowed back on the road to come home. So by Monday, the Summit had most of its on-site employees back, but not the usual workload for them. Heather and Santos talked to employees about taking vacation days or working shorter hours until the usual traffic resumed. They agreed.

Hector got busy catching up on maintenance inside and out. When he worked outside, he played the radio. One afternoon, he was working near the coffee shop but walked over to the Patton Museum. When he got back, he told his crew. "I could hear that radio all the way to the museum." He realized that the traffic hum probably obscured some sounds at the Summit. "It's nice," he added, "but I will be glad to hear the traffic again."

On Thursday Heather got a troubling call. "We can't get there. There's no way. CHP won't let us through." It was the payroll carrier. Heather called CHP to no avail. She got in her car and drove to Palm Springs to pick up the payroll herself. Before she started back a construction truck spilled a load on the freeway. She sat on the road for hours, but she made payroll.

On Friday, the bridge reopened after Caltrans made some repairs that allowed them to reroute traffic. What a pleasant sound to all those who lived and worked at the Summit; the traffic was humming again. By then, Margit was back. In conversation, she summarized the situation, "Yes, we lost business for several days, but some good came out of this. All the agencies came together fast. This is a model for handling emergencies. And because of the bridge collapse, our desert infrastructure is getting attention. That bridge was on a watch list, as are some others."

But what she also realized was something that would do Joe's and Ruth's hearts good. Family and employees could think on their feet and could count on each other. The third generation was ready. The fourth generation was learning.

In crisis or not, the Chiriacos kept a lookout for new opportunities. By fall of 2016, Margit was pursuing two new but different vehicle ventures. When ATV Experience, a company that provides tours in the desert for ATV enthusiasts was looking for space, the Summit leased them a new building and the land it stands on. ATVs are not allowed on Joshua Tree National Park land, but like the Broads on Quads, they are allowed on other desert terrain around and near the Summit. She also worked with ChargePoint, Inc, to win a California Energy Commission award for the property to receive electric vehicle charging stations. She involved Victor and together they came up with an idea to make the charging area uniquely appealing. They planned to integrate it with the Classic Car Garage and open it as soon as compliance issues were met. In the meantime, Victor, like his great-grandfather, started his own company. He purchased Red's Headers & Speed Equipment, a business specializing in manufacturing and sales for early Ford parts. His plans are to move the business from Thousand Palms to the Summit and integrate it also with the Classic Car Garage. Again, the Summit, with its long past, is meeting the future head on.

*Photo 87: Concept of the Future Electric Vehicle Recharge Station at Chiriaco Summit, 1930 Ford Roadster and 2017 charger.*

Back to the question posed at the beginning of the story: what has sustained this family and its business for eight decades so far? Sweat equity? The immigrant work ethic? Keeping ahead of the times? Yes to all, but that's still not enough to keep anyone going indefinitely.

*Photo 88: The Chiriaco Four from L-R: Norma, Robert, Pauline, Margit.*

The deeper answer is the many-faceted effects of love. Ruth wrote to Joe that the operating room was a steam box and then turned playful in the same letter. Joe told Ruth that he was trying so hard because she inspired him. It all started with the partnership between the young Italian fellow, Joe Chiriaco, and the stalwart, beautiful Norwegian nurse he married, Ruth Bergseid, and before that with the influence of family values that came across the Atlantic with their European immigrant parents. And then came the infusion of folks from Oaxaca to the Summit, bringing their own love stories. The combination of the hard-work ethic of the Chiriacos and the driven character of the Mexican immigrants added to the success factors. The immigrants saw a better life. They were willing to work hard to achieve the American dream for those they loved. They saw potential. Add to that factors that came from the hearts of the Chiriacos themselves now over generations: providing a safe and comfortable environment, hosting celebrations that connect communities, and treating employees like family.

"But then love was never smart," wrote Ruth usually right about things, but on this she was wrong.

*Photo 89: Ruth with her four children at Shaver Summit, 1940s.*

Love was smart after all. It drove this 1930s couple to learn what they needed to learn, to fight the fights they needed to win, and to teach the lessons their progeny needed to carry on successfully in the future. The wall was threatened but stood. The bond was strained but strengthened. As a result, the business based on Joe's slogan lives on.

When Chris asked Joe in his later years, "What do you see, Grandpa?" Joe answered without hesitation, "A city. A city to keep the family close and to keep our family business from generation to generation." For a long time to come, the *world on wheels* can expect:

*All of the necessities and some of the luxuries*
At Chiriaco Summit.

# Epilogue

# Epilogue

*Perspective on Chiriaco Summit,*
*an American Success Story*

**Howard N. Stewart, President/CEO**
**AGM Container Controls (AGM), Tucson, Arizona**
**AGM was recognized by the US Chamber of Commerce as**
**"America's Best Small Business, 2009."**

In 1958, my family started taking long drives across the desert that separates Los Angeles and Tucson. The drive was over five hundred miles each way, and it was filled with stark contrasts, including treeless, barren mountains that lifted steeply against cloudless blue skies and empty riverbeds that seemed to meander aimlessly across a thirst-quenched landscape.

At the time these drives began, I was just a baby, loaded up in an old Ford Fairlane station wagon with my parents and two older sisters—no seat belts or air conditioner. In the dusty, desert pueblos along the way, the temperature sometimes soared to over 120 degrees Fahrenheit, so when the family got out of the car to gas up or take a lunch break or something, we felt like we'd been dropped in a toaster oven.

Such discomfort frequently resulted in crying; however, my mother had a reliable solution to this inevitable grievance. She would pop one or two ice cubes into my mouth from the white Styrofoam cooler that she always brought along for the trip, and my tears would momentarily cease until the rising temperature inside the car would start the cycle all over again.

The purpose of these long drives was to help my dad, a manufacturing representative based in Los Angeles, to stay connected with a Tucson-based company, Arizona Gear and Manufacturing, that he had just begun representing.

The primary routes from Los Angeles to Tucson in those days are still in use today. The southern route travels through San Diego and Yuma, while the northern route cuts through Indio, Blythe, and Phoenix. The primary difference between then and now is the quality of the roads. Most of the roads then were only two-lane US highways, with one lane for eastbound and westbound traffic. While there wasn't a lot of traffic on those roads, I remember that the cars would whiz by one another at dangerously high speeds, and over the years, our family saw more than our share of deadly accidents, including burned-up or rolled-over wrecks. Joe may have salvaged some of these wrecks to park in his junkyard.

Of course, nowadays, these two old US-highway routes have been replaced with much safer, high-speed interstates, where traffic in a single direction is always a minimum of two lanes, occasionally expanding to three, four, or more lanes through the sporadic larger towns and cities along these routes.

Whenever our family took the northern route from Indio to Blythe, we must have occasionally pulled over to gas up at Chiriaco Summit. However, those gas stops faded from my memory long ago. As such, I don't have any specific memories of stopping there—that is, until I began to make long drives on my own, beginning in my late teenage years.

I liked to stop at Chiriaco Summit because, over time, it had become more like a big friendly travel stop, although it was far more modern and up-to-date than most. I also liked that it had a restaurant and store, the latter having all sorts of amenities and goods for sale.

To this day, Chiriaco Summit is the best place to stop between Phoenix and Indio. It's clean and welcoming. Due to its relatively high elevation, it's a little cooler in temperature than the competing gas stations one might see along the route in towns like Quartzsite, Blythe, and Indio. It's also strategically located, in that there's absolutely no other gas station—or virtually anything else—along the 92.9 grueling miles between Indio and Blythe.

When starting a retail business, it's widely agreed that the three most important decisions are as follows: location, location, and location. Joe Chiriaco, who had no formal business training, intuitively understood this premise. As such, Joe saw something that no one else could see: Tons of people would travel past this area. So Joe decided to provide the gas, food, water, lodging, and auto repair that these people would need, while his wife, Ruth, provided the outstanding customer service that travelers can still experience to this day.

So how does the Chiriaco Summit business story relate to the two businesses, AGM Container Controls and Stewart's Ice Cream 'n More, that my family owned and operated?

In 1960, my father, Roger Stewart, left Earl S. Condon, the Los Angeles manufacturing representative company that he had worked for the previous eight years. He left to start his own manufacturing representative firm that he named Aztec, taking the Arizona Gear and Manufacturing account along with him.

My dad started Aztec on a card table in my parents' master bedroom, and within a year, seeing Aztec's potential, my mother, Joyce Stewart, gave up her part-time position as a piano teacher to help my dad build Aztec. Just like the Chiriaco Summit story, our family business was started by a husband who was joined by his wife, which is how many businesses, then and now, are built.

My parents eventually acquired Arizona Gear and Manufacturing and later renamed the company AGM Container Controls (AGM) to better reflect the mix of products they were manufacturing—just as Joe and Ruth had moved from leasing their land, to ownership, and later to changing the name of the Summit for practical reasons.

AGM started with just seventeen employees but has since grown to roughly 110 employees, which means its headcount is approximately the same as the Chiriaco Summit operation. Similar to Chiriaco Summit, AGM has grown primarily as a result of our owners constantly being on the lookout for new and different ways to serve our existing customer base.

In June 1971, just nine months after AGM began, I joined the company as a part-time summer worker—I was just twelve years old. My parents chose to pay me only $1 per hour, having witnessed my not so great work ethic on previous family projects. Frankly, I was elated to be making $1 per hour! Today, if I had to select the one reason I came back to work summer after summer—and Christmases—I would have to say that it was the money. The Chiriaco kids seemed to have liked both the work and the overall environment. Perhaps in this case the desert was a plus.

In my early twenties, I visited a very successful ice cream store in Cambridge, Massachusetts, which ultimately led me to think about opening a similar franchise in Tucson, Arizona. Although I knew almost nothing about business at the time, I started to read a lot about retail in an effort to overcome my lack of business experience. In addition, I also used to spend entire days parked across the street from numerous ice cream stores, counting customers from open to close. I would note whether customers were men or women, as well as if they were adults or children. I also noted the proximity of other businesses or public events that seemed to influence each store's traffic patterns.

Realizing that young people, especially college students, ate a lot of ice cream, and that movie patrons frequently visited ice cream stores after seeing a movie, I ultimately set my sights on a boarded-up building near the University of Arizona that was within a mile of five movie theaters. I also learned that this building was on the corner of one of the five busiest intersections in Tucson, and that most of the university's sororities and fraternities, not to mention the basketball arena and football stadium, were within walking distance.

Of course, fifty years earlier, Joe had done something quite similar, locating his business smack-dab in the middle of nowhere, along the planned new US Highway 60.

My parents and I invested in the ice cream venture, and for each of the five years that we owned this ice cream store we were voted the "Best Ice Cream in Tucson" by readers of the *Tucson Weekly*. At the time our store was probably the busiest ice cream shop in the Southwest. Unfortunately, the store fell victim to eminent domain, as the city of Tucson had determined that they needed to take down the building that housed our store to accommodate ever-increasing traffic at this busy intersection.

When this occurred, I assumed that my days as a business owner were over. But things didn't turn out that way. By this time, I had a wonderful wife who was enrolled in a full-time doctoral program. Accordingly, I needed to find employment that would keep us afloat financially. So after a hiatus of six years, I returned to AGM as a full-time buyer.

Shortly thereafter, AGM ran into serious economic problems, resulting in a massive layoff and a need for the company to reinvent itself in order to survive. However, these challenges ended up serving as opportunities for me to prove myself as an employee who could make a positive difference at AGM. In turn, I was able to prove my value, passion, and capability to the company. I was named president and CEO of AGM on January 1, 2000.

Just as AGM has become everything to me, the Chiriaco Summit business became everything to Joe, his wife, and two of Joe's four children. Most people will never build this kind of connection with their work. They will never let their work define their success or who they are; however, this is exactly what can happen to a small business owner. You see, business owners frequently become just as married to their business as they are to their spouses. For comparison's sake, when one starts a small business, it's a little like birthing a baby. And parents become obsessed with their baby's survival and growth.

Thus, without Joe's keen vision, the place we now call Chiriaco Summit would have never become anything more than a desolate piece of real estate along the interstate, but Joe was undeterred by the stark conditions. He started his business in 1933, growing it through sheer will to provide the products and services that no one else could provide.

How many times would Joe take arduous hikes into the mountains behind Chiriaco Summit in order to fix a leaky pipe miles away, knowing that failure to repair such could spell the difference between whether or not his business would survive, let alone thrive?

Some business owners are like that. They're willing to do whatever it takes to make their business a success. Why does this happen? It's because the business has become a part of them.

That said, it's clear that the one person Joe needed most for his business to succeed was his wife, Ruth. The author, my friend Dr. Mary Gordon, makes it very clear that Ruth was the archangel in Joe's life for many, many reasons. For example, Ruth seemed to know when to listen to Joe and when to tell him no.

A vital part of what made Joe successful was Ruth's constant steadfastness. Despite Joe's occasional anger issue or sporadic faulty decision, Ruth was always there for him—sometimes serving as his rock of salvation, but at other times serving as his rock of resistance, such as when he occasionally made a decision that needed to be reversed.

I'm a widower, and the best friend that I have ever had was my late wife, Beth, who both served as my rock of salvation and as my rock of resistance. Even though Beth has been gone more than a decade, I still think of her as the one who has given me the greatest amount of support in my life.

This is true for my parents as well. From the beginning, they were partners in both Aztec and AGM, and their love for each other, as well as for their two businesses, was intertwined and inseparable.

Not many businesses survive to be handed down to a second generation, but Chiriaco Summit was able to achieve this honor, in part because their children and grandchildren have developed a great deal of passion about their oasis in the desert, as well as an appreciation for the native desert that surrounds them.

Switching gears, any kid who is raised in a family that operates a family business grows up differently from a kid who doesn't experience this particular dynamic in life. Such children often join the family business early, beginning as the low man on the totem pole, and they struggle with the distinction of seeing their parents as bosses instead of parents. Likewise, their parents must struggle with the distinction of seeing their children as employees instead of as their children.

Joe and his son, Robert, had similar conflicts. As the founder and patriarch of Chiriaco Summit, Joe worked hard and smart, gradually growing the business from almost nothing into something of which anyone would be proud. However, he struggled with the thought of his own mortality, as represented by the fact that he had a difficult time coming to terms with the professional capabilities and the valuable contributions that his son, Robert, and his daughter, Margit, were making to the business.

More so than Margit, Robert went through his own struggles, wanting both his father's approval and the ability to run the business his own way. On one occasion, when Robert was totally frustrated with his father's unwillingness to accept and recognize Robert's contributions, Robert ran away. It was only Ruth who had the ability to navigate the distance between Joe and Robert in an effort to bring Robert back into the fold.

Throughout my years growing up in a family business, I have also experienced the joys and frustrations of being an employee in the family business. Even well into my late forties my parents would question the wisdom of my actions as the leader of "their baby," the business that they had founded together. Fortunately for me, their confidence in my ability to do the right thing has grown—or did they just soften with age?

Regardless, my father has often referred to me as his son who failed his way to success. While I've never perceived this fatherly statement as a ringing endorsement of my abilities, it's a comment on my life that has a strong ring of truth, but that's a tale for another day!

Home life and work life were virtually inseparable for the Chiriacos. The four children had a front-row seat, watching how their parents operated the business on a daily basis. They saw the outcomes of their father's ideas, for better or worse. They witnessed their father's unrelenting drive, as well as their mother's exceptional people skills. And between Robert, who initially succeeded Joe, and then Margit, who brought the Summit into the modern era, they absorbed a good deal of both. This almost uninterrupted, informal business education would serve the two of them immeasurably well when the time came for them to provide their second-generation leadership to Chiriaco Summit.

Likewise, I had the good fortune of watching my parents operate our company for many, many years. And while my parents maintain to this day that my second-generation leadership has been more successful than their own, truth be told most of what I have achieved in my career has been the direct result of witnessing their successes and failures here at AGM.

The Chiriacos saw their parents work through tough situations. One was hiring. Most nonbusiness owners don't know what a struggle and expense it is to find and replace a terminated employee. The business operator has to advertise the open position, read through all the submitted applications, interview all viable applicants, and then drug test the prospective employee. When an applicant fails the drug test, we have to repeat the aforementioned process with a new person. Once an applicant passes his or her drug test, the long and arduous task of training the new employee begins. Over the years, both AGM and Chiriaco Summit have hired hundreds, if not thousands, of employees. Some have worked out, but some have not. Because Chiriaco Summit is almost fifty miles from the nearest labor force of any size, its owners managed an extremely challenging hiring condition during its eighty-plus years, a situation that AGM has never had to face.

Fortunately, Ruth saw the immensity of their employee challenges. She knew it was usually better to nurture an employee, which included helping every employee feel at home rather than to dismiss anyone out of hand. However, she only nurtured to a point, knowing that the practical side of Joe would see when it was time to encourage any failing employee to move on.

Like many successful business owners, I feel that I relate to both Ruth and Joe, in that my "Ruth side" totally commits to my employees and their families, as I know that they are counting on me for continued employment and career opportunities, as well as earnings and benefits. As such, I'm pleased to report that I've yet to lay off a single employee in my twenty-four years of management at AGM. That said, my "Joe side" is ever present, and it falls upon me to tell a given employee that it's time for them to move on down the road for the good of our business.

There's one reason and one reason only that most companies stop growing between forty and fifty employees, and that is the founder or subsequent owners' inability to delegate. This condition is especially true of founders, as they're the ones who got the given enterprise up and going on his or her own, and due to their overall involvement in every aspect of their business, they just can't let go.

Joe was this kind of founder. He couldn't let go. He had to be involved in everything. Whatever broke (pipes, cars, generators), he would fix it. He had trouble delegating decisions to others within the business. However, as Joe aged, he realized that he couldn't do everything, and he begrudgingly relinquished control as his body gradually gave out. Robert and Margit ran things differently than Joe. Starting with Robert and then accelerating with Margit, the business really took off, breaking through the forty to fifty employee ceiling.

Chiriaco Summit has lasted into its fourth generation. It has weathered some hard times, as most businesses do. It's my assessment that Joe had a more positive impact on Chiriaco Summit than any subsequent family member or employee. It's my opinion that the Summit would not have been able to get to where it is today had Joe stayed in good enough health to remain at the helm. However, Joe ran out of time, just as we all will, and he was forced to hand over control, which has proven to be a really good thing for the business.

The second generation of leadership, including Joe and Ruth's two other children, Pauline and Norma, who have been on the board since young adulthood, moved away from Joe's model of direct control and constant oversight toward a more inclusive direction, allowing others within the business to help make decisions. I'm sure that it also helped that they all had spent years watching the impact of Joe and Ruth's decisions, including what worked and what didn't.

Over the years, most of the Chiriaco family and many employees have developed a passion for the business and the desert that surrounds it. The desert presented a dichotomy: sowing the seeds of possible failure while simultaneously creating opportunities to flourish, reminding one of the challenges that any living thing (e.g., flora or fauna) faces in the unforgiving desert.

In closing, *Chiriaco Summit* is a story that should appeal to anyone who wants to increase his or her understanding of how a modern business is founded and developed, despite incredible challenges along the way. Due to the passion and innovation of the family who founded it, Chiriaco Summit has ultimately gone on to survive against all odds.

Howard N. Stewart is the president and CEO of AGM Container Controls, a company that was founded by his parents, Roger and Joyce Stewart. He began to work at AGM as a teenager in 1971. He was named president and CEO in 2000. The US Chamber of Commerce named AGM Container Controls as "America's Best Small Business" in 2009. Mr. Stewart currently chairs the board of directors for the United Way of Tucson and southern Arizona. He serves as a member of the board of directors for both the Tucson Metro Chamber and Greater Tucson Leadership. He climbed Mt. Kilimanjaro in 2011, so he'd like to think that he might be able to make the treks that Joe Chiriaco made in order to repair his water pipes along the arduous mountain trails of Joshua Tree National Park.

# Appendices

# Appendix A:
## Family and Business

# Family Tree: Family Mentioned and to the Fourth Generation since the Summit was Founded

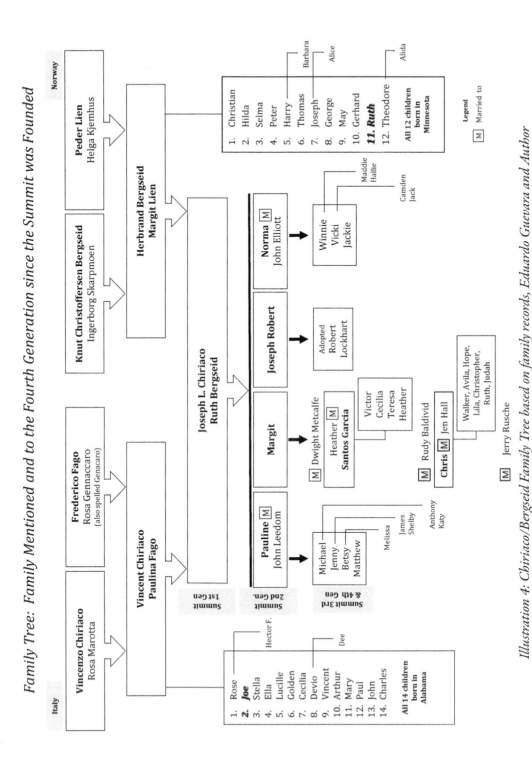

*Illustration 4: Chiriaco/Bergseid Family Tree based on family records, Eduardo Guevara and Author*

## Recipes from Ruth's Kitchen

This is not a cookbook. These recipes are Ruth's historical and charming recipes, unique to her era, but not all tested for today. Most are in her own words.

# ❧ Grandma Ruth's Pot Roast ☙

One nice piece of beef roast, salt and pepper and pat with flour, place in roast pan. You can brown in a little oil if desired and you can add a packet of Lipton's onion soup too.

Cut fresh onions and place around meat and add a cup of water, cover with a lid and then bake roast in a 350 oven until meat is tender. Remove meat and add more flour mixed with water, pour into pan juices (if there is too much liquid in pan, pour some out, then add the flour and water. It should be a paste). Cook over flame until a thick beautiful brown gravy.

Serve the meat with boiled potatoes, cooked carrots in chunks, or mashed potatoes and biscuits *and the yummy gravy.*

# ❧ Stuffed Quail ☙

Six or more little birdies. Clean bodies and cavity and mix a simple bread stuffing or corn bread stuffing, and you can add onions, celery or raisins or cranberries. Stuff the cavities of the bird. Spread butter or oil on skin of bird and place in 350 oven until crispy brown and done

Serve with fresh vegetables, potatoes, salad, and a delicious french bread, *and dine under a mesquite tree in the desert with a bottle of wine.*

# ❧ Mattie's Tacos ☙

Deep fry corn tortillas and form into taco envelopes, and drain. Put a couple of pounds of hamburger in pan with small amount of Crisco, salt and pepper, diced onions, and a pinch of chili powder, and cook well until brown. When cooked, place large spoonful of meat in taco shell. Add shredded lettuce, diced tomatoes, grated cheese, and top with sour cream and fresh salsa.

**Beans and Rice:** Add some refried beans (refried beans in can) and if desired Mexican rice (white rice, almost browned in oil in big skillet). Add small slivers of onions, plus water (two cups water to one cup rice), and add diced tomatoes, or a can of crushed tomatoes, or V-8 juice. Then cover and cook until rice is done and all is a nice rosy color.

**Fresh Salsa:** diced tomatoes, minced fresh chilies of your choice, diced onions and cilantro. *Mix in a small slice of heaven.*

# ❧ Norwegian Meat Balls ☙

Take two pounds of hamburger meat, mix with an egg, 3/4 cup milk, six pieces of bread, and squish together. Add salt and pepper and onion or Lipton onion soup mix. Form into little balls and place in a fry pan with hot oil in bottom. Cook until brown and done inside. Then drain the meatballs. Add a little flour to the drippings and one-half cup milk and a carton of sour cream, and create this heavenly sauce. Return meatballs to sauce, then spoon over a mound of cooked white rice or brown, or noodles or mashed potatoes.

Serve with cooked carrots or green peas, and a pear and cottage cheese salad, and a dinner roll. *Eat like a farmer just in from the field.*

**P.S.** These meatballs can be used in spaghetti also. Add some Italian seasonings.

# ❧ Barbeque Ribs ☙

Slabs of pork or beef ribs, cook covered in 375 oven. Salt and pepper and cover with barbeque sauce, either purchased or homemade. Cook until well done, brown and tender until smells delicious.

Serve with baked beans and coleslaw ... maybe french fries and french bread.

**Homemade Sauce:** tomato sauce, teaspoon Worcestershire sauce, half jar of plum jam, three-quarter cup of brown sugar, two teaspoons of vinegar, plus hot sauce or chilies.

**Coleslaw:** slice cabbage finely, add finely sliced apples or pineapple or carrots or all.

**Dressing:** one cup mayonnaise, sugar and vinegar (should be sweet and tart). *Now tie a bandana around your neck and get out your guitar and pretend it is the wild west.*

# ❧ Baked Ham ☙

One large ham with bone in. You can score fat and put in cloves, then smother with sauce and put in covered pan and bake until brown and crispy on top and smells delicious.

**Sauce:** one jar plum jam, with one cup brown sugar, with splash of vinegar, two teaspoons mustard and some hot fire pickles sliced very fine, plus some of the juice. Mix all together and spread over ham.

Serve with cooked yams, can be with brown sugar, marshmallows and butter, green beans, scalloped potatoes and a Waldorf salad.

**Scalloped Potatoes:** take off skin of potatoes, slice and place in pan, add butter, and a white sauce and cover with grated cheese ... also salt and pepper to taste.

**Waldorf salad:** mixed cut apples, cocoanut, pineapple, marshmallows, celery, and pecans and top with a mayonnaise and sugar dressing.

Serve with sweet Hawaiian rolls. *Say a prayer of Thanksgiving and enjoy.*

# ➢ Lady Baltimore Cake, Chiriaco Summit Style ℭ

You need a lot of egg whites for this cake. Check the chicken coop to make sure the hens are laying. Once ready, scoop out 1/2 cup of shortening (½ of this can be butter). Put in a mixer bowl and add 1 ½ cups of sugar and cream until fluffy. Now in another bowl, sift together 2 ½ cups of flour, 2 ½ tsp. baking powder, and one tsp. salt. Mix the flour combination into the sugar-shortening mixture. Combine a cup of milk with 1 tsp. vanilla flavoring and mix in alternately with the flour combination. Beat 4 egg whites until they are stiff and fold into batter. Pour into 2 round cake pans. Bake in 350 oven for 30–35 minutes. To test, poke with a toothpick. If it comes out clean, the cake is done. Cool about 10 minutes and then turn out on racks another twenty minutes When cool, spread some Chiriaco Summit Jam of your choice on each cake layer. You can find many fruit flavors of this jam in the coffee shop store. Finish with the filling and then icing.

> **Filling:** Scoop 1/3 of the icing into a small bowl. Add your choice of dried fruits such as 1/3 cup each chopped figs and dried raisins or dried berries. Add ½ cups chopped walnuts.

> **Icing:** Beat 2 egg whites until stiff; fold in 1 tsp. vanilla and put aside. Boil together until stringy 1 ½ cups sugar, 1 tsp. light corn syrup and 2/3 cup of water. Pour slowly into beaten egg whites and beat until mixture is fluffy

> **Finishing:** Spread filling on bottom layer of cake. Put top layer on and then ice the whole cake. *Hide until ready. Surprise the birthday guest with a cake sparkling with candles reminiscent of a desert night.*

*Photo 90: Sugar cookies made by Chiriaco employee, Kim Jones, served at the reception after the Palm Springs Walk of Stars Ceremony, March 3, 2015. Inset Heather and Santos Garcia, Chiriaco Summit General Managers.*

## Historical numbers related to the business

Original Café and Pump Prices: The table below shows some entries from Joe's handwritten ledger of November 8, 1933. Lunch was listed as 15 or 20 cents. It may have been a bologna sandwich. Annotations are in parenthesis.

| | | |
|---|---|---|
| 1 | beer | 0.20 |
| 1 | lunch | 0.20 |
| 1 | candy | 0.05 |
| 20 | Union 76 (gallons of gasoline) | 3.50 |
| 1 | fan belt | 1.00 |
| 13 | ethyl (gallons) | 2.54 |
| 1 | pop | 0.10 |
| 6 | magic (could be a snack) | 0.95 |
| 1 | tire repair | 0.25 |
| 1 | coffee | 0.05 |
| 1 | candle | 0.20 |

*Illustration 5: Selected entries showing café and pump prices from Joe Chiriaco's ledger, November 8, 1933.*

Ramp volumes: Traffic volumes at Chiriaco Summit on and off ramps were last counted in 2008 with the most updated listing in the *Caltrans Freeway Ramp Volumes on the California State Freeway System, District 8*, Issue 2015, page 6. See 2001 and 2005 volumes for pre-2008.

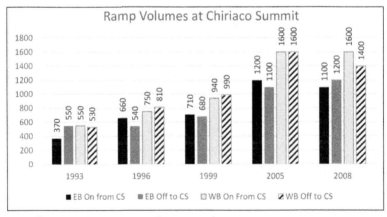

*Illustration 6: Ramp Volumes at Chiriaco Summit, 1993-2008.*

Samples are obtained from short periods of time and then factored to find the annual average daily number. There are no newer ramp numbers for Chiriaco

Summit since 2008 as verified with Caltrans. (emails of April 3 and 6, 2017). Vehicle counts in and out while visiting the site and official volume counts past Chiriaco Summit last reported in 2015 indicate continuous increases over the years.

Gasoline sold at Chiriaco Summit: Over 100,000 gallons per month as reported in AAA's June 1978 issue of *Shop Talk*. In 1978 Chevron installed the Summit in its elite 100,000 Gallon Club. Sales have been on the rise ever since.

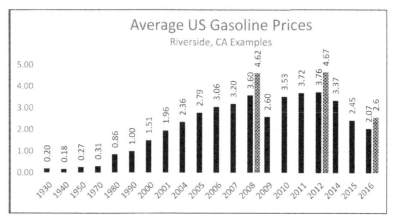

*Illustration 7: US Gasoline Prices as of September 2016. Regular leaded to 1989. Regular unleaded from 1995 on. Regular Unleaded for California. Not adjusted for inflation Not all years are recorded in the sources cited.*

Fourth generation helping out serving the twenty-first century world on wheels.

*Photos 91: Joe and Ruth's great grandchildren, sisters Teresa and Cecilia Garcia, who help out when home from school, 2015 and 2016.*

# Appendix B:
## A Family Business Checklist

### Foresight, Fortitude, Family

## The Checklist[**]

Love had a lot to do with the Chiriaco Summit success, but is that replicable?

Some statistics about family businesses indicate that only about 30 percent outlast the third generation. Other statistics suggest the second generation is the end. Some do not make it past the first. So what have the Chiriacos been doing right that other small family businesses can emulate?

Many sources present success factors to emulate and problems to avoid. Problems can be deduced from success factors, but one is worth mentioning with a chuckle: "Lack of ambition for competition with the best in the world." (*Economist*, November 1, 2014 edition) Joe took on General Patton and marched on from there.

The success factors listed in a number of sources are here made into a checklist with examples from the Chiriaco story. The list is grouped according to foresight, fortitude, and family, although it can be argued that they overlap.

## Foresight

✓ Having a strong sense of purpose, a smooth succession plan, and definition of roles.
- The Chiriacos have had a defined mission from the start: *All of the basics*

---

[**] The checklist and analysis of the business aspects of the story are based on the author's experience coaching leaders in large corporations and small business entities, some of them family businesses.

*and some of luxuries for the traveling public.* Their succession was specific: Robert would take over with a board made up primarily of family members. The next succession was up to Robert and the board.

- Each generation grew into roles defining and redefining them as the business expanded and the environment changed.

✓ Sending family to business school, insisting on proper training, and/or acquiring expertise.

- Robert got a business degree from NAU. Margit learned through on-site and community involvement. She understood the importance of impressions so put to good use her UCLA BA in art, making the Summit visually appealing inside and out. Heather learned on the job from babyhood.
- Victor is rotating through the business positions. He is beginning to see the need for a business degree.
- The company reached out for expertise that was not within the family or for which the family did not have time. Diana Ragsdale (bookkeeping), Hector Sanchez (maintenance), and Eduardo Guevara (Office Manager taking on the roles of IT Manager, Webmaster, Photographer, and Certified Water District Operator) are some examples of this.

## Fortitude

✓ Managing risk.

- Ruth and Joe balanced each other. He was more risk averse than she was. One could be convinced by the other's reasoning. Thus they averted mistakes like Mr. Colby's triangle.
- Robert and Margit also had this juxtaposition, with Robert being more the risk taker and Margit, a fast study who moved smartly to action. This combination allowed them to get into new ventures but also to course correct even in a storm such as the MacDonald's to Foster Freeze example.
- The leaders from Joe on were resilient enough to recover from risks that did not work out. Some of that resilience came from having each other, from creativity, but also from being well connected in their community.
- Unspoken risks are poor health and addictions. Joe instilled the mindset against these risks. Robert is an example of winning against both the obesity and alcohol threats, not only to his health but also to the business.

✓ Managing change rather than letting it happen:

- Note the constant vigilance to the off-ramps, water, and power.

## Family

✓ Thinking in terms of generations.
  • Right at the start, Ruth was determined that they build that solid bond that no one could tear apart.
  • Joe saw a city that became the Summit's well-knit community where some of the fourth generation are starting to take up residence.

✓ Developing good performance
  • Joe and Ruth learned on the job; then they taught others.
  • They and their successors monitored and mentored performance by being right there with the learners. They encouraged good workers to stay and others to move on.
  • Their successors worked in almost every aspect of the business on their way up.
  • Chiriaco employees (family and nonfamily) are given opportunities to advance into leadership roles.

✓ Passing on to prepared, capable, and willing family members. Not falling into the trap that there is a place for everyone.
  • Ruth and Joe understood that all four children might not see the Summit as their long-term career. They exposed them to the world outside the Summit, even living near Indio for two short periods. All the Chiriaco Four went away to college. They were allowed to venture out and come back if the business and the place were right for them or move on if not. Two came back and stayed on.
  • First Robert, then Heather and Santos, were purposely mentored for leadership roles.
  • Margit learned by staying involved in the business and by standing up to take a lead on projects when she saw a need, often ones that were full of challenges. The family supported her in taking the lead in these difficult situations.
  • The fourth generation is trying out. This generation includes family and nonfamily.
  • Nonfamily members are playing significant roles.

✓ Volunteering—sense of community. The leaders of small family businesses volunteer, which engages the next generation early in partnerships. These partnerships or connections matter to the reputation of the immediate business and to reaching long-term goals.

- Recall Joe and Robert volunteering during the Korean War for civil air defense. Volunteering much more than that was very difficult for Joe and Robert, whose days and sometimes nights were filled with serving customers, flipping burgers, fixing pipes, and fueling the generators.
- The family agreed to have Margit represent them in the community.
- Her most visible project was and is the General Patton Memorial Museum. As of 2016 she chairs the board of directors.
- Not so visible but vital are the civic committees Margit sits on, such as DACE and California Women for Agriculture (CWA), for which she is the Coachella Valley vice president. These committees help desert businesses.

    For example, DACE supports actions that lead to sustainable communities.

    CWA informs members on agricultural issues and works to resolve them.
- Margit also volunteers with Catholic Charities, Salvation Army, Community Foodbanks, the Desert Advisory Committee for BLM, and the new Agriculture Academy for high school students under development in Coachella Valley. She serves as a model for her family and employees.
- Heather, as busy as she is 24-7, volunteers for the church and CWA.
- Eduardo gives time to environmental causes and is the treasurer for the General Patton Memorial Museum Board.

## At the heart

The checklist based on expert reports offers insights but does not get to the heart of what is Chiriaco Summit (for expert sources see Appendix E: Checklist). The family and employees loved the place, loved the business, and loved the people involved. Replicable? Each family business has to examine the relevance for itself—find its own heart and soul.

➢ **The place:** Ruth and Joe gave their children and grandchildren the freedom to explore around their desert home—although these busy parents may not have known the extent of it. The Chiriaco Four hiked, they picnicked, they had friends overnight, and they had parties and grand celebrations. They did not take themselves too seriously. They scoured the junkyard. They locked each other in the big refrigerator—unsafe, don't do it. Some even walked naked one night on the airport tarmac—don't try this either. The gleeful enthusiasm in these pranks is the message, not the pranks themselves.

➢ **The business:** The place was so intertwined with the business. The children cared about the business enough to pitch in whenever needed, often with employees doing the same. The first and second generations hiked up difficult terrain to help fix emergency leaks. They went on midnight tow missions. Members of all the generations of family and employees stayed up all night helping with emergencies.

➢ **The people:** At their core, the Chiriacos have been continuously about people, be they family, travelers, employees, or the community at large. In regard to family, they have been nurturing and forgiving. Robert turned out to be a rock in turbulent business situations after being nurtured through his own turbulence. The family nurtured Margit through her failed marriages. Joe and Ruth were dedicated to making travel bearable back in the Dust Bowl days to downright comfortable in the new millennium, from finding impossible fixes for stranded motorists to delivering babies to creating a traveler's information center. They treated employees like family, making affordable living spaces available for them and contributing toward their children's education.

Talent, acquiring it and retaining it, is critical to business success. For the Summit, this talent involved learning and performing out of ambition but also out of gratitude for the opportunities the Summit provided. Employees use the word *love* when they talk about the Chiriacos. Recall dependable Bob Howe, a wanderer who became a grandfather figure, Nina who felt love for the first time in her life with a hug from Ruth, Rudy Montoya who got a second chance, and Santos who fell in love with Heather, starting a long marriage and business partnership.

Family dynamics, good and bad, played into the story. To prevent an unraveling, the pioneer Chiriacos prepared a transition in addition to a succession plan. That was why Robert and then Margit moved so seamlessly into the CEO role. That's why Heather and Santos have continually fulfilled their roles smoothly. The Chiriaco Four did not always agree, for example on details of the expansion; but because their parents modeled the ability to see past immediate disagreements into the future, they could set aside their differences, enabling them to agree on critical business decisions. The Chiriaco Four watched two very different personalities who together created success in the desert they came to love and respect.

In summary, their belief in a long-term business gave Ruth and Joe the endurance to overcome the water and power struggles, to adjust to regulations as they sprouted, and to meet crises head on whether they be business threats like MTBE, the I-10 closure, or a threat to family. Recall Ruth's determination not to let anyone steal her man. The children and grandchildren observed and absorbed that same endurance, especially Robert and Margit, who needed it to meet challenge after challenge as the twentieth century became the twenty-first, all the while being gracious to the travelers. It is not uncommon for the business to receive testimonials like this one:

Dear Chiriaco and Garcia families,

Not too long ago, my family was en route from Arizona to Long Beach, CA when our car signaled that it was going to break down. Out in the middle of nowhere, with 105°, 1 was afraid for my family's well-being. 1 did a search to see if there was anything close to where we were, and low and behold, Chiriaco Summit showed up on the map. 1 had never heard of this little place, but we were going to try to make it there. With God beside us, we made it and we discovered your beautiful little town.

In order to stay out of the heat, my family and I sat in the lobby of your cafe, waiting for the tow truck. No one asked us to leave nor did they ask us to buy anything. (We did end up buying a couple of muffins though.) As we waited, we walked around and read all of the stories about how Chiriaco Summit came to be. Never would I have believed that this little town would have taught me about an important part of US History. It was like we had discovered a treasure in the middle of the desert. The tow truck finally came and we were on our way. You probably won't remember us, but just wanted to thank your families for the hospitality you probably weren't aware you had extended to us.

With much gratitude,
Patricia Maahs
August 10, 2014

In the end, that "damned Italian" outlasted Desert Center, although Suzanne Ragsdale still holds out hope for a modern travel stop with a 1930s ambiance—even perhaps in partnership with Desert Steve's old rivals. The Summit also outlasted the mining town of Eagle Mountain that Joe found so troublesome. It became a ghost town. No ghosts at the Summit. It keeps on bustling with the life and livelihood established long ago by a strong bond of love.

# Appendix C:
## Displays, Resources at the General Patton Memorial Museum as of Summer 2017

Honorary Chair: Helen Ayer Patton

Original General Patton Memorial Museum Committee, which evolved into the original Board of Directors:
- Margit Chiriaco Rusche, Chiriaco Summit, cofounder
- Leslie Cone, BLM, cofounder
- Wally Hernandez, Indo American Legion Post
- Albert Hinijosa, Indio American Legion Post
- Betsy Morrison, Volunteer

On display in the Tank Yard, adjacent to the museum
- A memorial to several Medal of Honor recipients with ties to the Coachella Valley.
- A memorial naming all the units that trained at the DTC-CAMA
- A duplicate of one of the stone chapels made by the soldiers at the DTC in the 1940s
- One Sherman tank
- Pershing tank

- Three Patton tanks
- Five M60 (Vietnam era) tanks
- One Russian T-55 Firefighting/crowd control tank
- One 5-ton wrecker
- Two WW II 2.5 ton trucks
- One WW II Burma Jeep, which is actually a truck
- One WW II Command car (parts vehicle), three WW II 1.5 ton trucks
- Two Vietnam era 2.5 ton trucks
- One WW II era Dodge Fire Truck once used at the military facility at Desert Center
- One tracked vehicle recovery unit
- Simulated tank frames

  The three white simulated tank frames were donated to the museum by Joseph Chiriaco. They were mounted onto jeeps with four 's' hooks, then covered with tent material; paint was used to make the simulated tank canvas cover look more like a tank. They were used for training. These are very rare.

Memorial Walls Outside in front of the Museum

Families and friends can honor those who served with a Founder's or Donor's brick or black marble tile on which the Veteran's name and other relevant information can be inscribed and placed on these walls

- Word War II (brick wall)
- Korean War (tile wall)
- Vietnam War (tile wall)
- Defenders of Freedom: the Gulf Wars, the War on Terrorism, and First Responders (tile wall)

  *Families and friends can honor those who served with a Founder's or Donor's brick on the World War II Wall engraved with the Veteran's name and other relevant information. The information can be etched in white on black marble tiles on the other walls.

Vehicles inside the museum:
- One WW II Willy's Jeep and trailer
- One WW II Japanese Howitzer
- One Vietnam Era "Mule"

Displays inside the main section of the Museum

- A topographic map on loan from the MWD
- WW I trench art and a section about WW I (out of respect for General Patton and all those who fought during WW I)
- WW II displays that tell the story about the former Desert Training Center and the story about the California-Arizona-Maneuver-Area, first commanded by General Patton
- Displays that honor those who served in the Korean War era, the Vietnam War era, the First Gulf Wars (Desert Storm-Desert Shield), and the War on Terrorism, both in Iraq and Afghanistan.
- The Holocaust Room
- The Medal of Honor room
- Books for sale

Research materials: available by appointment.

Thank you to the following people not mentioned in the chapters about the Museum who gave considerable time and effort to the Museum
- John R. Kalish, Chief, Office of Renewable Energy Coordination, Bureau of Land Management (BLM)
- Michael Mitchell, BLM Archaeologist
- Curly Ulhorn, Volunteer

Edison volunteers pictured on the May 27, 1988, cover of *Edison News*:
Jerry Rusche, Jack Lapice, Glenn Canfield, Cecil Klopfeinstain, Jack Friebus

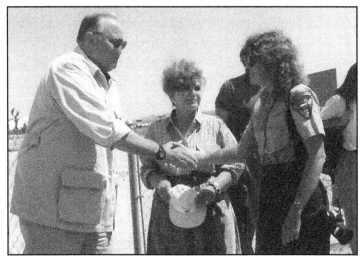

*Photo 92: General H. Norman Schwarzkopf with Patton Museum cofounders Margit Chiriaco Rusche and Leslie Cone (BLM), on his visit to GPMM, Chiriaco Archives, 1992.*

*Photo 93: General Patton Memorial Museum (GPPM), Chiriaco Summit, California*

New additions to the museum as of November 11, 2017:

- The six-thousand square foot Matzner Tank Pavilion. The pavilion funded by Harold Matzner, entrepreneur, humanitarian, and philanthropist, houses military vehicles that need to be kept indoors such as a restored Cadillac like one used by General Patton and an M60 tank which actually runs. Other vehicles from the outdoor yard will be moved into the pavilion as they become operational.
- The new Chandi West Wing. Kaiser Permanente donated portable buildings to the General Patton Museum for expansion purposes. The interpretive displays are made possible through a generous donation from the Donald and Coeta Barker Foundation. Nachhattar Singh Chandi is funding and undertaking the construction to complete the facility for the new displays. He is an immigrant from India who established himself in the Coachella Valley 26 years ago. He has become a desert tycoon from his humble beginnings as the owner of a single gas station, changing tires and sleeping at his small service station.
- The MWD Topographic Map in the Museum's entrance room. MWD has refurbished this map maintaining its geographic integrity but repairing damage such as cracks and adding new signage. MWD reinforced the building's foundation to better handle the five tons of what is also known as the Big Map. Interpretive panels are being added on the wall behind it to explain its history and significance.

# *Appendix D:*
# *Tables*

## Table of Maps

## Table of Illustrations

## Table of Photos

# Appendix E:
## Sources

Interviews, e-mails

Letters from Chiriaco Archives

Agency Research Contacts

Observations

Official Documents

Other Printed and Electronic Sources Listed by:

       Part One

       Part Two

       Part Three

       Part Four

       Part Five

       Checklist

       Historical Numbers

## Interviews, E-mails

- Baldivid, Chris (Margit Chiriaco's son)
- Beal, Ben (WW2 DTC veteran)
- Beal, Linda (Ben Beal's daughter)
- Campos, Jovita (RN, nursing information)
- Capp, Jimmy and June, (Customers)
- Chiriaco, Margit (Joe and Ruth's daughter)
- Chiriaco, Paul (Joe Chiriaco's brother, WW2 veteran)
- Chiriaco, Robert, (Joe and Ruth's son)
- Chiriaco, Shirley (Paul's wife)
- Chiriaco, Tom (Joe Chiriaco's nephew, Devio's son)
- Clark, Barbara (Ruth Bergseid Chiriaco's niece, Harry's daughter)
- Cote, John (PacBell technician assigned to the Summit, retired.)
- Cone, Leslie (Patton Museum, BLM retired.)
- Dilsaver, Lary (JT historian, professor, University of Alabama)
- Deorio, Rosemary (Customer)
- Elliott, Norma Chiriaco (Joe and Ruth's daughter)
- Franck, Hector (son of Joe's sister, Rose)
- Fariester, Eileen Heimark (Margit's friend)
- Garcia, Santos (Heather's husband)
- Garcia, Victor (Joe and Ruth's great grandson)
- Gilford, Steve (historian, writer, Sage productions)
- Gratz, Arch (school bus driver)
- Green, Daniel W.E. (Director, Central Bureau for Astronomical Telegrams at Harvard University)
- Green, John F. (field ornithologist)
- Grey, Jerry and Veronica (Customers)
- Guevara, Eduardo (Employee)
- Kalish, John (BLM)
- Keefe, John (Father Jack, Catholic priest)
- Krieger, Robert (CSWD's consulting engineer))
- Leedom, Michael (Pauline's son, Joe and Ruth's grandson)
- Leedom, Pauline Chiriaco (Joe's daughter)
- Lubitz, W. David (private pilot, small plane identification)
- Lubitz, Rebecca (MD, medical information)
- Maahs, Patricia (customer)
- Metcalfe, Dwight (Margit's first husband)

- Metcalfe-Garcia, Heather (Margit's daughter, Joe and Ruth's granddaughter)
- Michaelsen, Joel (Geography, UC Santa Barbara)
- Montoya, Beatriz (Employee)
- Montoya, Rudy (Employee)
- Ohlfs, Jeff (NPS)
- Pierson, Michael (Patton Museum)
- Quintana, Ernie (NPS)
- Ragsdale, Diana (Employee)
- Ragsdale, Suzanne (Desert Center)
- Ragsdale, Sidney (Desert Center)
- Ramirez, Richard (Patton Museum)
- Roberts, Dr. Dan and Diane (Customers)
- Rodebush, Alida (Ruth's niece, Ted's daughter)
- Rusche, Margit Chiriaco (See Chiriaco, Margit)
- Sanchez, Angelina (Employee)
- Sanchez, Hector (Employee)
- Sanchez, Leticia (Employee)
- Schindewolf, Jacque (Patton Museum)
- Schiavone, Dee Chiriaco (Joe's niece, Devio's daughter)
- Smith, David (NPS)
- Stewart, Howard (CEO, AGM—a family business, SBA Award Winner)
- Tapia, Nina (Employee)
- Tisdel, Steve (Employee)
- Williams, Paul and Elsie (Customers)

## Letters from the Chiriaco Archives

(Business related letters are under official documents or under the part of the story for which they are a source)

- *My Nurse,* Poem to Ruth Bergseid by O.H, c. 1929–30.
- Correspondence between Ruth Bergseid and Joe Chiriaco, October 2, 1932–April 1937
- Selected correspondence between Ruth and Joe Chiriaco, 1992, 1993, 1995
- Letter from Margit Bergseid to Joe Chiriaco, November 27, 1933
- Letter from Ella Chiriaco to Joe Chiriaco, December 14, 1933
- Letter from Harry Bergseid to Joe Chiriaco, June 6, 1934
- Letter from Fr. Michael Lee to Joe Chiriaco, January 11, 1936
- Letter from Joe Chiriaco to Pauline Chiriaco, October 11, 1953

## Agency Research Contacts

- California Department of Transportation (DOT, Caltrans): Lushbaugh, David (DOT Library), Kassinga, Terri (Chief, Public and Legislative Affairs, Caltrans District 8) Pribyl, Cindy (Research Analyst)
- California Regulatory Assistance Office (DTSC): Conti, Glori (Regulatory Assistance Officer)
- Chiriaco Archives: Rusche, Margit Chiriaco, (CEO, Joseph L. Chiriaco, Inc.)
- Edison Archives: Hume, Ed (International Corporate Communications), Netter, Paul (Southern California Edison Public Relations)
- Florence-Lauderdale Public Library Local History-Genealogy Department, Florence, Alabama: Freeman, Lee (Local Historian).
- General Patton Memorial Museum Archives: Shindewolf, Jacque (Conservator, retired). Pourtemour, Peggy (Archivist)
- Imperial Irrigation District (IID), Imperial, California: Champion, Marion (Officer, Media Communications)
- Joshua Tree National Park Archives: Spoo, Melanie (Curator), Most, Madison (GIS Specialist)
- Los Angeles Metropolitan Water District Archives (MWD): Acuna, Armando (Media Services Manager); Keller, David (Senior Analyst)
- National Centers for Environmental Information, National Oceanic and Atmospheric Administration: Online contacts
- University of North Alabama Archives (UNA): Huddleston, Louise (Archives Assistant)
- Riverside County, Environmental Health, HazMat: Crain, Nicholas (Hazardous Materials Management Specialist), Cauffield, Suzanne (Environmental Health, Hazmat Staff)
- Sharlot Hall Museum Library & Archives, Prescott, Arizona: Schmidt, Tom (Reference Desk Coordinator)
- United States Department of Agriculture (USDA): Peterson, Cliola

## Observations

The author made the following observations at or near Chiriaco Summit:
- Stops at Chiriaco Summit between 2002–2017 as a traveler two to three times a year
- Full days in 2009–2010 as an exhibitor at the Patton Museum
- Partial days from 2014–2017 interviewing at and visiting Chiriaco Summit and nearby sites

- Overnight stays interviewing and searching archives, April 24–26, 2015; October 5-6-7, 2015; February 20–26, 2016, July 8–10, 2016
- Site tour into Camp Young, along pipelines, and on old roads with Robert Chiriaco, February 13, 2014
- Stops at Joshua Tree National Park Visitor Center and at Desert Center, October 7, 2015
- Eight-mile hike in Joshua Tree National Park to see the oases and the pipelines used by Shaver/Chiriaco Summit. Guided by Dick and Phyllis Clawson, NPS Guest Hosts, February 25, 2016

## Official Documents

Anderson, Rick. "Letter to Margit and Robert Chiriaco confirming water rights donated by Joe Chiriaco to JTNM." Twentynine Palms, CA: National Park Service, Joshua Tree National Monument, 25 April 1986.

Articles of Incorporation of Joseph L. Chiriaco, Inc. No. 581250. Office of the Secretary of State, California. 2 October 1969.

*Biological Opinion of the Chiriaco Summit Electrical Transmission Line Project, Memorandum 1-6-00-F-11*. Carlsbad, California: United States Department of the Interior, Fish and Wildlfe Services, 2000.

Board of Supervisers, Riverside County, California. "Resoultion No. 2000-01. Ordering the Formation of the Chiriaco Summit Water District and Calling an Election on the Question Thereof." Riverside County, 11 January 2000.

Board of Supervisors, Riverside County. "Memo to Kreiger and Stewart, Incorporated regarding LAFCO 99-14-4—Formation of the Chiriaco Summit County Water District." Riverside County, 3 August 2000.

Califorinia-Arizona Manuever Area, Headquarters Comminications Zone. "Release of Real Estate, 601.53 (172) CNWZJ, Nicholson, Kennedy, Hammond & Halsall Tracts." San Bernardino, 10 April 1944.

Caltrans. "Department of Transportation, Sign Installation Order 08-08241." Comp. Chuck Favel. San Bernardino, California, 28 July 2008.

Chiriaco, Joe. "Shaver's Summit Payments to Cram Bros., Mentone, CA (Three pages of handwritten payment records)." November 1, 1942–Feb 3, 1946.

Chiriaco, Joseph L. and James E. Cram. "Lease Agreement, State Selection No. 9597, Los Angeles Land District, Serial 044168." County of Riverside, California, 15 July 1933.

Chiriaco, Joseph R. "Bill of sale, transfer of assets from Chiriaco Water Comany to Chiraco Water District." Riverside County, 13 February 2001.

Cone, Leslie. "Letter to Henri Bisson, BLM California Desert District Manager, regarding the Patton Museum." Roswell, New Mexico, 18 March 1995.

"Endangered…Desert Tortoise, Final Rule." 5 February 1994. *Federal Register, Vol. 59*, 5820-5866. 21 May 2015. <http://ecos.fws.gov/docs/federal_register/fr2519.pdf>.

Gastellum, Ronald. "Contract between the Metropolitan Water District of Southern California, the State of California acting by and through its Department of Transportation and Chiriaco Summit Water District relating to the Sale of Water." Los Angeles, 1 August 2002.

Krieger and Stewart, Incorporated. "Memo to Margit Chiriaco Rusche Re Water District Formation." Riverside, 9 August 2000.

McFadden, Joseph, Chair LAFCO, Riverside County. "Resolution No. 24-99 Approving Formation of the Chiriaco Summit Water District, LAFCO No. 99-15-4 (includes attachments of boundary descriptions and maps)." 28 October 1999.

"Metropolitan Water District Board Meeting." Los Angeles, California, 8 June 1964. (Accessed, MWD Archives, 2015).

Metropolitan Water District. "Colorado River Aqueduct Roads, Desert Center to Thermal, Map, File No. 300-6-109." Los Angeles, May 1933. (Accessed, MWD Archives 2015).

MLS. "Correspondence Related to Shaver's Summit Reservoir, Synopsis from December 30, 1930 to May 25, 1965." Los Angeles, California: Metropolitan Water District Archives, Box 47F023, 1965. Accessed 2015.

"Plan and Profile of State Highway between Shaver's Summit and Desert Center, Map, B-3206." Department of Public Works, Division of Highways, California, 21 December 1931. MWD Archives, Accessed 2015.

"Quitclaim Deed for Lost Palms Oasis from Joe Chiriaco to Joshua Tree National Monument." County of Riverside, California, 21 November 1986.

"Quitclaim for Shaver Reservoir from MWD to Federal Government, MWD Archives, Box 47F23." 1965 21 July.

"Shaver's Summit, Legal Description." (Appears to be description of purchased property), n.d. but c. October, 1942.

"Shaver's Summit, Purchase Agreement, James E. Cram et al and Joseph L. Chiriaco with attachment: Union Oil Agreement for Loan Arrangement." County of San Bernardino, 10 October 1942.

Skinner, R.A. "Letter to Joe Chiriaco Re: Shaver Summit Reservoir Site, MWD 132–9-11&15." Topics: Quitclaim of Reservoir to US Government, Right of Way to Joe Chiriaco. Los Angeles, California: Metropolitan Water District, 24 June 1965.

Sommerville, R.J. "Letter to Tom Cackette, ARB Executive Director: Agreements reached on

May 8, 1998 [in regard to the vapor recovery program]." Sacramento: Air Pollution Control District, 1998.

Spiliotis, George J., Executive Officer LAFCO. "Certificate of Completion. 2000-300849, Formation of Chiriaco Summit Water District." 3 August 2000.

"Statement of Escrow, No. 2579. Note re amount still owed, First National Bank in Coachella." 4 November 1947.

"Statement of Escrow, Chiriaco Purchase of Cram Property." October 28 1947.

Statement of Escrow, Total with payments due. No. 2579. First National Bank in Coachella: 28 October 1947.

Townsend, Michelle. Registrar of Voters, Riverside County. "Election Canvass for Chiriaco Summit County Water District Held on May 9, 2000." Riverside, 15 May 2000.

Townsend, Michelle. Registrar of Voters, Riverside County. "Certificate of Registration of Voters to the Results of the Canvass of Election Results." 15 May 2000.

Union Oil Company. "Letter to Joe Chiriaco listing checks received." Mentone, California, 10 December 1942.

"United States v 435 Acres of Land in Riverside County, etc. (Letter to Joe and Ruth Chiriaco regarding need for immediate signature)." 26 May 1946.

Wolfe, Raymond (Director, Department of Transportation, District 8). "Letter to Robert Chiriaco regarding termination of potable water contract with WMD." San Bernardino, 18 January 2011.

## Other printed and electronic sources

*Dates for websites include date published and/or date accessed.*

PART ONE: WINDING BACK TO THE PIONEERS, 2014–1800s

*About Twentynine Palms*. 2011. 29 April 2016. <http://www.ci.twentynine-palms.ca.us/About_29Palms.76.0.html>.

"Aged Negro Woman Dies (Aunt Jessie Simpson Thomas)." *Florence (AL) Herald* 27 January 1939: 8.

Ammenheuser, Maura. "San Jacinto Mountains: Tunnel a 1930s Engineering Feat." *Press-Enterprise* 2 March 2012. 23 April 2014. <http://www.pe.com/local-news/riverside-county/hemet/hemet-headlines-index/20120303-san-jacinto-mountains-tunnel-a-1930s-engineering-feat.ece>.

Anderson, Dave. "A bunch of farmers upset football tradition." 24 December 1962. *Sports Illustrated Vault*. A Time Warner Company. 8 May 2014. <si.com/vault/article/magazine/MAG1135109/index.htm>.

Bartholemew, Dana. "100 Years of Water: Los Angeles Aqueduct, William Mulholland helped create modern L.A." 11 November 2013. *Los Angeles Daily News*. 7 June 2014. <http://

www.dailynews.com/environment-and-nature/20131101/100-years-of-water-los-angeles-aqueduct-william-mulholland-helped-create-modern-la>.

Bisell, Chas H., ed. *The Metropolitan Water District of Southern California, History and First Annual Report (first published in 1939).* Commemorative. Los Angeles: Haynes Corporation, June 2011. 23 April 2014. <http://www.mwdh2o.com/mwdh2o/pages/about/AR/AR1928.html>.

*California Aqueduct Map.* n.d. 23 April 2014. <http://www.mwdh2o.com/mwdh2o/pages/about/AR/AR1928/Appendix/Map-and-Profile-Aqueduct.pdf>.

*California Highways.* n.d. 5 May 2014. <cahighways.org/057-064.html#060>.

"California Highways and Public Works." January-February 1933. *California Highways, Occidental College Archives.* 23 June 2014. <http://libraryarchives.metro.net/DPGTL/Californiahighways/chpw_1933_janfeb.pdf>.

*California State Assembly, John L. Collier, South Pasadena, 54th District.* Sacramento, California: California State Archives, Legislative Biographies, c. 1972.

Carney, Charlene. "Chiriaco Story and Timelines for Chuckwalla Valley History (draft)." 2014.

—. "M.W.D Aqueduct and the Men Who Built It." *The Tattler* March 1998: 5.

Chiriaco, Golden Virginia. "Ancestry of Joseph L. Chiriaco" unpublished document, Chiriaco Archives, 7 pages, nd.

Colley, Nevada C. *From Maine to Mecca.* Indio: Nevada C. Colley, 1967.

"Colorado River Aqueduct." n.d. *American Society of Civil Engineers.* 12 June 2014. <http://www.asce.org/project/colorado-river-aqueduct/>.

"Crash of 1929." 2012. *Amercan Experience.* PBS. 28 January 2016. <http://www.pbs.org/wgbh/americanexperience/features/primary-resources/crash-headlines/>.

"Desert Steve Ragsdale." *The Desert Magazine* 17 August 2012. 5 May 2015. <https://desertmagazine.wordpress.com/2012/08/17/desert-steve-ragsdale/>.

*Diseases and Conditions: Deviated Septum.* n.d. 7 June 2014. <http://www.mayoclinic.org/diseases-conditions/deviated-septum/basics/definition/con-20031537>.

Fagan, Brian. *Elixir: A History of Water and Humankind.* New York: Bloomsbury Press, 2011.

"Florence City Schools Timeline." 2015. *Florence City Schools.* 15 January 2016. <http://www.florencek12.org/>.

Gilford, Steve. *Transcript of Nonrecorded Interview of Joe and Ruth Chiriaco.* Chiriaco Summit, 1987.

Gruen, J. Philip. *Colorado River Aqueduct, HAER No. CA-226, Historic Engineering Record.* Washington, DC: National Park Service, 1998. 16 June 2014. <http://lcweb2.loc.gov/pnp/habshaer/ca/ca2400/ca2472/data/ca2472data.pdf>.

Harrrison, Randall. *Desert Steve Ragsdale*. 16 August 2012. 10 November 2015. <http://mydesert-magazine.blogspot.com/2012/08/decent-folks-are-welcomeenjoy-but.html>.

"Henry Ford Health System." n.d. *Psot-Op Instructions: Deviated Septum*. 21 June 2014. <http://www.henryford.com/body.cfm?id=52812>.

Herbrason, Nels. "The Bergseid Family." 1980.

Hiltzik, Michael. *Colossus: Hoover Dam and the Making of the American Century*. New York: Free Press, 2010.

"Historic Califorinia Highways." n.d. *US Highway 60*. 23 June 2014. <http://www.gbcnet.com/ushighways/US60/index.html>.

"Historic Endpoints of US highway 60/70 in Los Angeles." n.d. *US highway endpoints, photos, maps, and history*. 27 July 2014. <http://www.usends.com/Focus/LosAngeles/index.html>.

Holmes, Elmer Wallace. *History of Riverside County*. Los Angeles: Historic Record Company, 1912. 13 October 2015. <https://books.google.com/books?id=wm8UAAAAYAAJ&pg=PA138&lpg=PA138&dq=Riverside+County+Supervisor+Shaver&source=bl&ots=1u-Blt lFWz&sig=uPqoKD4CzOCq9QLzUeXdqYWVXlw&hl=en&sa=X&ved=0CDgQ6AEw A2oVChMIzqKQjprAyAIVipMNCh1ruAwG#v=onepage&q=Riverside percent20County percent20Supe>.

"IID History." n.d. *Imperial Irrigation District*. 31 July 2016. <http://www.iid.com/about-iid/an-overview/iid-history>.

"Information About the Lincoln Highway." 1999. *Lincoln Highway Association*. 16 June 2014.

Janczyn, George J. "Groksurf's San Diego: Local Observations on water, environment, technology. law & politics." 20 May 2013. *A Tour of Hoover Dam and the Colorado River Aqueduct System*. 7 June 2014. <http://groksurf.com/2013/05/20/a-tour-of-hoover-dam-and-the-colorado-river-aqueduct-system/>.

Laflin, Patricia. *Indio, Images of America*. San Francisco: Arcadia, 2008. <https://www.amazon.com/Indio-Images-America-Patricia-Laflin/dp/0738556181>.

"Lincoln Highway." 1998. *A Brief History, Origins, 1912–13*. 16 June 2014. <http://lincolnhigh-way.jameslin.name/history/part1.html>.

"Lincoln Highway Association." 1999. *Information About the Lincoln Hughway*. 16 June 2014. <https://www.lincolnhighwayassoc.org/info/>.

Metropolitan Water District of Southern California (MWD). "The Big Map (pamphlet)." n.d.

Michaelsen, Joel. "Colorado Desert Region Physical Geogrpahy." n.d. <http://www.geog.ucsb.edu/~joel/g148_f09/readings/colo_desert/colo_desert.html>.

*MWD, Metropolitan Water District of Southern California, A Short History*. April 2003. 31 March 2015. <http://mwdh2o.com/Aqueduct/april_2003/history4.swf>.

Norris, Floyd. "Looking Back, Crash of 1929." 1999. *New York Times on the Web*. 28 January 2016. <http://www.nytimes.com/library/financial/102929crashfront.jpg.html>.

*NYC Environmental Protection*. n.d. 6 September 2014. <http://www.nyc.gov/html/dep/html/drinking_water/history.shtml>.

Palo Verde Historical Museum, Sunkist Garage Photo. *Blythe and the Palo Verde Valley*. Bythe: Arcadia Publishing, 2005. <http://www.arcadiapublishing.com/9780738530727/Blythe-and-the-Palo-Verde-Valley>.

Pollack, Alan. *Grand Opening of the Los Angeles Aqueduct*. n.d. 25 July 2015. <scvhistory.com/scv/history/LW2401.htm>.

"Post-op Instructions: Deviated Septum." n.d. *Henry Ford Health System*. 19 June 2014. <http://www.henryford.com/body.cfm?id=52812>.

Powell, J.W. "A Report on the Arid Region of the United States with a More Detailed Account of the Lands of Utah." 1878.

Powell, James Lawrence. *Dead Pool: Lake Powell, Global Warming, and the Future of Water in the West*. Los Angeles: University of California Press, 2008.

Pratt, Bob. "Refusal to go into hole led 1 worker to summit." *The Press Enterprise* 7 September 1986.

Reisner, Marc. *Cadillac Desert, The American West and Its Disappearing Water*. New York: Penquin Books, 1993.

"Rush Work on Blythe Bridge (Information about the Sunkist Trail)." *Prescott Evening Courier* 9 January 1929: 3. 16 November 2105. <dcourier.com>.

*Rush's Traveler's Guide ... on the Sunkist Trail*. Rush Advertising and News Service, 1928. 1 September 2015. <https://books.google.com/books?id=1YdCywAACAAJ&dq=sunkist+trail&hl=en&sa=X&ved=0CCkQ6AEwAmoVChMI87Hmud3UxwIVxy-ICh1QnwE5>.

Schexnayder, C.J. *The 1927 Rose Bowl: Alabama Vs Stanford*. 22 December 2009. 8 May 2014. <www.rollbamorall.com/2009/12/22/1197979/the-1927-rose-bowl-alabama-vs>.

"Shaver's Well." 29 December 2011. *Historical Marker Database*. 5 May 2015.

Spence, Bob. "Steve Ragsdale." 15 March 2013. *The Desert Empire*. 26 October 2015. <http://thedesertempire.com/steve-ragsdale/>.

Taylor, Nick. "The Great Depression." n.d. *New York Times*. 3 October 2014. <http://topics.nytimes.com/top/reference/timestopics/subjects/g/great_depression_1930s/index.html>.

"The Story of the Los Angeles Aqueduct." n.d. *Department of Water and Power, City of Los Angeles*. 12 June 2014. <http://wsoweb.ladwp.com/Aqueduct/historyoflaa/>.

*The Surveyor's Basic Tools*. n.d. 7 June 2014. <http://www.surveyhistory.org/the_surveyor's_basic_tools.htm>.

"Thomas, Jessie: Records related to her and her family: Social Security Claims 1936–07, Census 1870, 1880, 1900, 1910, 1920, 1930, 1939; Death records for Florence, Alabama 1917 and 1939; Florence cemetery maps, Florence directories 1920–21, 26, 35, 39." Florence-Lauderdale, Alabama Public Library, Local History-Geneology Department, November 2015.

"Timeline of the Great Depression." n.d. *American Experience, 25 Years, PBS*. 23 June 2014. <http://www.pbs.org/wgbh/americanexperience/features/timeline/rails-timeline/>.

"UNC (University of North Carolina Libraries)." c. 1901. *Collection Number: 02813, Alexander Donelson Coffee Papers*. 15 January 2016. <http://www2.lib.unc.edu/mss/inv/c/Coffee,Alexander_Donelson.html>.

University of California, Davis, Department of Land, Air, and Water Resources. *Sierra Sea, California Water from the Sierra to the Sea*. Davis, n.d. 23 April 2014. <http://sierratosea.ucdavis.edu/ca.html>.

Ward, Erica M. *Coachella, Images of America Series*. San Francisco: Arcadia, 2014.

## PART TWO: PIONEERING COURAGE PAYS OFF, War Years, 1940s

*Berdoo Camp*. n.d. 6 May 2014. <www.ghosttowne.com/states/ca/berdoocamp.html>.

Books, Robert T. Elson and editors of Time-Life. *World War II, (series of books)*. New York: Time-Life Books, 1976.

Bortle, John E. "The Bright-Comet Chronicles." 1998. *International Comet Quarterly*. 5 September 2016. <http://www.icq.eps.harvard.edu/bortle.html>.

"Brightest Comets Seen Since 1935 (from the ICQ Archive and other sources)." List Updated 2016. *International Comet Quarterly*. 5 September 2016. <http://www.icq.eps.harvard.edu/CometMags.html>.

Bureau of Land Management. *World War II Desert Training Center*. n.d. 25 May 2014. <http://www.blm.gov/ca/st/en/fo/needles/patton.print.html>.

Calamandrei, Camilla. "Italian POWs held in Amercia during WW II." 2000. *Prisoners in Paradise*. 27 August 2016. <http://www.prisonersinparadise.com/history.html>.

*California State Military Museum, Historic California Posts: Camp Young*. n.d. 18 August 2014.

"Desert Training Center Sky Trail." n.d. *DTC History*. 7 July 2014. <http://skytrail.info/new/camp_young.htm>.

*Desert Training Center Sky Trail, Docent Narrative*. 20 March 2012. 12 February 2015. <http://skytrail.info/new/docent_narrative.htm>.

*Desert Training Center, Map 1*. n.d. 25 May 2014. <http://www.blm.gov/pgdata/etc/medialib/blm/ca/pdf/pdfs/needles_pdfs.Par.9ef47a7a.File.dat/map1.pdf>.

Dickens, Carol Beal. *Benjamin R. Beal Interview*. 25 November 2007. DVD.

Dighera, L. *Shaver's Summit Army Airfield (According to Margit Chiriaco Rusche the following errors are in this document: No such person as Gordon Chiriaco at the Summit. The Summit never fueled Army airplanes. The gas station in the 1940s was not a Chevron.* 28 August 2011. 30 April 2015. <http://skytrail.info/new/shavers_summit_airport.htm>.

Dracun, Joseph. *NOAA History (National Oceanic and Atmospheric Administration).* 8 June 2006. 19 September 2014. <http://www.history.noaa.gov/stories_tales/geod1.html>.

Henley, David C. *The Land That God Forgot. The Saga of Gen. George Patton's Desert Training Camps.* 4th edition. Western Military Association, 1989.

"John W. Hilton." n.d. *Bodega Bay Heritiage Gallery.* 25 June 2014. <http://www.bodegabayheritagegallery.com/Hilton_John_W_.htm>.

*Joshua Tree, History and Culture.* n.d. 14 May 2015. <http://www.nps.gov/jotr/learn/historyculture/index.htm>.

"Jukebox." 2000. *How Products are Made.* Gale Research, Inc. 20 October 2015. <http://www.encyclopedia.com/topic/Jukebox.aspx#1-1G2:2896900067-full>.

Kaufmann, K. "Mixed feelings over solar in Desert Center (includes history of Desert Center)." *The Desert Sun.* Palm Springs: Gannett, 2 May 2014. 30 April 2015. <http://www.desertsun.com/story/tech/science/energy/2014/05/03/desert-center-town-solar-development/8651961/>.

Kessler, Wayne (Lt. US Army). "History of the Communications Zone, C-AMA." US ARMY. May 11, 1944.

"Major Meteor Showers." n.d. *American Meteor Society.* 27 September 2016. <http://www.amsmeteors.org/meteor-showers/major-meteor-showers/>.

Martin, Jill. "The Greatest Evil, Interpretations of Indian Prohibition Laws, 1832–1953, paper 2432." 2003 1 January. <http://digitalcommons.unl.edu/cgi/viewcontent.cgi?article=3432&context=greatplainsquarterly>.

"Record of Climatological Observations, Hayfield Pump Plant." January 1949. *National Center for Environmental Information, National Oceanic and Atmpospheric Administration.* 24 June 2015. <http://www.nws.noaa.gov/os/coop/>.

*Riverside County, Airport Land Use Commission.* n.d. 25 May 2014. <http://www.rcaluc.org/>.

Rizzo, Johnna. "National Geographic." 27 May 2013. *Japan's Secret WWII Weapon: Balloon Bombs.* 28 June 2016. <http://news.nationalgeographic.com/news/2013/05/130527-map-video-balloon-bomb-wwii-japanese-air-current-jet-stream/>.

Rodenberg, Eric. "Antiqueweek.com." 27 February 2009. *Out of the desert comes a treasure trove (Brigadears).* 4 November 2015. <http://www.antiqueweek.com/ArchiveArticle.asp?newsid=1093>.

*The California State Military Museum, Historic California Posts, Desert Training Center.* n.d. May 25 2014. <http://www.militarymuseum.org/CAMA.html>.

"The Desert Battalion (Brigadears)." 4 April 2009. *Toons at War.* 4 November 2015. <http://toons344.rssing.com/chan-13131499/all_p1.html>.

United States Department of the Interior, Bureau of Land Management, California Desert District. "Desert Training Center, California-Arizona Manuever Area, Interpretive Plan." 1985. *Bureau of Land Management Library.* 26 January 2015. <https://archive.org/details/deserttraining-ce00unit>.

Weeks, Linton. *Beware of Japanese Balloon Bombs.* 20 January 2015. 28 June 2016. <http://www.npr.org/sections/npr-history-dept/2015/01/20/375820191/beware-of-japanese-balloon-bombs>.

Wurlitzer. "History of the Jukebox." n.d. 20 October 2015. <http://www.history-of-rock.com/history_of_the_jukebox.htm>.

## PART THREE: PUTTING CHIRIACO SUMMIT ON THE MAP, 1950s, '60s, '70s.

American Automobile Club of Southern California. "Chiriaco Summit, C/S 626, Celebrates 20 Years With the Club." *Shop Talk* June 1978: 1–2.

Baxter, James. "55 MPH Speed Limit is unenforceable and counterproductive." 26 July 2009. *US News and World Report.* 27 October 2014. <http://www.usnews.com/opinion/articles/2009/07/27/55-mph-speed-limit-is-unenforceable-and-counterproductive>.

"California Department of Transportation." n.d. *The History of Interstate Highways in California.* 1 May 2014. <www.dot.ca.gov/interstates/CA/htm>.

"California Department of Transportation." 1 November 2001. *Highway Design Manual.* 31 August 2014. <http://www.dot.ca.gov/hq/oppd/hdm/pdf/chp0500.pdf>.

*California Roads and Highways by AA Roads.* 6 February 2009. 19 September 2014. <http://www.aaroads.com/california/i-010wa_ca.html>.

Chiriaco, Joe. "Letter to Jonathan Thompsen re 1932 Cadillac." Chiriaco, Summit, CA, 16 August 1959.

"Energy Crisis (1970s)." n.d. *History Channel.* 25 September 2014. <http://www.history.com/topics/energy-crisis>.

Faigan, Daniel P (webmaster). *Califorinia Highways, Routes 9–16, Interstate 10.* 12 February 2015. 12 February 2015. <http://www.cahighways.org/009-016.html>.

"Freeway 60 Route to Get Air Survey." *The Daily Enterprise, Riverside California, Desert and Pass Edition* November 23 1956: B1–2.

*From Bust to Boom to Bust: Eagle Mountain, CA.* 8 February 2012. 27 October 2016. <http://sometimes-interesting.com/2012/02/08/from-boom-to-bust-eagle-mountain-ca/>.

*Gas Lines Evoke Memories of Oil Crises in the 1970s.* 10 November 2012. 17 September 2014.

<http://www.npr.org/blogs/pictureshow/2012/11/10/164792293/gas-lines-evoke-memories-oil-crises-in-the-1970s>.

Harris, Bobbie. "The Story of Purple Glass." *Unpublished flyer from Bobbie's Antiques*. n.d.

"Highway Water May Soon Be Abandoned." *Kingman Daily Miner* 15 August 1975. <http://news.google.com/newspapers?nid=932&dat=19750815&id=90NTAAAAIBAJ&sjid=y4UDAAAAIBAJ&pg=4881,2601116>.

*Historic Highway 99*. 30 April 2013. 15 January 2015. <http://www.gbcnet.com/ushighways/US99/index.html>.

Jackson, Helen. "Shaver's Summit Girl Fair Queen." *Clipping from unidentified newspaper, location of story given as Hemet, California* 21 August 1954.

Jones, Patricia A. and Thomas S., Plunkeet, eds. *Annual Average US Steel Prices*. Washington, DC: US Government Printing Office, US Department of the Interior, US Geological Survey, 1999. 10 December 2014. <http://minerals.usgs.gov/minerals/pubs/metal_prices/metal_prices1998.pdf>.

Kelley, David. Los Angeles Times Staff Writer. "Shavers Summit Where Four Children Grew up, Draft." 24 August 2008.

Lyneis, Dick. "In 48 years, Joe Chiriaco has seen the desert bloom." *The Daily Enterprise, Desert and Pass Edition* 1 February 1974: C1–2.

"Mainstream Drug Use in America, pre-1980s, Analysis of Drug Use in Modern America." n.d. *William and Mary College, Research*. 29 September 2014. <http://web.wm.edu/americanstudies/370/2007/sp5/Main_drugs.htm>.

*Milestones: 1969–1976, Oil Embargo 1973–1974*. 31 October 2013. 17 September 2014. <https://history.state.gov/milestones/1969-1976/oil-embargo>.

Nace, Aprille. "What causes the varied purple hues in old glass bottles." 11 August 2014. *Corning Museum of Glass?* 1 October 2014. <http://libanswers.cmog.org/a.php?qid=283712>.

"Nelson appointed new director of Patton Museum." *Los Angeles Times* 3 April 1993: D1.

"Nixon signs national speed limit into law, January 2, 1974." n.d. *History Channel, This Day in History*. 2 October 2014. <http://www.history.com/this-day-in-history/nixon-signs-national-speed-limit-into-law>.

*Plane Spotting in the 1950s*. n.d. 31 January 2016. <https://bissella9.wordpress.com/plane-spotting-in-the-1950s/>.

"President Johnson Signs the Highway Beautification Act." n.d. *History Channel*. 14 January 2016.

"Proposition 14, State College System." 1974. *State College Sytem, Legislative Constituional Amendment Analysis, John "Bud" Collier signer*. 19 June 2014. <http://librarysource.uchastings.edu/ballot_pdf/1974/1974g14.pdf>.

"Publication 100 - The United States Postal Service - An American History 1775 - 2006, Postal

Reorganization Act." 2012. *United States Postal Service.* 8 January 2014. <https://about.usps. com/publications/pub100/pub100_035.htm>.

Ray, Michael. *Trans Alaska Pipeline System.* 16 May 2014. 30 August 2014. <http://www.britan-nica.com/EBchecked/topic/602272/Trans-Alaska-Pipeline>.

Ritter, Eric W. ed. *A Cultural Resources Overview of the Colorado Desert Planning Units.* Riverside, California: California Desert District, US Department of the Interior, Bureau of Land Man-agement, 1981. 19 September 2014. <http://www.blm.gov/pgdata/etc/medialib/blm/wo/ Planning_and_Renewable_Resources/coop_agencies/new_documents/ca1.Par.88876.File. dat/A.9464.71>.

Rizzo, Anthony. *Duck and Cover.* Federal Civil Defense Administration and Archer Produtions. 1951. film. 31 January 2016. <https://archive.org/details/gov.ntis.ava11109vnb1>.

*Satin's Sadist.* Film Released, 1969. 30 August 2015. <http://www.imdb.com/find?ref_=nv_sr_ fn&q=Satin percent27s+Sadist&s=all>.

"The Cornell Lab of Ornithology." n.d. *All About Birds.* 26 August 2014. <http://www.allabout-birds.org/guide/scotts_oriole/lifehistory>.

*The Ground Observer Corps.* n.d. 31 January 2016. <http://www.radomes.org/museum/docu-ments/GOC/GOC.html>.

Thompsen, Jonathan. "Letter to Joe Chiriaco re 1932 Cadillac." Baldwin Park, CA, 11 August 1959.

"Yearly Traffic through Blythe Shows Increase." *Unidentified newspaper clipping, Chiriaco Archives (story location given as Blythe, reports 1948 statistics)* 1950.

## PART FOUR: TRANSITIONING, 1980s, 1990s

*American Business Brokers, Gas Stations and Convenience Stores.* n.d. 30 April 2015. <http://www. abbunitedstates.com/glossary_gas_convenience.asp>.

Berry, Kristin H. and Timothy A. Duck. "Chapter 2: Important Laws and Regulations Protecting Tortoises." Winter 2010. *Answering Questions about Desert Tortoises.* Bureau of Land Manage-ment. 21 May 2015. <http://www.deserttortoise.org/answeringquestions/chapter2.html>.

Chevron. "25 Years with Chevron USA, Presented to Joe Chiriaco referencing being a Chevron dealer since 1961." n.d.

*Chevron University, version 3.4.10.* 2005-2015. Chevron Products Company. 28 July 2015. <https://businesspoint.chevron.com (requires login)>.

Chiriaco, Joe. "A story about a boy named Joe by a man named Joe." Chiriaco Summit, California, 23 April 1993. Chiriaco Archives.

"Desert Tortoise." n.d. *Joshua Tree National Park.* 15 May 2015. <nps.gov/jotr/learn/nature/ tortoise.htm>.

*DesertUSA, George S. Patton Memorial Museum.* n.d. 12 February 2015. <http://www.desertusa.com/desert-people/patton.html>.

Dilsaver, Lary M. *Joshua Tree National Park: A History in Preserving the Desert, NPS Task Agreement #P11AC90959.* National Park Service, Joshua Tree National Park. Twentynine Palms, California, March, 2015. <http://www.nps.gov/jotr/learn/historyculture/upload/JOTRAdministrativeHistory-web.pdf>.

"Events." *Newsletter, General Patton Memorial Museum* 4 May 1990: 1.

Fish, Peter. "Western Wanderings: Forgotten Land, Remembered War." *Sunset* October 2000: 22. print.

*General Patton Memorial Museum.* n.d. 25 May 2014. <http://generalpattonmuseum.com/patton-history/>.

Hamaker, Sarah. "Self-serve Evolution." *NASC Magazine Online* October 2011. 12 September 2014. <http://www.nacsonline.com/MAGAZINE/PASTISSUES/2011/october2011/Pages/Feature8.aspx>.

Henry, Mark. "Summit reaches higher." *The Press-Enterprise, Desert and Pass* 21 June 1998: B1&B4.

Henstridge, Fred. *The Big Map.* n.d. 13 February 2015. <http://henstridgephotography.com/Newsletter percent20PDF percent20Files/Vol percent201 percent20No. percent203_Web.pdf>.

Hillinger, Charles. "V-E Day Plus 40—GIs Return to Patton's Camp." *Los Angeles Times* 9 May 1985. <http://articles.latimes.com/1985-05-09/news/mn-6727>.

—. "What's Progress?: Desert Center's 75-year Old Owner is Cool to Change." *Los Angeles Times* 15 October 1990. 19 September 2015. <http://articles.latimes.com/1990-10-15/news/mn-1950_1_desert-center-cafe>.

Johnston, Francis W. *The Wonder of Guadelupe.* Charlotte, N.C., Tan Books, 1993.

"Joshua Tree." n.d. *National Park Service.* 25 August 2014. <http://www.nps.gov/jotr/index.htm>.

"Joshua Tree National Park, Maps." n.d. *National Park Service.* 23 June 2014. <http://www.nps.gov/jotr/planyourvisit/upload/jotrmap.pdf>.

*Our Lady of Guadalupe.* n.d. 10 June 2015. <http://www.sancta.org/>.

Power, Robert H. "The Best Advice I Ever Received." Draft Copy of article for Nation's Restaurant News, attached to letter to Sandra Elder, Assistant Executive Secretary, State Histotial Resources Commission, Scaramento, CA, 2 May 1989.

"Rest Area Commercialization." 2015. *NACS Online, the Association for Convenience and Fuel Retailing.* 15 May 2015. <nacsonline.com/Issues/Other/Pages/RestArea Commercialization.aspx>.

Rosenberg, Jennifer. "1980s Time line, 1990s Timeline." 2015. *Timeline of the 20th Century.* 8 January 2015. <http://history1900s.about.com/od/timelines/tp/1980timeline.htm>.

Silva, Andrew. "Golden Arches to Greet Chiriaco Visitors." *The Desert Sun* 6 June 1998: B1.

Standard Oil of California. "Presented to Joe Chiriaco in recognition of dedication and service to the motoring public as a Chevron Dealer since 1961 (award plaque with no date of presentation)." n.d.

*The 6th Armored Division (Super Sixth)*. 20 June 2014. 1 November 2014. <http://www.ushmm.org/wlc/en/article.php?ModuleId=10006136>.

"Threats to the Desert Tortoise." 2012. *Endangered Species International*. 17 May 2015. <engangeredspecies international.org/deserttortoise>.

*Underground Storage Tank Cleanup Fund*. 28 October 2015. 1 February 2016. <http://www.waterboards.ca.gov/water_issues/programs/ustcf/>.

*Underground Storage Tank Cleanup Fund, History*. 20 August 2009. 29 January 2016. <http://www.waterboards.ca.gov/water_issues/programs/ustcf/history.shtml>.

## PART FIVE: THE TWENTY-FIRST CENTURY COMES TO THE SUMMIT

"75 Years in the Dust, Chiriaco Summit." *Los Angeles Times*. 2008 24 August. 11 May 2014. <articles/latimes.com/2008/aug/24/local/me-chiriaco24>.

About Us, Our Mission and Vision for the Future." 15 June 2010. *Desert Alliance for Community Empowerment (DACE)*. 10 June 2015. <http://www.dace-rancho.org/About_DACE.htm>.

"Ad with menu, Chiriaco Summit." *Chuckwalla Buzzz*. June 2000.

"Ad, Chavez Truck and Tire." *Chuckwalla Buzzz*. June 2000.

Atagi, Colin. *Tex Wash Bridge to be Completely Demolished*. 28 July 2015. 31 July 2015. <http://www.desertsun.com/story/news/traffic/2015/07/28/tex-wash-bridge-collapse/30785609/>.

*Automobile Driving Museum*. 13 September 2013. 14 September 2104. <http://www.automobile-drivingmuseum.org/2014/09/13/the-history-and-collectability-of-gas-pumps/>.

Chiriaco Family. "Letter to customers regarding projected opening of new facilities." 2004.

Chiriaco Summit. "Come for the Food (poster)." c. 2004.

"Chiriaco Summit ideal stop for those flying by or worth a visit on its own." *Pacific Flyer* March 2007: A23.

"Civil Aviation Post-9/11/01, Reverberations of the Attack in Civil Aviation and Beyond." 16 January 2007. *9–11 Research*. 30 October 2015. <http://911research.wtc7.net/post911/aviation/civil.html>.

*Coachella Valley Water District*. n.d. 5 May 2014. <www.cvwd.org/about/whrewater.php>.

*Crash Course: The Origins of the Financial Crisis*. 7 September 2013. 9 June 2015. <http://www.economist.com/news/schoolsbrief/21584534-effects-financial-crisis-are-still-being-felt-five-years-article>.

Donovan, Emily. *I-10 Closed at Collapsed Bridge in Desert Center*. 21 July 2015. 27 July 2015. <http://www.desertsun.com/story/news/2015/07/19/#desert-center-bridge-collapse/30395123/>.

Four Chaplains Award Flyer, General Patton Memorial Museum. Chiriaco Summit, 11 November 2015. Flyer.

Galli, Joe. 21 July 2015. KESQ News. print and video. 27 July 2015. <http://www.kesq.com/news/i10-closure-cuts-off-chiriaco-summit/34269516>.

Gilford, Steve. "A History of Total Health, Thieves abscond with bronze historical marker at Desert Center." 8 August 2013. *Kaiser Permanente*. 25 May 2015. <http://kaiserpermanentehistory.org/tag/chiriaco-summit/>.

Goolsby, Denise. "Bridge Collapse Recalls Earlier Desert Flood Disasters." *The Desert Sun*. 29 July 2015. 31 July 2015. <http://www.desertsun.com/story/news/2015/07/29/history-coachella-valley-flooding/30860197/>.

—. "Chiriaco Summit Coffee Shop to celebrate 83 years of community." *The Desert Sun* 30 July 2016. <http://www.desertsun.com/story/news/2016/07/30/chiriaco-summit-gen-patton-memorial-museum-1933/87763396/>.

—. "Chiriaco Summit Museum Pays Homage to Gen. George Patton." 19 July 2014. *The Desert Sun*. 20 July 2014. <http://desert.sn/1msxz5A>.

—. "Desert pioneers Joe and Ruth Chiriaco get 380th star." *The Desert Sun* 7 March 2015. 9 March 2015. <http://www.desertsun.com/story/news/2015/03/07/palm-springs-walk-stars-chiriaco-summit/24516789/>.

"LAFCO." 27 October 2007. *Local Agency Formation Commitee: LAFCO 2006-145-4—SPHERE OF INFLUENCE REVIEW.* 29 August 2014. <http://www.lafco.org/opencms/monthly_hearings/agenda/pdf/2007/October/4.i.2006-145-Chiriaco_Summit_CWD_SOI.pdf>.

Lech, Steve. "Back in the Day: Chiriaco Summit became a popular desert outpost." *The Press-Enterprise* 27 August 2015. 12 September 2015. <http://www.pe.com/articles/chiriaco-778219-summit-shaver.html>.

Lee, Barbara A. *EPA ID Profile, Department of Substances Control, ID#CAC002275769 (Gives one inactve date of Desert Center Gas Station)*. Sacramento, California, October 25, 2000.

Moore, Steve. "Joshua Tree National Park's annual wildflower show delivering extra punch." *Press-Enterprise* 1 March 2008.

—. "Revamped rest area in desert to reopen." *The Press-Enterprise* 26 November 2007: B1&B4.

"Our History." 2015. *Kaiser Permanente*. 26 May 2015. <http://share.kaiserpermanente.org/article/history-of-kaiser-permanente/>.

*Pilot Getways, Chiriaco Summit*. 2000–2013. 25 May 2014. <http://pilotgetaways.com/search/node/Chiriaco%20Summit>.

Ramirez, Richard, President General Patton Memorial Museum. "Letter to Jim Kidricikis, President Air and Space Museum, San Diego, Regarding the Da Vinci Acquisition." Chiriaco Summit, California, 10 January 2013.

Rushe, Margit Chiriaco. "Letter to employees regarding secret shopper, Chiriaco Summit." c. 2004.

Sullivan, Jim. "Places That Were." 18 May 2015. *The Sprawling Ghost Town of Desert Center-Part One-The Main Drag*. 27 October 2016. <http://www.placesthatwere.com/2015/05/desert-center-part-1.html>.

—. "The Sprawing Ghost Town of Desert Center-Part 2-Abandoned School and Junkyard House." 26 May 2015. *Placces That Were*. 27 October 2016. <http://www.placesthatwere.com/2015/05/desert-center-part-1.html>.

*The Recession of 2007–2009*. February 2012. 9 June 2015. <http://www.bls.gov/spotlight/2012/recession/pdf/recession_bls_spotlight.pdf>.

## A FAMILY BUSINESS CHECKLIST

Caspar, Christian, Ana Karina Dias, and Heinz-Peter Elstrodt. *The Five Attributes of Enduring Family Business*. January 2010. 9 June 2015. <http://www.mckinsey.com/insights/organization/the_five_attributes_of_enduring_family_businesses>.

*Chiriaco Summit, About Us*, 18 February 2017. <http://www.chiriacosummit.com/about-us/>.

"Family Companies, Relative Success." *The Economist* 14 November 2014: 12–13.

"Forbes." 23 April 2015. *New Survey Pinpoints What Keeps Family Business Going for Generations*. 4 August 2015. <http://www.forbes.com/sites/chasewithorn/2015/04/23/new-survey-pinpoints-what-keeps-family-businesses-going-for-generations/>.

Groysberg, Boris and Deborah Bell. "Generation to Generation: How to Save the Family Business." 10 April 2014. *Harvard Business Review*. 4 August 2015. <https://hbr.org/2014/04/generation-to-generation-how-to-save-the-family-business>.

Lang, Eugene: Columbia University Business School. "The Owner's Journey, Experiences Shared and Lessons Learned from Entrepreneurs who Successfully Sold or Transfereed their Businesses to Family Members." Case Studies. 2015.

"Lasting Family Businesses—How to Get Past the Third Generation." 12 August 2014. *Business Families Foudation*. 4 August 2015. <https://businessfamilies.org/read/lasting-family-businesses-how-to-get-passed-the-third-generation/>.

Small Business and Entrepreneurship Council. *Small Business Facts and Data*. 2015. 17 July 2015. <http://www.sbecouncil.org/about-us/facts-and-data/>.

Stalk, George and Henry Foley. "Avoid the Traps That Can Destroy Family Businsses." *Harvard*

*Business Review* January-February 2012. <https://hbr.org/2012/01/avoid-the-traps-that-can-destroy-family-businesses>.

Stewart, Howard. "E-mail to Mary Gordon Regarding Family Business Success." Tucson, Arizona, 9 June 2015.


## HISTORICAL NUMBERS

California Department of Transportaion (Caltrans) and US Department of Transportation (USDOT). *Ramp Volumes on the California State Freeway System, District 8 (Chiriaco Summit*, p.6). 2015. 7 April 2017. <http://www.dot.ca.gov/trafficops/census/docs/2015-ramp-vol-district08.pdf>. See also Ramp Volumes issued in 2001 and 2005 for 1993 to 2005 numbers.

California Department of Transportation (Caltrans). "California State Highway Log, page 16, Chiriaco Summit Off-ramps, D08_RT10_p16_ocr." Department of Transportation Library (Librarian David Lushbaugh), 2003.

California Gas Prices, Riverside City." 12 April 2017. Gas Buddy California, Historical Price Charts. <http://www.CaliforniaGasPrices.com/retail_price_chart.aspx?city1=Riverside&city2=&city3=&crude=n&tme=132&units=us>.

Chiriaco, Joe. Handwritten Ledger of November 8, 1933, Chiriaco Archives.

ERS, US Department of Agriculture. "Red Meat Yearbook." 2015. <http://usda.mannlib.cornell.edu/MannUsda/viewDocumentInfo.do?documentID=1354>.

"Fact #835, August 25, Average Historical Gasoline Pump Price, 1929–2013 (Table 9.4 to Nov. 2015)." n.d. *Energy.gov.* 13 January 2016. <http://energy.gov/eere/vehicles/fact-835-august-25-average-historical-annual-gasoline-pump-price-1929-2013>.

"Fact #943, Fuel Economy." 19 September 2016. *Energy.gov.* 9 October 2016. <http://energy.gov/eere/vehicles/fact-943-september-19-2016-fuel-economy-being-chosen-most-important-vehicle-attribute>.

Pribyl, Cynthia. "Email to Mary Gordon correcting WB Off in 2008 Ramp Volume from 2200 to 1400." 6 April 2017.

—. "Email to Mary Gordon verifying that 2008 was the last year Chiriaco ramp data was charted by Caltrans." 3 April 2017.

# *Acknowledgments*

I am honored that the Chiriaco family and business entrusted me with their story, a story representative of the dreams and struggles of many who settle in challenging terrain to start and run businesses that make up the fabric of America. This story has many historical backdrops, which required me to learn and fact check constantly; but I didn't mind at all. I got to communicate with fascinating people: family members and their friends, World War II Veterans, business associates and experts, suppliers, employees, customers, historians, scientists, medical experts, archivists, and representatives of public and private agencies. At times I thought I might drive all these people crazy by drilling down from their initial input to get the story behind the story or to get details related to fact checking. But they put up with me, especially the family members who bore the brunt of my questioning.

## The initiator:

Margit Chiriaco Rusche, the current CEO of Joseph L. Chiriaco, Inc., initiated this book. She helped me make initial contacts. She scoured Chiriaco archives for photographs, thoughtfully reviewed drafts, and gave feedback throughout the process. She was the eyes and ears on the ground that I could contact anytime. Her willingness to hunt down details for me was a key to the historical integrity of this story.

## More family:

I could not have done without Robert Chiriaco who answered many technical questions, especially about the arduous work on the water pipelines. He took me on desert tours, which helped me place incidents correctly in time and location. Pauline Chiriaco Leedom, the oldest of the Chiriaco Four, shared stories and photos of the early years at the Summit. Norma Chiriaco Elliot, the youngest of the four, described fun and adventure in desert summers and winters that added to the charm of the childhood years. Heather Metcalf Garcia, Margit's daughter, was especially helpful with the business aspects of the 1990s. She put me in touch with her father, Dwight Metcalf, who described the law enforcement environment in his days as the only officer in the Summit area. Victor Garcia, Margit's grandson, and Heather's son, brought me into the twenty-first century with a new venture he planned to integrate with the past. My late husband Bob's and son Greg's fondness for old cars helped me appreciate young Victor's work and enthusiasm for the Classic Car Garage with its electric car charging unit. Chris Baldivid, Margit's son, brought Joe and Ruth's long term vision into view by quoting Grandpa Joe's statement about his city on the hill. Michael Leedom, Pauline's son, shared what it was like for several of the grandchildren who worked summers at the Summit. Cousins Barbara Bergseid Clark and Alida Bergseid Rodebush helped me round out Ruth's character. Two Chiriaco cousins, Hector Franck, living in Alabama, remembered his visits to the Summit and sent historic photos; and Dee Schiavone, helped clarify the times her father, Devio, spent there.

Suzanne Ragsdale, not a Chiriaco but from the Desert Center family, helped me bring the rougher, tougher desert and its business competition alive. Her brother, Sidney Ragsdale, verified locations for me.

### The Patton Effect:

One of Joe's youngest siblings, Paul Chiriaco helped me round out Joe's character. He remembered many fascinating tales of the early years at the Summit, especially in regard to General Patton's presence there. At the age of 96 and losing his sight, he read and gave feedback to the drafts with the help of his wife Shirley. His memories, some back to the 1920s, fact checked again and again. Ben Beal, who had actually served under General Patton, added his experiences at Camp Young. His daughter, Linda, helped navigate my appointments with him and sent historic photos. General Patton's effect has been long-lasting at the Summit as shared by those involved with the museum. He was the reason Santos Garcia came to the Summit and started an influx of dedicated, permanent workers. Leslie Cone, cofounder of the General Patton Memorial Museum, Michael Pierson, past director, and Richard Ramirez, past president of the board all contributed information that painted the picture from the start of the museum to the present. Jacque Schindewolf, curator at the time I started the research, lent me copies of military documents that made clear the tremendous undertaking of the DTC. Peggy Pourtemour, museum employee, found information that verified the Brigadears, ending my long search on that topic. Ed Hume, Edison International Corporate Communications, and Paul Netter, Southern California Edison Public Relations, located the photo and names of the Edison volunteers who helped build the Museum.

### Employees and Customers:

Thank you to the many employees and customers who shared their stories and impressions with me. I spent time at the Summit, on the phone, and in e-mail chains with many of them. I bent Rudy Montoya's ear the most. Often he'd tell me he was serving a customer and would get back to me. He did, helping me make additional contacts, verifying information, and rounding out one of the love stories in the book. Other stories came from employees: Diana Ragsdale, Angelina and Hector Sanchez (another love story), Leticia Sanchez, Nina Tapia, and Steve Tisdel. Heather's husband and co-general manager, Santos Garcia, was one of the first persons I saw on early mornings. He was already hard at work in the coffee shop predawn. I was able to observe the industriousness of his crew already bustling at the coffee shop, on the grounds, at the Food Mart, and at the gas station. Over in the office Eduardo Guevara and Leslie Nunez, later in the day and after I left, did the arduous task of scanning over 100 photos. Eduardo started scanning some tough photos before I arrived. He also created some of the composites in the book and improved the illustrations. I talked to customers, especially truck drivers, in the early morning to ask why they stopped at the Summit. They were always pleasant as they shared their good experiences. Coffee shop customers, Jim and June Capp, Jerry and Veronica Grey, Dan and Diane Roberts, and Paul and Elsie Williams, talked to me in person and/or by e-mail. The Capps gave me one of the classic car stories. Out in the parking lot around lunch one day, I encountered the Broads on Quads, who explained to me they tour the desert together. They continued their conversation with me inside the coffee shop around a large table the staff had set up for them. They added zest to the desert story I was writing.

## Experts (historians, scientists, medical professionals, business associates):

Except for Mr. Krieger and Mr. Gilford, these people are not mentioned in the story but communicated with me back and forth to help me make its background accurate. Robert Krieger, a consultant to the Chiriaco business, was one of the first experts I contacted. He described the 1920s-30s surveying methods and clarified some of the water issues that arose several times in the story. Joshua Tree National Park Historian, Lary Dilsaver, pointed me in directions to clarify some of the vagaries around the desert water issues. Steve Gilford, the Kaiser historian, helped me understand some of the local history. John Green, field ornithologist, Daniel W. D. Green, astronomer, and Joel Michaelsen, geographer, helped me with the natural desert environment on the land and in the sky. Rebecca Lubitz, MD and Jovita Campos, RN, helped me understand the medical details in the story. John Kalish, BLM, explained BLM connections with the area, the Summit, and the Museum. John Cote, retired from PacBell, explained the Summit's unusual phone system to me.

There were surprising finds in the process of writing this book. I will mention two. I was able to pinpoint an exact snow date in 1949 by e-mail and phone conversations with the National Oceanic and Atmospheric Administration. There was a note giving the date on the back of the photo of an old small plane gassing up at Joe's gas station, but nothing else. David Lubitz, a private pilot of the kind that would have landed at the Summit Airport, identified it as a model he had flown some twenty years before as a teenager in Canada.

## Archivists:

Archivists are listed with sources, but I will mention their roles in ending some of my frustrating searches especially to do with water, roads, the environment, and a possible former slave. Armando Acuna, MWD, sent me a 1939 report which gave me the aqueduct story, and he led me to David Keller who had boxes of relevant files ready for me when I arrived at headquarters, some folders even marked as especially relevant. David Lushbaugh, Terri Kassinga, and Cindy Prybyl, of Caltrans all helped find the exact dates of the opening of the Chiriaco I-10 ramp, of later signage changes, and increases in traffic volumes. Glori Conti, of the California regulatory assistance office and Nicholas Crain, of Riverside County Hazmat, clarified some of the environmental issues that businesses needed to deal with in the late '90s. Marion Champion, Imperial Irrigation District clarified water, power, and related environmental issues. Restaurant food was a part of the story. I was curious about how prices changed over time. Cliola Peterson, USDA, helped me find the history of restaurant meat prices.

Paul Chiriaco suggested I check his memory about "Aunt Jessie" who was a nurse to the fourteen Chiriaco children and to a very famous person. Louise Huddleston, University of North Alabama Archivist started the search about the possible former slave and then referred me to the person who she believed could find the needle in the haystack. She was right. Lee Freeman, from the local history department at the public library in Florence, Alabama, kept digging into records over several months until he finally found the information that proved Paul Chiriaco was correct: Jessie Thomas, possibly a former slave who had worked as a nurse for the Alabama Chiriacos, had also been a nurse to Helen Keller. The information he sent also verified her son, Jim, whom Paul had also described to me, even the fact that he operated a horse and buggy livery service.

## Joshua Tree National Park:

Ernie Quintana, the park's first superintendent, shared the park's conservation mindset in such a way that it melded into the story. Chief law enforcement officer, Jeff Ohlfs, told me of incidents that illustrated the sparse lifestyle that both the rangers and their Chiriaco neighbors lived. Melanie Spoo and Melinda Most, park specialists, found maps and information to help talented cartographer James Mansfield with details that were important to the Chiriacos. Not at the park, but map related, Tom Schmidt at the Sharlot Hall Museum Library and Archives, explained details regarding a map from their collection. The current superintendent, David Smith referred me to NPS sources throughout and gave his part of the story, which involved removing old pipes. More about him in another section.

## Special Situations:

Father Jack Keefe so eloquently expressed the spirit at the Summit that his is one of only two e-mail quotes in the story. The other is from Michael Leedom, Pauline's son, who shared the surprise and awe of discovering the old pipes on a mountain hike, pipes he had helped Joe repair as a youngster. Margit's longtime friend, Eileen Heimark, verified information in the story and gave me the hilarious driving incident. Arch Gratz, the school bus driver, let me in on his way of dealing with the lively desert youth of the day so that their long trip was fun but safe.

## Interim Reviewers:

Helen Patton, General George S. Patton's granddaughter, an extremely busy person with worldwide interests, found time to read the manuscript, and then wrote the foreword. She did this while on the road to honor military service past and present and to foster the goals of the Patton Foundation and its related organizations. Howard Stewart, CEO of AGM Containers, Inc., which won the US Chamber of Commerce Small Business First Place Award in 2009, met with me at the beginning of this project and periodically to discuss the business aspects of this story. In the end he read the entire manuscript and then wrote the epilogue. Tara Turek, his assistant, spent many an hour, working the document back and forth. Thanks also to Crystal Barker, technical writer who read one of the early drafts, to Leslie Cone, retired from BLM, who read one of the last drafts, and Sister Diane Pekarek, a Notre Dame Nun, who read one of the chapters I kept rewriting. Her helpful feedback stopped my spinning. Also, thanks to Tim O'Connor, Sara Chen, and Dan Gordon who reviewed sections.

## The Founders, Joe and Ruth Chiriaco:

All through my research I kept thinking, I have to see for myself what it was like to maintain the pipes. Joshua Tree Superintendent, David Smith, made that possible by arranging to have NPS guest hosts Dick and Phyllis Clawson guide me on an eight-mile hike through gorgeous but rough terrain. Without the Clawsons I never could have found my way. For a full day they led me back onto disappearing trails, over sizable boulders, and finally back to the Summit in the dark.

That hike did it! It gave meaning to *you have to see it to believe it!* Yes, the hike pulled together the many facts, but it also let me glimpse the mindset, heart, and soul it took to be pioneers in this area. I was in awe of the beauty but also the challenges faced then and now. So the biggest thank you goes to Ruth and Joe Chiriaco for setting in motion what it takes to keep alive the inspiring, fascinating story of Chiriaco Summit.

Gratefully,
Mary Contini Gordon
Author

# Index

This index covers people, organizations, places, and related historical events in the story itself. It does not cover the epilogue or the appendices except for GPPM. It includes items not easily found in the extensive table of contents or in other tables.

# *About the Author*

**Dr. Mary Contini Gordon** became fascinated with the Chiriaco story after one of her first trips on the I-10 to the Los Angeles area after being moved to Tucson by her employer in the early 2000s. She wondered how this business started and survived in what was at first an isolated area. As she came to know the business and the people involved, she not only learned the story but deepened her appreciation of what the Chiriacos symbolize today—the significant contributions of many small businesses to the well-being of individuals, communities, and the country as a whole and the fascinating pioneering spirit that showed itself again and again through so many challenging changes over decades.

Mary's credentials gave foundation to the rigorous research, to the making of connections among the business facets, and to finding the underlying human aspects of this history. Mary is a meticulous researcher with years of examining organizational issues in the public and private sectors. She was the executive director of the Hughes Institute for Professional Development responsible for internal research; and directly relevant to this book, she oversaw professional and executive development across all five Hughes Companies. After Raytheon bought Hughes, she developed and then led an innovation-services group that worked with leaders of emerging programs and technologies, in a sense small ventures. After retiring at the end of 2008, she became the facilitator for the Arizona Technology Council's CEO Network in Tucson, mostly small companies, some family businesses.

Her degrees and background in theater, TV production, and educational psychology contribute to her use of vignettes to bring the reader into the heart of the story. Her previous book, *TIQ SLO'W, The Making of a Modern Day Chief* is also a book about leadership. It is used at UCLA and a subject of over thirty talks. Dr. Gordon's research method, employed for both books, which she refers to as ***Her-His***tory™ Method is featured on the Great Lakes College Association's Oral History in the Liberal Arts Initiative Resource Site. (Search OHLA, Mary Gordon Indexes.) Her work in the leadership and innovation arenas is as of this writing featured on the current Idea Connection Systems, Inc. website. (Search Idea Connection speakers, Mary C. Gordon.)

Dr. Gordon is dedicated to telling the stories of those who may not be famous but who contribute mightily to the fabric of our country. In addition to writing, Mary enjoys nature trips with the families of her four children, Greg, Dan, Sara, and Rebecca, who beckon from places across North America.

Mary is honored that the Chiriaco family and business put their story in her hands.

CPSIA information can be obtained
at www.ICGtesting.com
Printed in the USA
BVOW09s1724280717

490182BV00002B/7/P

9 781627 874656